AN INTRODUC͟   ͟ ͟ ͟ ͟ ͟ ͟
MUSEUM ARCHAEOLOGY

An Introduction to Museum Archaeology provides a comprehensive survey and synthesis of all aspects of current museum practice relating to the discipline of archaeology. This book is divided into four separate, but related parts. It begins with a discussion of what is meant by museums, archaeology, and museum archaeology and includes a brief survey of the history, legal foundation, and global geographic spread of museum archaeological practice.

The second part of this book deals with collections in all of their aspects. This includes subjects such as the looting of illicit antiquities, the major challenges posed by the ever-mounting quantity of material from archaeological excavations, and the very recent debates over the place of human remains in museums. It also discusses conservation and research.

The third part deals with the use of archaeological materials and methods in displays, exhibitions, and public and educational programmes. Drawing heavily on examples, it deconstructs the different challenges posed by trying to tell archaeological stories in museum buildings and on related sites.

The final section sums up the state of museum archaeology in the early twenty-first century and discusses the major issues that museum archaeology is currently confronting. There is also a detailed list of every museum and exhibit mentioned in the book, each with a Web address and an exhaustive list of references.

An Introduction to Museum Archaeology provides an essential text for anyone studying museums, archaeology, or cultural heritage, and it is a reference for those working in these fields. It is full of detailed information, and it discusses concepts and provides the context for current debates.

Hedley Swain is Head of Early London History and Collections at the Museum of London and chair of the British Society of Museum Archaeologists. He is an honorary lecturer at the Institute of Archaeology, University College London, and a tutor at Birkbeck College, University of London. Swain has published widely on museum and archaeological matters and is the author of several major surveys of museum archaeology in Britain.

AN INTRODUCTION
TO MUSEUM ARCHAEOLOGY

HEDLEY SWAIN
Museum of London

CAMBRIDGE
UNIVERSITY PRESS

CAMBRIDGE UNIVERSITY PRESS

Cambridge, New York, Melbourne, Madrid, Cape Town, Singapore, São Paulo, Delhi

Cambridge University Press
32 Avenue of the Americas, New York, NY 10013-2473, USA

www.cambridge.org
Information on this title: www.cambridge.org/9780521860765

First published 2007

Printed in the United States of America

A catalog record for this publication is available from the British Library.

Library of Congress Cataloging in Publication Data

Swain, Hedley, 1961–
An introduction to museum archaeology / Hedley Swain.
     p. cm.
Includes bibliographical references and index.
ISBN-13: 978-0-521-86076-5 (hardback)
ISBN-13: 978-0-521-67796-7 (pbk.)
1. Archaeological museums and collections. 2. Archaeological muse-
ums and collections – Management. 3. Antiquities – Collection and
preservation. 4. Museum techniques. I. Title.
CC55.S93   2007
930.1074 – dc22   2006103440

ISBN   978-0-521-86076-5 hardback
ISBN   978-0-521-67796-7 paperback

For Bryony and Finlay

At the end of the lawn was a large summer or Moss House (the subject of many a poetic lay). The walls were constructed of sturdy limbs of trees ranged side by side, and covered on the outside with dry heather, while the inside was lined with moss. Shelves were fixed around formed of elm branches cut so as to leave the bark on the front edges; and on these appropriate supports were arranged the numerous urns and larger objects found in the barrows. On either side were smaller cells constructed on the same plan, but more open; in these were many of the larger fossils, notably a very fine slab of coal measures shale's with very beautiful remains of fossil plants. On the floor of the centre compartment was a plan of the temple of Avebury, formed of large pebbles to represent the stones and form the main circles. The two avenues branched off right and left leading to the smaller cells mentioned above. In the centre of one of these was a circle of the pebbles to represent the head of the serpent, according to Stukely and others.

(A description by his daughter Elizabeth of the display of William Cunnington's collections in his garden at Heytesbury, as quoted in Annable and Simpson 1964, p. 5.)

CONTENTS

List of Figures, Tables, and Illustrations

Figures

Tables

Illustrations

PREFACE

This book tries to capture the nature of museum archaeology (the discipline of archaeology as it affects museums) as it exists at the beginning of the twenty-first century. This is a huge and amorphous subject. It includes great museums, such as the Louvre and the British Museum, as well as small district museums. It deals with the conservation and ordering of excavation archives and the looting of cultural heritage. It deals with major political quandaries such as the fate of the Parthenon Marbles and prosaic practical problems such as how to write display captions. From this, the idea that emerges is that museum archaeology has a rather strange double existence. Two personalities inextricably linked by history and a shared vocabulary but otherwise largely distinct. One half is that of the classic archaeology of Carter and Schliemann with its Egyptian mummies and Greek vases displayed as decorative arts, denuded of context and brushing shoulders with a world both of classic scholars and also of private collectors and auction houses. The other half is that of the local archaeological contractors uncovering vast assemblages of mundane domestic pottery sherds and contributing to local authority museums. Such museums try to provide contextualised galleries replete with reconstructions and dioramas, content for national archaeology days, and for young archaeology clubs, to try and make archaeology relevant to modern communities.

The book is divided into four parts. Part 1 gives the background, history, and context for how museum archaeology currently operates. Part 2 deals with collections – the things dug up by the antiquarians, archaeologists, and looters. Part 3 looks at how these collections are communicated through museum galleries and programmes. Part 4 includes a list of every museum and gallery mentioned in the text.

The book tries to deal with the subject globally. If you look hard enough, you will probably find museum archaeology of one form or another in every town in the Western world and in every city in the world. However, inevitably, it is primarily a story of Britain, Europe, and North America because this is where the most museums, the most money, and the most museum archaeologists are located; and this is where the museum archaeological tradition developed. As such, the "West" is referred to often. It is a descriptor that is much used and abused but has relevance within the context of museum archaeology. It is used to describe a geographical location, a philosophical and cultural outlook, an economic grouping, and a state of mind.

However, in many of its examples, this book is unashamedly London-centric. I have spent most of my life living in London and a good proportion of it working for the Museum of London. Since its creation in 1976, the Museum has always had field archaeologists undertaking excavation in London; has always had permanent galleries drawing heavily on archaeological finds and methods; and has always had public and educational programmes, including temporary exhibitions, that make use of archaeological discoveries and knowledge. In the last 10 years, we at the Museum have grappled with many, although not all, of the issues facing museum archaeologists. The major exception is that despite London's multicultural, multiethnic nature, we have not dealt directly with Indigenous peoples. However, in 2005, I spent most of the year working on guidance for British museums dealing with human remains and claims for their return. Hopefully, this has given me an insight into this particular world.

Archaeology, particularly outside the United Kingdom, and for a whole series of historical, cultural, and practical reasons, blurs disconcertingly with other subjects, most notably history, ethnography, and fine and decorative arts. The same object might be categorised, curated, interpreted, and displayed under any one of these headings depending on its history and circumstances. This will be discussed further in later pages, but it also gives me the opportunity to be liberal with my examples and to follow where the discussion is allowed to lead me.

Throughout the world, a series of very loaded terms have developed historically to describe archaeological and historic periods. These include such terms as *Classical, Stone Age, Roman, Viking, Neolithic, First Nation*, and so forth. All of these terms are specific to particular times and places and, most importantly, to those who have invented them and use them. But they remain the only easy way we have of describing certain archaeological periods and cultures in a way that most will understand. For this reason, I have tended, throughout the book when describing sites, objects, galleries, and theories, to use the most commonly used descriptor. Occasionally, this will jar: what is the point of identifying how false the term *classical* is in one chapter, if I then use that very term to describe an archaeological gallery in the next? However, as they say, life is too short.

Museums are unreal, almost surreal creations. They have created a place for themselves in the world, where, through a slow process of self-authentification, they have come to be authenticated by wider society. Scratch the surface and it is easy to identify the weaknesses of that authenticity. One wonders if museums would be created if they did not exist. Similarly, archaeology, along with its near relative palaeontology, has a strange position amongst academic disciplines. A subject of complex, often tedious, scholarly research, it has also caught the widest public imagination. In popular culture, it has cross-fertilised, for better or worse, with treasure seeking, tomb raiding, and the supernatural. Nevertheless, there is something special about museums and about archaeology. I have a passion for both. I hope this book will make a contribution to their particular and shared mythologies.

Hedley Swain
Summer 2006

ACKNOWLEDGMENTS

I would like to thank Simon Whitmore who supported this project when at Cambridge University Press and Beatrice Rehl for seeing it through to completion. I am also grateful to Maggie Meitzler for her help in the editing process.

For inspiration over the years in things archaeological, museological, and museum archaeological, my deepest gratitude goes out to Peter Addyman, Duncan Brown, David Clarke, Moira Gemmill, Rachel Hunter, Nick Merriman, Janet Miller, Susan Pearce, Tim Schadla-Hall, Harvey Sheldon, and Simon Thurley.

A number of friends and colleagues have been extremely generous with their time and expertise in providing specific information for this book. Others have simply made comments in conversations (sometimes many years before the book was commissioned), or responded to my ideas in ways that have helped me think differently about the subject. I am very grateful to Dave Allen, Adrian Babbage, Nicola Burdon, Andy Calver, John Chase, Terry Childs, John Clark, Jon Cotton, Maurice Davies, Robin Densem, Torla Evans, Katherine Edgar, Hazel Forsyth, Brett Galt-Smith, Helen Ganiaris, Francis Grew, Jenny Hall, Mark Hall, Sophie Hall, Dave Heslop, Dan Hicks, Pete Hinton, John Jackson, Meriel Jeater, Andrew Jones, Penny Kalligerou, Jackie Keily, Suzanne Keane, Morag Kersel, Christine Kyriacou, Jane Lawrence, Henrietta Lidchi, Elena Lioubimova, Jack Lohman, Sally MacDonald, Carolyn MacLulich, Angelika Marks, Xerxes Mazda, Siorna McFarlane, Darryl McIntyre, Mary Miller, Judy Mills, Diana Murray, Tim Murray, Lisa O'Sullivan, Janet Owen, Deidre O'Sullivan, John Paddock, Deborah Padgett, Norman Palmer, Helen Persson, Laura Peers, Andrew Reid, Alan Saville, Garry Shelley, Margaret Serpico, John Shepherd, Faye Simpson, Robin Skeates,

Mike Smith, Sonia Solicari, Bob Sonderman, Kate Starling, Roy Stephenson, Bly Strube, Bryony Swain, Kathy Tubb, Claire Valerino, Blaise Vyner, Elizabeth Walker, Sarah Williams, Philip Wise, Barbara Wood, Rob Young, Konstantinos Zachos. And finally, my thanks go out to all colleagues, past and present, at the Museum of London.

ABBREVIATIONS

ADS   Archaeological Data Service
AHPA   Archaeological and Historic Preservation Act
             (USA)
AHDS   Arts and Humanities Data Service
AIA   Archaeological Institute of America (USA)
AMA   Associate of the Museums Association
APPAG   All-Party Parliamentary Archaeology Group
APVA   Association for the Preservation of Virginia
             Antiquities (USA)
ARC   Archaeological Resource Centre, York.
ARPA   Archaeological Resources Protection Act
             (USA)
BCRPM   British Committee for the Reunification of
             the Parthenon Marbles
BM   British Museum
CBA   Council for British Archaeology
CIA   Congress of Independent Archaeologists
DCMS   Department of Culture, Media, and Sport
DES   Department of Education and Skills
DIG   Detector Information Group
DoE   Department of the Environment
EH   English Heritage
ERA   Education Reform Act
GEM   Group of Educators in Museums
HEFCE   Higher Education Funding Council for
             England
HERs   Historic Environment Records
IAA   Israel Antiquities Authority (Israel)
ICOMOS   International Council on Monuments and
             Sites (International)

ICOM	International Council of Museums (International)
ICON	Institute of Conservation
IFA	Institute of Field Archaeologists
INAH	Instituo de Nacional Antropologia y Historia (Mexico)
LAARC	London Archaeological Archive and Research Centre
MA	Museums Association
MAP2	Management of Archaeological Projects, 1991 English Heritage publication.
MDA	Museums Documentation Association (now known as MDA)
MLA	Museums, Libraries, and Archives Council
MoRPHE	Management of Research Projects in the Historic Environment, 2005 English Heritage publication
NAGPRA	Native American Graves Protection and Repatriation Act (USA)
NMAI	National Museum of the American Indian (USA)
PACE	Palestinian Association for Cultural Exchange (Palestine)
PAS	Portable Antiquities Scheme
PPG16	Planning and Policy Guidance Note 16, Archaeology and Planning
RAO	Registered Archaeological Organisations
ROB	Rijksdienst voor het Oudheidkundig Bodemonderzoek (Netherlands)
RCAHMS	Royal Commission for Ancient and Historic Monuments Scotland
RCAHMW	Royal Commission for Ancient and Historic Monuments Wales
RPA	Register of Professional Archaeologists (USA)
SAA	Society of American Archaeology (USA)
SHA	Society of Historical Archaeology (USA)
SMA	Society of Museum Archaeologists
SCoPA	Standing Conference on Portable Antiquities

SMRs	Sites and Monuments Records
SOPA	Society of Professional Archaeologists (USA)
SSN	Subject Specialist Network
STOP	Stop Taking Our Past
UNESCO	United Nations Educational, Scientific, and Cultural Organisation (Int.)
UNESCO 1970	Convention on the Means of Prohibiting and Preventing the Illicit Import, Export, and Transfer of Ownership of Cultural Property (Int.)
UNIDROIT	Institute for the Unification of Private Law (Int.)
UNIDROIT 1995	Convention on Stolen and Illegally Exported Cultural Objects (Int.)
VTC	Virtual Teaching Collection
WEMACRU	West Midlands Archaeological Collections Research Unit
WHAM	Women, Heritage, and Museums
YAT	York Archaeological Trust

PART I

INTRODUCTION

*Today archaeology is in fashion. In the following pages we shall
seek to establish the reasons for the somewhat belated popularity of a
subject which was long regarded as tedious and even slightly absurd.*
Gilbert Charles-Picard (1972, p. 6)

*The massed weight of archaeological storage boxes demonstrate
daily the success of archaeological investigators in convincing
museum staff of their claims for institutional immortality.*
Susan Pearce (1997, p. 48)

CHAPTER 1
WHAT FOR WHOM?

What is archaeology, what are museums, and what is museum archaeology? What is their value and purpose within wider politics, society, and culture?

Introduction

Ask members of the public what it is they might see if they visited a museum and, along with paintings and dinosaur bones, most would say archaeology. They might not use that word. It might be to see treasure, or old things, or mummies, or old stone tools. Museums are, and have always been, associated with the objects unearthed as evidence of ancient civilizations and peoples. These objects are considered to be treasures: valuable, rare, and vulnerable.

Like the great world art galleries, the "great ancient civilization" museums, such as the British Museum, the Louvre, and the Metropolitan Museum of Art (to name the most obvious three), are global tourist sites whose identity is deeply rooted in the global psyche. They hold items that everyone has heard of: (The Elgin (or Parthenon). Marbles, the Rosetta Stone, the Venus De Milo, Winged Victory). These objects are considered treasures because they are from the ancient world, were made by somewhat mysterious ancient civilizations, and were dug up from the ground or recovered from the bottom of the sea by great adventurers from the past. But more than this, they are tangible evidence that "we" had a civilized past, and by displaying them and visiting them, "we" have a civilized present. Their power has grown *because* they are in great museums behind thick glass and are protected from thieves or even from being touched. They were once great symbols of power, and they have been transformed into symbols of power once more. These symbols somehow reflect power onto those who come to view them.

The great national and regional museums, almost all designed to look like classical temples, are a key component of the Western world-order that is based on a linear progression of civilization from the Middle and Near East of Egypt, Babylon and Assyria, through Greece and Rome the Middle Ages, and the Renaissance to the Enlightenment (and, as discussed in Chapter 2, archaeology has not only helped create this past but has couched its own mythology in this past). Other world cultures, however complex, sophisticated, or important in the story of humanity, have traditionally been seen as side shows to this grand narrative. And largely, this is, as it still is in museums, often literally with artefacts from other cultures occupying basements, annexes, or not present at all.

This is one facet of museum archaeology. There are others. Museums are also the place where many people initially, and most often, come into first-hand contact with real archaeology, the archaeology of stratigraphy and stone tools, and broken pots and skeletons. The irony of this is that archaeological study is all about context, association, and assemblage: what is found gets most of its value from where it is found and what it is found with. Yet, by studying and preserving archaeology for others, archaeologists remove these meanings. Objects are taken away from their sites and away from the things with which they were found. They are cleaned, conserved, given labels, and put in glass cases. Archaeologists are then irritated that visitors do not easily understand their "true meaning."

Finally, museums are where local pasts are explained. Local museums display local archaeology for local audiences. Community archaeology takes place, as do educational and public programmes. The past is "brought to life" by actors and craft demonstrations.

But much archaeology does not go on in museums, or is in any way closely linked to museums. Similarly, most of what museums do has absolutely nothing to do with archaeology. A model has emerged for archaeology (see Chapter 3), where money, resources, strategy, and direction has minimised the role of museums and the vision of archaeology that they might espouse. Similarly, it could be argued that in the early years of the twenty-first century, in seeking a socially inclusive, contemporary, and "relevant" role for museums, archaeology has been pushed to the periphery as a main museum subject: a complex dead subject about the long dead. Despite this, and possibly because of the challenges this poses, some incredibly innovative and considered museum archaeology is now taking place.

Archaeology will not go away now that it has been created. An interest in the past seems universal – how it is negotiated by different presents may change, but the raw material will maintain its fascination. Only time will tell whether museum archaeology is actually changing. In 1981, Barry Cunliffe wrote about regional museums that still offered "a slice through time," about blockbuster exhibitions that wowed visitors, possibly by offering "gold and gore," and about new "real-life simulations" that were "all good family fun" and were "catching a corner of the public imagination." He went on to muse on the contribution of TV and publishing to the public's experience of the past. Its patrician manner aside, is this much different to what a modern survey would find? New political dogma and new theory are changing things at some levels. Merriman (2000, p. 22) has argued for a new museum archaeology that acts as a "transaction" in which communities are much more actively involved both in the curation and exploration of the archaeological resource and in the discussion of its interpretation with professionals who see their role as enablers and educators in the widest sense.

Museums and archaeology are now global phenomena, as described in Chapter 5, although both originated practically and philosophically in Europe and "The West." Western Culture is still the dominant force in world museum archaeology, but museums and archaeology will now be found everywhere. Museums and archaeologists can be found in places even McDonalds has so far failed to penetrate. As such, this is also a subject that is bedevilled by the sheer range of its scope.

Archaeology, as described in this chapter and in Chapter 3, covers everything from the excavation of Tutankhamen's tomb to a survey of Cold War remains in the British countryside. A museum archaeology experience can be anything from a visit to the Louvre, to a demonstration of prehistoric basketry at a small local museum.

Definition of Museums

Museums have been a common part of modern Western life for more than 150 years and a common part of global life in the last 100 years. Every town has a museum, every city has several, and every major city has many, including very large and impressive ones that often act as a key communication node or focus. Like libraries, shops, and sporting arenas, they are so much part of the fabric of human geography that they are more-or-less taken for granted, whether they are used or not. The majority are publicly funded, a reflection of how they developed, but also of their role as keepers of a culture's collective and tangible past and as credentials of a peoples' civilized values.

A definition of museums is quite easy to find as the museum profession, itself, has found a need to provide one. The UK Museums Association (MA) defines museums as "institutions that collect, safeguard and make accessible artefacts and specimens, which they hold in trust for society" (agreed by the MA in 1998). Whereas, the International Council of Museums (ICOM) define museums as thus: "a non-profit making, permanent institution, in the service of society and its development, and open to the public, which acquires, conserves, researches, communicates and exhibits, for the purpose of study, education and enjoyment, material evidence of man and his environment" (ICOM 1996).

These definitions provide useful summaries. They also tell us what museum professionals think museums are not. Perhaps most importantly, if there is no collection, then there is no museum. Where the definition fails is by not recognising any sort of dynamic. Museums must surely be not just collections, although these are essential, but must also include

6

the people who manage and interpret these collections and a public who respond to this interpretation. This is a two-way dynamic. The collections are nothing unless the people who manage them are active in trying to understand them and interpret them for a public. Similarly, the public, whoever they are (See Chapter 11) must be active in receiving the interpretation of the collections and must also, through active involvement and criticism, influence not only the interpretations that are being created but also, at a very fundamental level, the collections that are being formed, and how they are being managed. So a museum should be a dynamic set of negotiations. Unfortunately, it too often remains a one-way process.

Just as museums can only exist with a public whose interaction justifies their existence, Susan Pearce (1997, p. 47) has observed that museums are a manifestation of their time and place, and, as such, need to redefine and reexplain themselves for each age. However, as Pearce also notes, museums have a certain gravitas that does manage to transcend passing trends. For her, museum authority is based on "the power to arbitrate upon material culture, to decide what is 'valuable' or 'interesting' and what is not." This goes to the heart of the place of objects within human culture and the way we place values on these objects. A society that did not think objects could have more than a purely functional role would have no place for museums as museums are currently perceived. Of course, public museums and museum collections are only one way that valued artefacts from the past have been and are dealt with. Egyptian mummies were once ground down as medicines, cathedral treasury exhibitions hold holy relics, and many artefacts are held in private collections and traded for profit.

Definition of Archaeology

Museums are perhaps more easy to define than archaeology, which is less tangible and seems to be expanding with time. Museums are things, entities. The term "archaeology" is often used as a general description for the ancient past, particularly prehistory and classical civilization, whether revealed through excavation and fieldwork or not. Archaeology is not a period in the past, however, vaguely defined, it is a methodology used to try and understand human behaviour in prehistory (the period before historic records), history, and for some, the present. For prehistory, it is arguably the only method. For the historic period, it is one method used alongside historic records, personal testimonies, photographs, and others. So, as I discuss in the next section, strictly speaking, there are very few, if any, archaeology museums or museum archaeology displays and exhibits. But there are many museums that tell prehistories and histories that use material recovered and understood using archaeological methods.

A definition of archaeology and what it encompasses is not as simple as it once was. The dictionary definition of archaeology (archaeologists themselves seem not to have worried too much about self definition) gives us "the excavation and subsequent study of the physical remains of earlier civilizations" (*Chambers 21st Century Dictionary*) or "study of human antiquities, especially of the prehistoric period and usually by excavation" (*Concise Oxford Dictionary*). These definitions rightly highlight the centrality of material culture – objects, things, to archaeology. They also both highlight the idea of the past. This seems straightforward, but some would argue that archaeological methods have a relevance to any period including the present. Nevertheless, it is the case that archaeology is of most relevance to prehistory because, for this period, archaeology is the only prime evidence. Using the emergence of anatomically modern humans this means that archaeology is the only evidence for about 200,000 years of a human past for which history can contribute about 5,000 years of evidence. Going back as far as the emergence of the hominid ancestors of modern people, archaeology contributes some 3,000,000 years of evidence. Yet, picking up any written "history of mankind" shows that it is only with the arrival of historical records that human history gets serious – most such books give the first 200,000 or 3,000,000 years an introductory chapter before getting down to the business of history.

The *Oxford Dictionary* definition also emphasises the importance of excavation, the prime method of the archaeologist. Excavation is at the actual and romantic heart of archaeology. Archaeologists dig in the ground to uncover evidence, and the finds that they piece together by making a painstaking logical analysis of what they find. That these uncovered finds are occasionally great treasures from the past gives archaeology its romantic allure. It also sets up the first tension in the relationship between the archaeologist and the museum. Museums are all about things and as such the finds of archaeologists are perfect for them. But archaeology and archaeological meaning is all about association and context. It is almost impossible for the museum not to take away this association and context and create new ones as part of the process of collection and display.

Most new definitions of archaeology move beyond a simple study of the past through excavation. Archaeology has become so much more than just digging. It involves the study of human landscapes and human material culture (artefacts) in all of their manifestations. It has developed many ways of studying, categorising, and thinking about the past. Many of these are borrowed from other disciplines but are often given a new perspective, and many overlap with other subjects. It has become purer, more theoretical: "the objective study of the material remains of the past in order to lead to a greater understanding of past human societies" (Merriman 2000, p. 20). Although Merriman dismisses this definition in favour of a postmodern model by accepting that rather than accumulating more and more truth, archaeology carries out an ongoing negotiation between past and present through the study of material culture. As with museums, any definition of archaeology should include a dynamic process. One that involves review within the profession but also one with the public for whom archaeology is undertaken. Again, for museums, this dynamic is often missing.

The study of material culture leads to observations about the past. But archaeology has always been more than this. It has always sought to understand what was happening in the past and how human society developed at different places and at different times. And, for this reason, throughout the history of archaeology, there has seen a central conflict at the heart of the discipline that is particularly relevant to museums, and their purpose to educate and entertain. Archaeology has built its reputation on delivering scientifically verifiable facts that help develop prehistories and histories about a past that can never be proven. As Gathercole and Lowenthal (1990, p. 3) stated, "There can be no archaeologically achieved final truths or wholly objective interpretations." Year-after-year, its methods become more complex and detailed, and it reveals more and more fascinating things about the past. But we all know that many of its biggest questions will never be answered definitively. Whatever archaeologists do, whatever new discoveries are made, no one will never know exactly what Stonehenge looked like in 2,500 B.C. or what the exact motivations were of those who built it.

This is relevant to museums that need to decide what they are going to tell their visitors. Should they communicate the past to the public as "tablets of stone" (James 1999, p. 128) or as an open question to the visitor? The less that is known about the past, the harder curators have to work, and, therefore, often the more imaginative they are in thinking about the past and how it can be interpreted and explained. So, for example, thought on prehistory has often led archaeological theory and display practice. But again, how should intepretations of the past be communicated to the public? Most archaeologists would agree that their discipline is about the study and understanding of people. As such, the obvious way for museum archaeologists to connect with their audiences is by telling personal stories. But is it possible to empathise with someone living 5,000 years ago? Were the people in the past "just like us," or "other," or were they both similar and different? And how is this communicated to a public through museums? One of the things that makes museum archaeology so challenging and thrilling is that it forces archaeologists to confront the limitations of their evidence.

Archaeology, as a discipline, also overlaps uncomfortably with other disciplines, and this blurring is often emphasised in museum displays and categorisation, and through the language used. "Classical" archaeology often strays into the world of decorative and fine arts and also ancient and classical history. The archaeology of the nonclassical, non-European world is often blurred with ethnography and anthropology. Local archaeologies blur with local and social histories. This blurring is often confused further by different uses of these terms in different places. In North America, *anthropology* and *archaeology* are often more-or-less the same thing, archaeology objects turn up in ethnography displays and vice versa, and no need is felt to distinguish between the two. Cultural or social anthropology has an incredibly powerful, but often unspoken, influence on archaeological interpretations. All of these terms in their normal lazy use also perpetuate colonial, racist, and Eurocentric value sets.

Finally, and despite all of the above, archaeology has the ability to do three things: (1), reveal things about the past, and possibly the present that were not previously known; (2) to help to understand the world better through the study of these things; and, finally, (3) through its physicality and methodology to make people think differently about the world around them, and to interact with it. It is often the failing of archaeologists and museum archaeologists that they too often mistake the first for the second and often ignore the power of the third altogether.

Definition of Museum Archaeology

So, museums are institutions that collect material culture, manage it, and interpret it for a public. Hopefully, this takes place in a dynamic fashion where the public has an influence on what is collected and how it is interpreted. Archaeology is the study of past, and occasionally present, human cultures through its material culture and the use of the material culture to create new prehistory and history. Again, this should also include, but often does not, a dynamic link to a public who influence what is studied and how, and the interpretations that are put on it. The common link is the material culture, the interpretations, and the public. Museums take the things that archaeologists dig up, keep them and put them on display, and interpret them for a public. This also should be a dynamic process (between the archaeologist and the museum) but is too often a linear one. Too often, the museums act as a repository for archaeological material once the archaeologists have finished with it, and museums accept this role passively.

A traditional interpretation often pictures archaeologists providing new antiquities for museums on a supply and demand basis, where museums hungry for new acquisitions to study, and to tempt visitors, send archaeologists out into the world to collect for them (as immortalised in the Indiana Jones movies) and show the great museums competing for the best objects. Although such a situation was known in the nineteenth and early twentieth century, and is perhaps not completely unknown now, museums have always been, and continue to be, a relatively peripheral player in archaeological motivation. In the late twentieth and early twenty-first century, where so much archaeology has been undertaken by private contracting firms as part of the development process, or as part of university research, museums often have hardly any involvement at all except as a final repository for the finds. Over time, there has been a trend towards a greater separation between the archaeological "makers," the diggers, and the "carers," the museum curators (Sullivan and Childs 2003, p. 5). The universities might be added as the "thinkers."

The nature of archaeology has also given the public a largely peripheral and passive role. Most archaeology is done by and for archaeologists, or as part of a development process where the archaeologist is saving the archaeology from destruction. The public have no real place in this process other than providing some form of passive background support and acting as the passive receivers of bestowed wisdom or entertainment. One of the challenges of museum archaeology in the twenty-first century is to build an equitable relationship between the two worlds of archaeology and museums, and between the worlds of museum archaeology and public. Merriman has stated, "As museum archaeologists, we are uniquely concerned with the interface between the discipline of archaeology and the public through one of its main public manifestations, the museum" (Merriman 2000, p. 20).

For Whom?

Why is archaeology undertaken? Why do museums exist? If they did not exist, would they be invented? The sheer fact that archaeology exists as a academic discipline, profession, and hobby across much of the world; that museums with archaeology galleries and public programmes exist; and that there is a healthy trade in archaeological books and magazines and a regular flow of TV programmes would suggest that there is a demand for it amongst people. Archaeology and museums also have a firm founding in popular culture in different forms. But is this enough?

Museums and archaeology would seem to be a manifestation of humans' natural curiosity about the world around them and their place in it, and a desire to collect and classify the physical evidence for that world. Detailed studies have been undertaken of both these phenomena (e.g., Daniel 1978; Pearce 1995). But neither archaeology nor museum collecting are common to all people and all times. Superficially, both would appear to be more prevalent in materially "richer" societies and in what is termed the "affluent West." This would presuppose that both are relative "luxuries." This is not to downgrade either, but although it would be nice to believe that wishing to have an understanding of the past and putting a value on collective memory through material culture are universal and basic needs, observation would suggest otherwise. They only become important when they can be afforded. It would also appear that they are associated with a particular philosophical mindset (see Chapter 2).

It can also be observed that although archaeology would appear to be a popular subject with, at a relatively superficial level, a large public, this interest in the past is not universal in terms of places and periods and cultures (Merriman 1999, p. 3). For example, in British museums there persists a somewhat bizarre fascination with the ancient Egyptians and Romans out of all proportion to these cultures' relative importance to world history (no doubt natural historians take a similar despairing tone on the subject of dinosaurs). This would suggest, rather obviously, that interest in archaeology is largely a cultural construct.

The limited number of public surveys undertaken, itself an indictment of museum complacency, show that, perhaps unexpectedly, most of the public have a low level of understanding of archaeology and the periods archaeology covers. Surveys by the Museum of London for their 1994 prehistory gallery *People before London* (Cotton 1997) showed that when asked what the word "prehistory" meant to them, in a survey of 1,836 visitors, 28 percent cited dinosaurs (perhaps very reasonably as dinosaurs are indeed prehistoric), 9.6 percent cited cavemen, 5.7 percent gave "before written history," and 4.5 percent gave "very old" (Wood and Cotton 1999, p. 43). In all, forty-eight different responses were given, the majority by only a few individuals. A smaller survey at the Alexander Keiller Museum, Avebury, gave similar responses (Wood and Cotton 1999, p. 36). Surveys for the new *Medieval London* gallery at the Museum of London to garner what the public knew and felt about the period after the Romans revealed a similarly vague range of responses (Swain 2005a).

Chapter 11 explores the nature of the "public" or audiences for museum archaeology in all of its manifestations. It is enough here to state that although it is probably a justified aim to hope that museum archaeology should be for all, in fact, it has very specific audiences with specific expectations.

A Wider Relevance?

It has been popular to give archaeology and museums, particularly within the wider "heritage debate," a political dimension. This can perhaps be overstated. Archaeologists are fond of reminding the world of the weight of responsibility on their shoulders for effecting political change and avoiding the political abuse of their power. The use of archaeology and its representation in museums by the Nazi's are well-rehearsed (see McCann 1990, pp. 81–86 for a general background). However, is there any aspect of German culture in the 1930s and 1940s that was not abused in some way by the Nazis? On the whole, museums and archaeology reflect and are influenced by political activity rather than setting any particular agendas of their own. But that is not to say that they have no political part to play.

Museum archaeology displays have been used for explicitly political purposes. A much-referenced example is the *Celts, the Origins of Europe* exhibition held at the Palazzo Grassi, Venice, in 1991 (Kruta et al. 1991), which was used as an attempt to bind the European Union together with common cultural roots as it went through a renewed bout of growing pains. Museums have also been used in Israel to strengthen links between the West Bank and its new Israeli settlers (Skeates 2005, p. 310). A similar approach was taken in Gibraltar where, until recently, there was no mention in the museum of its Spanish history (Claire Valerino, personal communication), and on Chatham Island in the Pacific where local Moriori display makes no mention of the period of Maori dominance (Vanessa Bunton, personal communication). These are relatively clumsy and obvious examples. The wider debates about the role of Western museums and archaeologists in the empowerment of Indigenous peoples and the looting of archaeological sites are a more complex issue (e.g., Ucko 1987 in relation to the World Archaeological Congress and Apartheid). UNESCO (1970) and others claim that all humanity has contributed to a shared past and, as such, all share a common heritage. This might sound very noble, but has everyone been asked as to whether they want to share this particular past? Many have had their past shared whether they like it or not.

More recently, a political dimension for museums and archaeology has been seen within the "West against the rest" debate. If museums and archaeology are products of, and thrive best in, the Western world, are they appropriate to non-Western societies? Particularly because the colonial and imperialist pasts from which they derived are still so recent? Do they have too many associations with a particular worldview? Do they work against the role of objects in many cultures and societies? They are a physical realisation of the dualism of the West, where beliefs, meanings, and even ethics can be separated from day-to-day life. See, for example, Ucko (1994, pp. 260–262) for how museums and museum ideas have struggled against Indigenous cultural values in Africa, particularly Zimbabwe.

The destruction of historic Bucharest by Ceausescu (Done 1997), the destruction of the Buddha's of Bamiyan in Afghanistan by the Taliban, and the loss of heritage in Palestine and Africa through looting are reminders that the position in the West where history and heritage is revered, is protected, and is primarily about presenting a product to consumers is not universal. Beyond the safe West, heritage still, perhaps, has a more urgent meaning and value. Indeed, perhaps Western heritage needs to be threatened a little more often to retain its value.

The concept of values is also important here. To want to undertake archaeology, to build museums, and to visit museums in order to see archaeology presupposes that society has put some set of values onto the past, understanding it and wishing to interact with it (however passively). Stanley Price (1990, pp. 285–286) summarises a set of values derived from site preservation, conservation, and display:

Aesthetic/artistic values: things as having aesthetic appeal.
Economic/utilitarian values: the past as having an ability to raise money.
Associative/symbolic values: the past's ability to symbolise political meaning.
Historic/informational values: the past's ability to teach us new things.

All of these values, which might at different times and in different circumstances be seen as beneficial or sinister, combine in confusing computations within the world of museum archaeology.

Museums and archaeology are products of a particular history and a particular present. They create, and arbitrate over, values and, perhaps most powerfully, over the value of past objects. As such, archaeologists and curators have a responsibility to ply their trade within an ethical context.

Key Texts

Gathercole, P., and Lowenthal, D. (Eds.). (1990). *The politics of the past.* London: Unwin.

Merriman, N. (1999). (Ed.). *Making early histories in museums.* Leicester: Leicester University Press.

Renfrew, C., and Bahn, P. (1991). *Archaeology, theory, methods, and practice,* London: Thames and Hudson.

Skeates, R. (2000). *Debating the archaeological heritage.* London: Duckworth.

CHAPTER 2
MUSEUM ARCHAEOLOGY, ORIGINS

How museums and archaeology, and the ideas associated with them, developed and how, historically, they have related to each other.

Introduction

All subjects have their origin myths, and these are normally comfortable and legitimising. Archaeology and museums are no different. In recent years, these myths have begun to be questioned within the wider postmodern reanalysis of ortho-doxy. A new consensus on how the two disciplines developed and arrived in their present form is yet to fully emerge. This chapter is therefore built on the familiar myths, but it also identifies some of the parts of the story that have begun to be reassessed and questioned.

The story that emerges is overwhelmingly of Britain, Europe, and the United States. When writing about the West, it is dif-ficult not to promulgate the view that the world is centred on the West. However, both modern archaeology and museums do come firmly out of the Western tradition (Scarre 1990, pp. 12–13), and, inevitably, this has a profound effect on how these disciplines are currently placed in the world (see Lewis 1992 for a traditional history of museums).

Pre-Renaissance

Both archaeology and museums are traditionally seen as being borne out of the Renaissance and Enlightenment (e.g., Scarre

1990, Daniel 1978; and Evans 1981). Although there is some reference to collections of "antiquities" before this time in the early civilizations of the Near and Middle East and Mediterranean, there is no evidence that they are considered as anything other than souvenirs, heirlooms, and possibly as bestowers of cultural or sacred capital. There is some evidence of trying to understand the past through references to antiquities in China as long as 2,000 years ago (see Evans 1981 for a discussion) but elsewhere it might be considered strange that the antiquities and monuments that surrounded so many cultures were not used to enquire about the past and its nature. It has been suggested that this was a reflection of the pre-Enlightenment mindset (see the next section).

However, there is plenty of evidence of pre-Enlightenment and pre-Renaissance cultures recognising the symbolic and political value of objects, made manifest in the way certain objects, dress, and architectural styles become highly symbolic as part of the process of conquering or dominating foreign powers. This can be seen, for example, in the way the Romans adopted Greek style. This cult of the object can be seen in another form with the importance of Christian relics in medieval Europe. So, Western culture was familiar with the notion of the valuable object, sometimes from the past, holding cultural power and value well before the Renaissance. This may not have been museum archaeology, but it can be found lurking in that disciplines later manifestations.

Renaissance and Enlightenment

During the European Renaissance, for the first time, conspicuous personal and communal wealth was displayed through the commissioning, collection, and display of works of art (e.g., Jardine 1996). This was combined with a reverence for the past, in the particular form of ancient Greece and Rome that led to an interest in seeking out the antique.

It was during this period, with the idea of the *Studiolos* and cabinet of curiosities that make up the multiple function of the museum collection, that has been developed ever since, arrived. These were not just collections, but these were collections for study and learning. An element of display, or show, was also involved. And, in turn, this show was given both an entertainment value and an educational value. These different facets are now taken for granted, but they are not necessarily always compatible and lead to many of the contradictions and difficulties that modern museums find themselves in: Can they preserve and display? Can they entertain and educate? Another observation from this period is how the accumulation of collections of antiquities and curios was driven by the desire to be seen to be refined and part of an *intelligentsia*, whereas the main entry qualification was wealth and power.

The concepts that give the world both the modern museum and the discipline of archaeology, as opposed to antiquarianism, would appear to originate in the early eighteenth century with the ideas associated with the Enlightenment. Pearce (1999, p. 12) has suggested that the idea of archaeology emerged along with scientific rationalism out of recognising the value of material evidence, and reasonable deduction and the use of these to construct narratives of time and space and difference "which had a bearing on the notion of the essential self whose existence could be fixed within the intersecting configurations they constructed." The birth of the public museum can be dated to the same period as "an institution . . . featuring the rational individual with his assured place in the scheme of things, rendered intelligible by language referring to apparently external material evidence for its verification" (Pearce 1999, p. 13; see also Impey and MacGregor 1985 and Arnold 2006 for a discussion of the types of early collections and their influence on later museums). This model would appear to see museums as a form of comfort blanket rather than museums as actually contributing to the furtherance of knowledge.

Biblical orthodoxy that stated the whole realm of nature had been designed in perfection, and, famously, according to Archbishop Ussher (in 1650), had been created in 4004 B.C., provided one block to seeking a more complex and ancient past. But lack of philosophical horizons may have been a greater block. It has also been suggested (Evans 1981) that it was only concepts born in the European Enlightenment in the work of such as Kant, Descartes, Newton, and Buffon, and the nineteenth-century scientific breakthroughs that followed, that allowed people for the first time to conceive of a distant past, and a narrative of long-term history that could be navigated through material culture, and thus lay the foundations for true archaeological thought. In other words, for the first time there was a curiosity about a past that could be discovered and constructed, and this could be done by observing the remnants of the past that survived into the present.

The recently installed gallery, *Enlightenment: Discovering the World in the 18th Century*, at the British Museum sends a clear message: the British Museum is the child of Enlightenment values, and these are values that can be appreciated by all humankind, have given us the way we think, are valuable, and are not open to criticism. In a recent discussion paper on the future of museums by the British government (DCMS 2005a), the Minister for Culture Tessa Jowell states that museums "tell the story of this nation, its people and the whole of humanity . . . through . . . teaching, education and scholarship available to all: the values of the Enlightenment kept alive for each generation" (DCMS 2005a, p. 3). By laying claim to the Enlightenment for its inspiration the British Museum, and assumedly the British Government, is also stating that our museums are not based on, for example, Colonialism, Imperialism or Western elitism?

The introduction of the concept of educating a wider public through museums, and the need to make the displays accessible and even entertaining can also be dated to the Enlightenment period of the late eighteenth century and it has been argued was driven by individuals such as Charles Wilson Peale in North America (Moser 1999, p. 96) whose museum in Philadelphia opened in 1772. Amongst other methods, Peale included dioramas and painted backgrounds for his displays including that of an excavated Mastodon. Waterhouse Watkins's displays of concrete dinosaurs "in their habitat" at Crystal Palace can be seen as an evolution from Peale's dioramas, and, in the later nineteenth century, whole ecosystems were reconstructed as museum dioramas (Moser 1999). This method has been reborn recently in the powerful Ice Age ecosystem diorama at the National Museum of Scotland. It is still the key component of most natural history museums and a feature of many archaeology museums. Such displays both reconstruct the context that has been lost by removing objects from their find spots, and provide a method by which the complexity of archaeological interpretation can be made simple and attractive for the lay audience.

Alongside the establishment history of museums as a pure-born child of Renaissance and Enlightenment values must be set a slightly more murky set of relatives. Pearce notes that any creation of the Enlightenment should have a Gothic and a Romantic element and both of these can be found in the subject and methods of display within museums but also in other types of institution. Parallel to the growth of museums in the eighteenth and nineteenth century was such phenomena as freak shows and a tradition for illusions and reconstructions, particularly waxworks (e.g., Jordonova 1989), and also the great international exhibitions (e.g., Greenhalgh 1989) that operated to a voyeuristic, populist, and profit-orientated agenda. This almost certainly had an effect on the thinking of museum managers and curators and arguably does today through such institutions as The London Dungeon, Madame Tussauds, and the recently staged *Body Worlds* exhibition. Such shows are openly derided by establishment museum figures, but the exact dividing line between these shows, and their motives, and museum exhibitions are difficult to define.

The very first British museums to display archaeology, or at least archaeological objects, date to this period and all remain of importance: the Ashmolean Museum, Oxford, in 1683, the British Museum in 1759, and the Society of Antiquaries of Scotland (now the National Museum of Scotland) in 1780. All of these museums initially displayed classical antiquities rather than native finds.

Although museum collections, and the tentative moves towards their later function, where being developed, archaeology was also being born. This period is normally associated with the "antiquarians" (see Sweet 2004 for a discussion of British eighteenth-century antiquarians), although a clear definition of the difference between *archaeologists* and *antiquarians*, as might be expected, normally breaks down on detailed analysis. However, borne out of the new upper-middle classes, and the Enlightenment wish to observe the world, came a series of individuals who begun both to record the ancient monuments that littered the countryside and also to collect the objects that were occasionally released from them. This led in turn to the first "excavations" of monuments, such as barrows, and the accumulation of the first sizable collections of objects.

Throughout this period there remained a clear distinction between material from the classical world, Greece and Rome, that could be referenced in terms of the classical authors, and native material that remained meaningless and "barbaric." The period sees the beginnings of cataloguing and display methods were dominated by series and type that would dominate later museum displays, although there are occasional exceptions. In the early nineteenth century, William Cunnington displayed his collection of antiquities and grave goods from Wessex barrows in a small hut in his garden, and a description of it is worth repeating. "At the end of the lawn was a large Summer or Moss House.... Shelves were fixed around formed of elm branches cut so as to leave the bark on the front edges; and on these appropriate supports were arranged the numerous urns and larger objects found in the barrows.... On the floor of the centre compartment was a plan of the temple of Avebury, formed of large pebbles to represent the stones and form the main circles" (quoted in Annable and Simpson 1964, p. 5, the passage is given more fully as the frontispiece). Collections, such as Cunnington's, of course, were later to found the basis of key museum collections.

Nineteenth Century

Artefacts that had been kept as mere curiosities in the Renaissance were transformed into collections that could be studied to throw light on the past during the Enlightenment. In the nineteenth century, these collections were transformed again into typological series and housed in new public institutions that reflected local regional and then national pride (e.g., Skeates 2005, pp. 305–306 for Mediterranean countries).

By the late nineteenth century, national museums of antiquities had been created in France (the Musée des Antiquités Nationales de Saint Germain en Laye, Paris), Spain, and Italy (Skeates 2005, p. 305). Collections also took on the role of public educators, a role they have clung on to ever since.

While Western nation states were using archaeology and museums to help develop national identity, as colonial powers they were also beginning a great diaspora (Skeates 2005, p. 307) of antiquities from particularly the Mediterranean and Near and Middle East to European and U.S. museums. Roots were also laid for later national museums and for archaeological services in imperial colonies.

The late nineteenth and early twentieth centuries saw the major excavations by Americans and Europeans of the Classical and Mediterranean and Near and Middle East that were to shape the standard image of the birth and growth of civilization and were also to lay the foundations for the great Western museum collections and the model for collecting and displaying material from these cultures as decorative arts. These were often multinational projects in terms of funding and were tied up with colonial, imperialist and free-market sensibilities. The excavations at Ur by Leonard Woolley in the 1920s were undertaken by the British but funded from America. As a result, the subsequent artefacts are divided between the British Museum, the University of Pennsylvania Museum of Archaeology and Anthropology in Philadelphia, and the National Museum of Iraq in Baghdad.

By modern standards, the anarchic nature of this process is perhaps best exemplified by General Luigi Palma di Cesnola. As the U.S. Consul in Cyprus, he plundered that island of its antiquities and developed the concept of a pre-Hellenic Civilization. He then sold these finds to the highest bidder, the naisant Metropolitan Museum of Art in New York. Di Cesnola was then charged to conserve the finds and, eventually, ended up as the Museum's first director (Skeates 2005, p. 307). It was Cesnola and his contemporaries Schiemann and Evans, and those who came after, such as Petrie, Carter, Layard, Woolley, and Mallowen, who created many of the parameters of Classical archaeology that still exist. These remain the heroes of the archaeological creation myth. Evans excavated at Knossos, Crete, from 1900 until World War II, uncovering and controversially reconstructing what he found (see also Chapter 13). Schlieman was at "Troy" and then Mycanae between 1874 and 1876, famously looking into the face of Agamemnon and displaying his wife in Trojan treasure found in 1873. Layard excavated at Nimrud between 1845 and 1847, and from the 1890s Petrie was in Egypt and then Palestine. Most famously of all, Howard Carter was in the Valley of the Kings, which culminated in the discovery of Tutankhamen's tomb in 1923. These figures still dominate the archaeology of popular culture and, for many, what it is to be an archaeologist. Their collections, so the myths go, were obtained in blistering heat by gangs of pliant native labourers and under the noses of rivals and incompetent local bureaucrats for the greater good of humanity and to be kept as treasures in great museums. The American addition to the myth is temples lost in jungles, and cities forgotten on mountain tops. The most famous example of this was the rediscovery, in 1911, of the Inca city of Machu Picchu high in the Peruvian Andes by Hiram Bingham, an explorer, an academic, and, later, a politician.

These archaeologists were digging in the Near and Middle East because they had inherited a belief in the importance of these areas as the cradles of civilization from both the Biblical and the Greek traditions. Their heroic excavations reinforced this importance and their finds stocked Western museums and created the "classic" archaeology collections that are still with us today. They are only the most famous of a huge number of Western archaeologists, collectors, adventurers, looters, and colonial civil servants who stocked Western museums with the material culture of the ancient Near and Middle East and Mediterranean. Those collections remain and perpetuate the story of this areas' preeminence in human development and as the birthplace of Western civilization.

This period also saw the great diaspora of material from Egypt. This was fuelled by an academic obsession with ancient Egypt that spread into mainstream culture across Europe and North America and was set alight by Carter's discoveries in the Valley of the Kings. Collecting strategies did not help. For example, Petrie funded his work based on investment from regional museums and organisations on the understanding that they would then receive objects from his excavations. It has been estimated (Margaret Serpico, personal communication) that about 200 museums in the United Kingdom have Egyptian collections of some kind originating from about the same number of excavations. The twenty-first-century museum curator and archaeologist must live beside these different origin myths in the knowledge of their false origin, but be mindful of their popular power.

In terms of archaeological methodologies, the nineteenth century started with the antiquarian digs of the likes of Cunnington and Buckland and finished with Pitt Rivers and his excavations at Crambourne Chase and their publication (Daniel 1978; Pearce 1990). Several midcentury breakthroughs furthered the process begun with the Enlightenment of freeing archaeologists to use physical evidence to explore the antiquity of humanity. Prior to Darwin, Lyell, and the Three Age system, the development of archaeology had been impossible because it lacked any chronological framework except for those Mediterranean civilizations and the later periods covered by historic records. It is very difficult even with hindsight to grasp this barrier. People are now familiar with a prehistory that takes anatomically modern people back about 200,000 years and hominids back about 3,000,000 years. Before the nineteenth-century breakthroughs, both conceptual and practical, for example, in Britain all prehistory was compressed into a "before the Romans" period with elsewhere the only chronologies available coming from the Bible and classical histories. From the mid-nineteenth century onwards, real chronologies could be built and with them an attempt could be made to make sense of the deep past.

The work of Charles Darwin gave us *deep time* and a concept of the evolution of humanity. This model made sense of nature but also offered powerful European men, through the concept of natural selection and survival of the fittest, a justification for the world they were building through empire. Charles Lyall and the geologists developed the ideas of deep time through the study of rocks and also gave archaeologists the concept of stratification and association, two concepts that remain foundations of archaeological thought. Finally, the Scandinavian museum curators led by Christian Thomsen and Jacob Worsaae created the Three Age system that still dominates prehistoric archaeology today. Freed of the Roman occupation that allowed most Europeans to at least classify material into a pre-Roman, Roman and post-Roman periods, the Danes needed to interrogate their material in more detail for meaning. Thomsen observed that there appeared to be a basic chronological separation between the bladed objects of stone, bronze, and iron that could then be extended by association to other objects. This scheme was applied to the displays of the National Museum of Denmark in Copenhagen between 1807 and 1837 and published in the catalogue to the collections in 1836. Translations of the catalogue into English and Worsaae's *The Primeval Antiquities of Denmark* came in 1849.

The last breakthrough in archaeology that was made in the nineteenth century was that of disciplined recorded excavation. The figure most associated with this is Augustus Henry Pitt Rivers (Thompson 1977). His detailed excavations at Cramborne Chase resulted in the, now almost mythical, seven volumes of excavation reports. The importance of Pitt Rivers's work was to recognise the importance of the stratified record and how this becomes a collection, or archive, in its own right as important as any artefacts.

Pitt Rivers is also a key figure in the development of museum displays, collections, and theories about the place of material culture in understanding human societies. He developed ideas concerning the way objects "evolve," thus supporting the concept of typology. And these methods were used to display his collections of social history, archaeology, and ethnography. Those collections survive and in the case of the collections at the Pitt Rivers Museum in Oxford are still displayed to his original plan, thematically by culture rather than chronologically.

The Three Age system and the Pitt Rivers's displays, and their application to museum archaeology, continue to be a huge influence. It could be suggested that display of material by typology and series, or by themed function, remains the primary legacy of archaeology to display technique. Almost all archaeology galleries tend to negotiate with, and around, this kind of approach. An update of the typological display can be found in the "River Wall" display at the *London before London* gallery at the Museum of London or the gun display at the National Museum of the American Indian (The Pitt Rivers Museum also includes a typology of firearms). The thematic approach is seen at the *Early Peoples* gallery at the National Museum of Scotland (see also Chapters 12 and 13).

If waxworks and freak shows were the uncomfortable twins of museums in the Enlightenment era, in the later nineteenth and early twentieth century, it would have been the great international shows and exhibitions, seen at their most grand in France but also an important part of the scenery of London and American cities (Greenhalgh 1989). Their influence on museums was sometimes direct, as in the foundation of the Victoria & Albert Museum but was also present at a philosophical level in helping frame the debate between education and entertainment, and high art against popular art, both also seen in terms of social class. These are all very Victorian British concepts, indeed it has been argued that the *Great Exhibition of 1851* was the point at which Britain embraced the concept of educating the masses (Cunliffe 1981, p. 192).

The nineteenth century saw the founding of most major British local authority museums, many prompted by the 1845 Museum Act that gave authorities with large populations the power to use rates to found and run museums. The early nineteenth century had also seen the founding of philosophical societies that took an interest in archaeology, and these developed, in the later nineteenth century, into archaeological societies, often county based. These county societies remain an important if sometimes fringe part of the museum archaeological community today. Many of them own important archaeological collections and sometimes (as, for example, in Sussex and Wiltshire) play a part in running museums. The county societies also continue to play an important role in publishing archaeological reports (see also Chapter 11).

In the United States in 1873, Otis Mason used Lewis Henry Morgan's version of the Three Age system: Savagery,

Barbarism, and Civilization to organise the Smithsonian collections (Sullivan and Childs 2003, pp. 5–6). In the United States, native archaeology and anthropology collections became part of natural history collections and displays rather than part of cultural history collections, reflecting white elitism in relation to native peoples. The United States did not follow the European model of national and local authority museums, although interestingly a public service and educational role for museums was present from the beginning and was seen to be more important than the research function that dominated European museums.

In the United States during the late nineteenth and early twentieth centuries, the most influential archaeological institutions were the Smithsonian Institution (Englishman James Smithson had left funds in his will of 1826 to allow Congress to create a U.S. institution for the furtherance of knowledge); the American Museum of Natural History in New York; the Peabody Museum of Archaeology and Ethnology at Harvard; and the Museum of the American Indian (or Heye Foundation) also in New York (Sullivan and Childs 2003, p. 7; see also Jameson 2004 for a general summary of the development of U.S. archaeology).

Elsewhere in the world, if they existed at all, archaeology and museums tended to be imposed from above by imperial powers. For example, Indian museums originated in the early 1900s but most came later in that century to hold antiquities owned by national and state government. There were 12 museums by 1857, this had risen to 100 by 1937 and 360 by the 1990s, still a very small number considering the nations huge population (Momin and Pratrap 1994, p. 291). Digs generated large amounts of archaeological material in the early twentieth century. A call for a national museum would come on independence.

The late nineteenth century also saw the first legislation to protect archaeological sites. In Britain, this was the 1882 Ancient Monuments Protection Act. The year 1906 saw the first Federal archaeological law: the Antiquities Act that included wording about the need for the proper curation of finds (see Sullivan and Childs 2003, p. 9 and Chapter 4).

Early Twentieth Century

The first half of the twentieth century, in many ways, saw the continuation of trends identified for the nineteenth century but with the backdrop of the two World Wars and the European totalitarian regimes. The mid-twentieth century saw the use of archaeology and museums by the fascist states in Europe for propaganda and to develop their particular ideas of nationalism. The use of archaeological research by Hitler to both provide a distorted picture of German origins and to seek further evidence of Arian roots is well-recorded (see McCann 1990, pp. 81–86 and Skeates 2000, pp. 92–93 for a general background of Nazi use of archaeology, including the misuse of evidence to promote an image of German superiority), but archaeology and archaeological finds were also used by Franco and Mussolini (Skeates 2005, pp. 305–306).

Another major influence, and a more lasting one from this period, was the adoption by several avante-garde artists of traditional Indigenous art. This gave a new meaning to this material that has affected they way it is still displayed and considered in museums. Indigenous material went directly from being seen as evidence of primitiveness to high art without properly being articulated as evidence for social behaviour in-between. Thus, much ethnographic material sits uncomfortably between archaeology and art. For example, on a visit to many art galleries based on private collections, or previously private collections, such as the Burrell in Glasgow or the Sainsbury Centre for Visual Arts in Norwich, one will find ethnographic and archaeological objects displayed amongst, and as, fine art. At its best, this approach leads to traditional art being contemplated in new and exciting ways, as at the *Living and Dying* exhibition at the British Museum. This debate has taken on a new lease of life with the opening in Paris of the Musée du quai Branley that showcases "tribal art" and has led to accusations of French cultural elitism.

The early twentieth century also saw the first major museum exhibit on human evolution at the American Museum of Natural History. The first life-size reconstruction groups of "stone Age" people was also constructed in America shortly afterwards in Chicago (Moser 1999, p. 103) The early years of the twentieth century in North America saw greater interest in Native Indian origins and the linking of anthropology and archaeology. Theories on Indian origins were developed and tested through excavation. However, university anthropology departments undertook the majority of fieldwork, while museums were primarily concerned with public programmes.

Late Twentieth Century

The period after the end of World War II saw the end of traditional Colonialism and Imperialism and the aftershocks of this are still shaping the relationship between museums, archaeologists and anthropologists and the peoples of excolonial states. The War itself left the legacy of looted works of art spread across Europe that in some cases are only now being identified. For archaeology the period saw the arrival of scientific dating techniques, most notably carbon 14 dating. Theoretically it saw the "new archaeology" of structuralism or processualism championed by the likes of Lewis Binford and David Clarke whose book *Analytical Archaeology* (1971) argued that within a wider modernist philosophy, the collection and objective analysis of data could be used to make sense of the world. The early 1980s saw the arrival of postprocessualism or postmodernism to archaeology, with a parallel influence on museum theory with champions such as Ian Hodder (see Chapter 3). More prosaically, it has seen the arrival of market forces and commercialism to archaeological practice in North America and Europe with the subsequent professionalisation of the discipline. Museums have become players in the global political scene with calls for repatriation. They have also become part of the market place with blockbuster exhibitions and the need to find new even larger audiences.

A defining moment came for museum archaeology in the early 1970s. Slowly archaeologists became aware of the great destruction of archaeological sites and landscapes through redevelopment. In the United Kingdom, a campaign was launched, spearheaded, and now named after, RESCUE, The

British Archaeological Trust (see Rahtz 1974 and Mytum and Waugh 1987 for a history of RESCUE and its development into the 1980s). The net result was the birth of archaeology as a full profession and the huge growth in the number of archaeologists employed to undertake excavations in advance of redevelopment: to rescue the past from the bulldozers. But from the beginning, these new professionals and the organisations that employed them were not linked to museums and a split took place whereby museums and museum archaeologists became uncoupled from the archaeological decision-making process and from the generation of the finds and records that they would be expected to curate. As dealt with in more detail in Chapter 7, museums and the archaeological world, in general, are still grappling at a philosophical and practical level with both the huge amount of material that was generated as a result of the rescue boom and how it can best be preserved and accessed for the benefit of society.

The commercialisation and professionalisation of archaeology has dominated the discipline since the 1980s in North America and in Western Europe although it has yet to make a major impact on the rest of the world. *Rescue archaeology* has developed into the more considered "cultural resource management" and professional archaeological organisations have been formed in response to this new order. The Society of Professional Archaeologists (SOPA) was founded in the United States in 1976, the first attempt to professionalise archaeology, followed by the Institute of Field Archaeologists (IFA) in the United Kingdom (1982). The European Association of Archaeologists (EAA) was founded in 1994. October 1975 saw the first meeting of the UK Society of Museum Archaeologists.

A similar trend has been seen in museums. The late 1980s and early 1990s saw a new focus on increased efficiency and quality in museum services at the very time when budgets were often being cut as part of political expediency. Although there was a resistance to this from many in the sector (e.g., Schadla-Hall 1993), it became a reality as did an increased demand for quantifiable targets and results. These almost always fell back on a count of the number of people who visited a museum and the amount of money spent, saved, or raised. Only now in the early twenty-first century is the long-recognised failing of this system being addressed with the recognition of such concepts as cultural value (e.g., DEMOS/HLF 2004 and Clark 2006) that look to measure the success of museums and other cultural organisations by their value to society in qualitative terms rather than just quantity.

In Britain, the 1960s and 1970s had seen the first high-profile international "blockbuster exhibitions," including shows from Pompeii, China, Bulgaria, and Scandinavia (Cunliffe 1981, p. 193), and these included, most famously, the display of Tutankhamen's treasures at the British Museum. The following decade saw a number of high-profile temporary archaeological exhibitions of British archaeology. These included: *Capital Gains! Archaeology in London 1976–86* (Museum of London 1986) to celebrate the tenth anniversary of the Museum of London; *Archaeology in Britain since 1945: New Views of the Past* held, also in 1986, at the British Museum to show major British archaeological discoveries since World War II (and it included the display of Lindow Man, an Iron Age bog body) (Cherry and Longworth 1986); and most influentially *Symbols of Power at the Time of Stonehenge* (1985) at the National Museum of Antiquities, Edinburgh (Clarke et al. 1985).

Regional and local museums moved more and more to present accessible displays and programmes of relevance to larger audiences. As Merriman has noted (1993b, p. 10) "One of the most important trends in post-war museum development has been the thinning out of encyclopaedic displays and their positioning into some sort of interpretive framework, which has made displays more appealing to the non-specialist." The last two decades of the century also saw museums beginning to grapple with the challenges of stored collections (see Chapters 3 and 7).

The period also saw the development of international movements. ICOM was founded in 1946 to promote and develop museums and the museums profession at an international level. The European Union (EU) has funded a number of international projects, often with a aim of promoting pan Europeanism (Skeates 2005, pp. 311–312). Perhaps most significantly, the World Archaeological Congress, and most notably at its 1987 meeting in Southampton (Ucko 1987), explicitly accepted the Westo centric view of earlier archaeologists, and set out to try and redress this imbalance. However, despite the best intentions museums and archaeology would appear to remain a Western luxury. The direct relationship between national wealth and the museum and archaeological sector is clear. One measure is the number of museums in a country. For a stark comparison, see Skeates (2005, fig. 12.1) for the Mediterranean showing that although France has 5,305 museums and Italy has 1,897, Turkey has only 220, and Egypt has a mere 74. There was very little archaeological fieldwork in sub-Saharan Africa until the later twentieth century. For example, the first excavation in Botswana did not occur until 1938, and then there were no more until the 1970s (Kiyaga-Mulindwa and Segobye 1994). Museums and archaeology in the Third World remain a rare luxury or the result of external influences (see Chapter 5). Meanwhile, twentieth-century wars have continued to see museum archaeology and material culture, in general, suffer through accidental or purposeful destruction, looting for profit, and cultural theft. Large parts of the globe have their cultural property unprotected by legislation.

Key Texts

Arnold, K. (2006). *Cabinets for the curious, looking back at early English museums*. Aldershot: Ashgate.

Daniel, G. (1978). *150 years of archaeology*. London: Duckworth.

Evans, J. D., Cunliffe, B., and Renfrew, C. (Eds.). (1981). *Antiquity and man, Essays in honour of Glyn Daniel*. London: Thames and Hudson.

Merriman, N. (1999). (Ed.). *Making early histories in museums*. Leicester: Leicester University Press.

Vergo, P. (Ed.). (1989). *The new museology*. London: Reaktion.

Chapter 3
Current Aims, Methods, Practise, and Theory

Museum archaeology in the early twenty-first century: its organisation, and practical and theoretical basis.

Introduction

This chapter sketches out the current social geography of museum archaeology at the beginning of the twenty-first century and tries to identify its major theoretical and practical trends. This will hopefully create a backdrop for the chapters that come later, where the principle museum concerns: collections, display, and interpretation are dealt with in more detail. Chapter 4 summarises its legislative basis, and Chapter 5 provides a summary of museum archaeology in different parts of the world. Museum archaeology forms a subset of larger debates about cultural heritage in its widest sense (see Skeates 2000), about cultural objects and their ownership (see Vrdoljak 2006), about public archaeology (see Merriman 2004), and about museums and the museum experience (see Anderson 2004).

Museum' Archaeology's Current Scope

A survey of the current distribution of archaeology museums and displays would identify three principle types:

The Great Civilization Museums. These are museums, and displays within museums, that illustrate and celebrate the Mediterranean, Near Eastern, and Middle Eastern "classical civilizations" (Ancient Greece, Rome, Egypt, Mesopotamia).

These include the *Uber-museums*, the Louvre in Paris; the British Museum in London; The Museum of the Ancient Near East in Berlin; the State Hermitage Museum in St Petersburg; the Egyptian Museum in Cairo; and the Metropolitan Museum of Art in New York, and also many hundreds of regional museums throughout Europe and the Anglophone world. Such museums are very much a creation of European culture and a very particular European model of world history. The classical civilizations have the centre-stage and dominate, but these museums also often attempt to be "encyclopaedic" and include material under more generic titles representing other past civilizations: China, Japan, Europe, Central America. If other cultures are represented, they tend to be further grouped together as "ethnography." Many of these museums have collections that were largely amassed in the nineteenth and early twentieth century, in many cases from private collections. New acquisitions tend to be based on small-scale new research-based fieldwork or through occasional purchase.

Regional Archaeology Museums. These are museums, and displays within museums, that illustrate and interpret the prehistory and early history of a particular locality, region, or nation. These include the national museums of antiquities, such as in Paris and Stockholm, and again many thousands of museums throughout the world that display archaeological finds from their local region. Again, these are a particularly European phenomena. In North America and Australasia, the discontinuous link between modern, white-dominated culture and prehistoric Indigenous culture makes such museums more problematic, and also these become more often linked to ethnography. Similarly, in Africa the colonial origin of museums makes a comfortable link with the past less easy. Such museums also exist in Asia and South America, often as hand-me-downs from a colonial past. These museums tend to be actively collecting and tend to be the repositories for ongoing archaeological fieldwork in their regions. The rapid increase in fieldwork due to the linkage of archaeology to building development means that, particularly in Europe and North America, collections are often growing rapidly and in an unsustainable way (see Chapter 7).

SITE MUSEUMS. These are museums that are sited on and relate directly to a particular monument or, in some cases, particular excavation. As such, these could be seen as a subset of regional museums. Again, such museums are found worldwide and include such sites as the Jorvik Viking Centre in York, the Roskilde Viking Ship Museum in Denmark, Au Musée de la Civilisation Celtique in, Bibracte, France, Jamestown Settlement, in the United States, Ceren in El Salvador, and Chime Bells Museum in Suizhou, China. Because these museums are based around single sites, their collections are often static and, by definition, finite.

A fourth "subtype" of museums might be those displays dealing with human evolution and deep time. Such museums are relatively rare, although sometimes these are associated with specific finds spots such as Neanderthal. More often they appear as galleries within national natural history museums.

Objects tend to be presented very differently depending on the type of museum, and the reasons for this are discussed in more detail elsewhere (Chapters 2, 12, and 13). Objects in the great civilization museums tend to be displayed as decorative arts with minimal interpretation or context. The context has often been lost through the nature of how they were collected, but also because it is not directly relevant to their place in the museum as works of art. They also tend, for various reasons, to be most resistant to changing museological styles. These museums tend to be nineteenth-century foundations in nineteenth-century buildings. The buildings, interiors, and objects tend to send a very clear view of the world based on Western values and the West's model of the past. These museums are often founded in an imperialistic and colonial past. They are also often held up as arbiters of taste and civilization and are a draw to millions of tourists. This contradiction is recognised by many people who govern, staff, and visit these institutions, and attempts are now being made to rethink the place of such institutions. However, there is a long way to go, and a challenge for the museum community in the twenty-first century, if they are going to make the Great Civilization museums into institutions, that truly celebrate all world cultures and history, will be a need to find a completely new organisational, literary, and visual vocabulary. Perhaps a first faltering step has been made with the National Museum of Australia and the Te Papa Museum in New Zealand. More recently, the National Museum of the American Indian at the Smithsonian has been an example of dealing with this challenge, but the museum has not been without its critics (Pes 2005, Jenkins 2005; Chapter 15). The Museum of World Cultures, in Gothenburg, Sweden, is another attempt to break from the older tradition of ethnographic and archaeological museums. In contrast, the new Musée du quai Branley in Paris has been considered highly controversial for displaying "tribal art" separately from mainstream Western art.

The British Museum is also making moves to change its place in the world, from a holder of other peoples' culture to an institution that shares knowledge with peoples represented in its collections in a more dynamic way as witnessed by its Summer 2005, *Africa Now* programme and the 2006 exhibition on Kenya (Heywood 2006). The model is perhaps not unlike the transformation that zoos have gone through. From being institutions that go to a foreign place, capture an animal, and bring it back and display it in a totally false setting, most zoos now see their city centre sites as the fundraising shop windows for conservation programmes in natural habitats. Could the great museums go through a similar transformation?

The regional archaeology museums tend, depending on their age and location, to either resemble small versions of the *decorative arts*-based great civilization museums or to be more like social history museums. In social history museums, an attempt is made to provide a stronger narrative and greater context through a more varied and fuller use of display methods. These often include such props as models, reconstructions, and mannequins. Such museums tend to have a more comfortable place within an identifiable community and to be less politically contentious.

The site museums have the great advantage of being locked into a strong "sense of place," something that can continue even if, like at Jorvik or Roskilde, the original excavation has completely disappeared. A sense of place will encourage designers to use the landscape in which the museum sits and has the potential to create a strong sense of context for displays. What could be more dramatic than the full-height glass windows opening onto open water at the Roskilde Viking Ship Museum?

This rather "archaeological" characterisation of museum types may be too simplistic. Arguably, site museums and regional museums are one-in-the-same, just different in scale. A more anthropological approach might divide archaeology museums into those that tell the story of a culture that is directly appropriated by the tellers (most of the regional and site museums); those that tell a story about cultures that are now isolated but have been appropriated by the tellers (the "great civilization" displays); and those that tell the story of a culture that is not appropriated by the tellers (the social anthropology collections). The idea that some cultures collected by archaeologists and displayed in museums are now "culturally isolated," in that there are no living people who consider themselves their cultural descendents, is a useful one. The culturally isolated groups have no one to speak up for them so they can be acquired or adopted and used to build modern histories. All the great civilization cultures would fall into this category, as would groups such as the "Vikings" and "Celts" in Europe.

Archaeology Current Scope

The range of activities that it is acceptable to include under the heading of archaeology expands by the year. Shortly after World War II, in London, Professor William Grimes courted controversy by being one of the first to recognise the value that archaeology could contribute to the medieval period (Milne

2001, p. 1). It was then considered that digging sites could offer very little to a period that was so exhaustively (it was felt) covered by historic records (see Gerrard 2003 for a fuller discussion of the development of medieval archaeology). But in recent years, archaeology has begun to make a significant contribution to the understanding and interpretation of the two World Wars (e.g., Schofield 2005), as seen in the case of World War I exhibition (*Finding the Fallen*, at the National Army Museum). There is also a growing body of work on the archaeology of the Cold War (e.g., Cocroft and Thomas 2003). More generally, post-Medieval archaeology that was once reserved for the sixteenth and seventeenth centuries now covers all centuries up to the twenty-first. This work has been pioneered in the United States and Australia (e.g., Mayne and Murray 2001) but is now beginning to be explored in the United Kingdom at places like Stoke-on-Trent and in London and in some UK universities. This approach has perhaps reached its extreme in such projects as the archaeology of zoo's (Holtorf 2000), and the "archaeological" analysis of sites of recent political contestation such as the Maze Prison, Northern Ireland (McAtackney 2005) and the Greenham Common Airbase and peace camp (Anderton and Schofield 2000). These studies of recent historical sites show how, conceptually, archaeology has changed, at least in the eyes of its practitioners from a methodology for discovering the ancient past to a philosophical approach to understanding human activity through material culture (see also the definitions in Chapter 1).

Archaeology has also been influenced by the wider heritage and conservation movement and by the commercialisation of this process through development and planning control. The vast majority of archaeology as practiced in the vast majority of the Western world is now undertaken on a commercial basis by commercial or semicommercial organisations paid for by those who are destroying archaeology by development of some form. Publically funded archaeology is primarily aimed at seeking to protect archaeology from development; or seeking to record and characterise archaeological remains threatened by development.

Like the museums that collect and display archaeology, archaeological practice can be roughly divided up into the different sorts of organisation that undertake it.

DEVELOPMENT CONTROL OR CULTURAL RESOURCE MANAGEMENT ARCHAEOLOGY. The vast majority of archaeological fieldwork undertaken in the United Kingdom, Western Europe, and North America is now undertaken by commercial or semi-commercial organisations, often in competition, to mitigate the destruction of archaeological remains by development (residential and commercial building, road building, and gravel extraction to name the most common). Such work is normally underpinned by legislation or government guidance. This work is relatively well-funded, but it is within a commercial market-based framework and is seeing the "professionalisation" of archaeology and archaeologists. Huge amounts of new archaeology are generated through this work. However, because of its nature, it is often difficult to involve the general public or deliver direct community benefit. It is also more difficult to deliver primary research from such work as the funding seldom allows for this. As such, debate has begun as to how this work should continue into the future (e.g., British Archaeology 2006 and Schofield 2006).

This type of archaeology has produced a large number of practitioners who are now comfortable and proficient at working within the world of large scale engineering projects. Although this type of archaeology is unusual outside of the Western World, some large infrastructure projects in the developing world have seen archaeology of this type. Those involved in such work are normally peripatetic and need to rapidly move on to new projects. As such, the results of fieldwork, finds, and records are normally deposited in local museums and repositories as archives as soon as possible after fieldwork is completed (see Chapter 7).

UNIVERSITY RESEARCH AND TEACHING ARCHAEOLOGY. Once the main mechanism for undertaking archaeological fieldwork, university projects are now dwarfed in scale by development-led fieldwork. However, most university archaeology (and in the States, anthropology) departments do undertake fieldwork and because this can be purely research-driven, it continues to make a disproportionately large impact on new archaeological knowledge. Many U.S. and European universities also have active research projects in the Third World and are often the main archaeological practitioners in some countries. Where the results from such work end up often depends on local circumstances – much will go to local museums, but some goes back to university collections. Universities remain dominant in undertaking research, particularly theoretical research. And, of course, they teach archaeology. Teaching remains primarily academic as opposed to vocational, something that has become increasingly questioned as the need for a trained profession grows.

Museum Archaeology. In the West, few museums now undertake major fieldwork projects, being replaced, like the universities, in this role by the commercial firms. However, some active fieldwork remains and this is often research-, training-, or community-based. Museums (as explored in Chapter 7) remain the prime repository for the records and the finds from fieldwork and the prime mechanism for delivering first-hand contact with archaeology to the public.

State or Local Authority Sponsored Archaeology. Again, in the West, state and local authority archaeological endeavour has been scaled back and taken on a strategic, standard setting, and monitoring role. In the developing world, state and regional government archaeology is still often the main local archaeological provider.

Other Provisions. In different parts of the world, on occasion, other arrangements fund or support archaeological endeavour. These include charitable trusts and foreign schools of archaeology particularly in the traditional "classic" locations of the Mediterranean and Near East and Middle East.

The commercialisation of archaeology linked to conservation and heritage protection has led to the development of a whole new subdiscipline that has taken on a life of its own largely divorced from the more traditional archaeology of research, ancient civilizations, and public interpretation. It is also largely divorced from the world of museums (as is discussed in more detail in Chapter 7). Philosophically, there has also been a move away from a discipline primarily interested in digging up and understanding the past, to one interested in preserving and managing a finite resource.

The new commercial, management, and planning importance of archaeology in the United Kingdom has led to a huge increase in the amount of information available about archaeology and in the range of types of information. Schofield (2006) notes that for England in the period since 1989, the entries in sites and monuments records (SMRs) have increased from 516,000 to more than 1.43 million; these include the National Mapping Programme that has contributed possibly 56,000 previously unrecorded sites, and the Archaeological Investigations Project has recorded 16,000 archaeological evaluations. The sheer quantity of data now available is daunting. One solution has been a rush in the development of archaeological research frameworks that summarise current knowledge for an area or subdiscipline (see also Chapter 9). It has also seen the development of SMRs or, as they are now more commonly called HERs or Historic Environment Records. HERs are normally held by local authority planning departments and provide a map-based database of known archaeology for an area. Although primarily aimed at helping development decisions, through extra funding, they have emerged as an "alternative" source of public archaeological information to museums. Barrett (2001) summarises their role in comparison to museums and their potential for education and research. However, despite this new level of data management, some are questioning whether those wishing to make use of archaeological data can keep up with the increase in its creation (e.g., *British Archaeology* 2006).

Maritime archaeology has run a parallel history to the development of terrestrial archaeology. Here too, there has been the slow realisation of the richness and fragility of the resource and a move away from speculative research and "excavation" to an attempt to manage and research the resource. In parallel, there has been the need to come to terms with the rights of "hobbyists" and those seeking to make a commercial gain from salvage of material.

Funding and Governance of Museums

The norm is still for museums to be funded from public sources. This has developed from a long British and European tradition that took firm hold in the nineteenth century. Some museums are privately or independently funded, and this is the norm in North America. However, it is rare to find privately funded archaeology museums, particularly those associated with regional or site archaeology. The other funders of museum archaeology collections are universities and some of the most important and historic archaeology collections are held by such institutions as Oxford, Cambridge, and Yale universities.

The fact that most regional museums, and indeed overall most museums of all types, are funded and governed from public sources means that it is normally competing within a political agenda for resources, and it needs to be justified in terms of providing a public service. Being required to work to financial constraints and deliver a true public service must be good for the internal health of an institution. However, for the United Kingdom, in particular, and much of the West, in general, the arts and culture are seen as pleasant luxuries rather than core to government. Most museums find themselves trying to deliver improved public services, to a particular political agenda, with smaller and smaller budgets. This is not always the case. In some parts of Northern Europe, for example, Denmark, culture is seen as central to national life and legislation allows good funding levels. At other times and in other places, such as in China and Egypt, governments are using culture and the past to promote national unity and external tourism.

Despite the 1845 Museum Act, there has never been a compulsion on British local authorities to provide museums, and many still do not, which causes problems for the archiving of excavation collections (see Chapter 7). Those local authorities that do support museums do so in a discretionary way and are governed by elected members and officers. British national museums are covered by their own acts of Parliament that delimit their powers and duties. These have occasionally led to controversy, for example, the British Museum Act (a new Act in 1963 which replaced the original of 1753 [Caygil 1996]) has been used on several occasions to refuse the repatriation of objects and human remains (in the human remains case, it is now overcome by the 2004 Human Tissue Act; see Chapter 8). National museums are governed by boards of trustees or governors, and although they are funded and given targets by government, they are also often relatively independent. University-funded museums are often parts of academic departments which receive funding through academic funding councils.

Museums are also governed by professional and institutional organisations and associated codes. For example, in the United Kingdom, museums can be accredited by the Museums, Libraries and Archives Council (MLA), and museums can be members of the Museums Association which expects institutions and individual members to adhere to its code of ethics (Museums Association 2002). Accountability is also increasingly provided by funding targets. Hooper-Greenhill (1994, pp, 27–30) provides a summary of accountability initiatives.

Marketing, Branding, Press, and Commercial Opportunities in Museum Archaeology

A fundamental part of modern museums is how they go about selling their product to their audiences and stakeholders. The sophisticated process of branding helps an institution project its values and its product offer. This extends to how a museum markets itself and its different exhibitions and programmes. For archaeology, this can often mean the need to find ways of communicating complex ideas to mass audiences with the temptation to rely on the very misconceptions and clichés that a display or exhibition is trying to dispel. The Jorvik Centre in York is all about dispelling the myth of Vikings as nothing but aggressive raiders. However, some of its advertising used images of powerful looking Viking warriors. A similar situation exists when dealing with the media. Coverage on TV, radio, or in print is vital to museums as a means of free publicity. However, again there is a careful balancing act not to sensationalise a story in order to get it covered, or to make it too complex or "worthy" to lose out. (See Chapter 14 for a discussion of the use of the media for advertising new archaeological discoveries.) In both cases, there is a need for the museum archaeologist to be sympathetic to the needs and constraints of colleagues in press and marketing departments and hope that this will be reciprocal.

How a museum markets its product is both of practical importance (if they get it wrong, no matter how good the product is, people will not visit), and also of philosophical importance. When considering how to market a product, there is a need to distill down its core elements and decide to whom these elements will appeal. It is a worthwhile exercise when developing an idea for an exhibition or public programme to imagine very early on how it will be sold on a poster or an events leaflet. Hooper-Greenhill (1994, pp. 24–25) provides a brief summary to the introduction of marketing to museums with a summary of literature.

Archaeological material has always been, is, and probably always will be bought and sold by private individuals, corporations, and public bodies. This is discussed in more detail in Chapter 6. That antiquities have a market value is a reality that museums and archaeologists have had to come to terms with. A few yards from the main entrance of the British Museum, there are a number of shops selling archaeological objects. Inside the Museum, only accurate replicas can be purchased. Very occasionally, museums and archaeologists become involved in the sale of actual artefacts. In China, some museums sell artefacts in their shops (Solicari 2005) and, at different times, British museums have dabbled in selling archaeological material of no real monetary or academic value such as unstratified building material. Bromwich (1997) is one of the few to have undertaken an analysis of archaeo-logical museum shops in a work that compares museums in Britain and France. He makes the somewhat obvious observa-tion that the more space and products a museum shop have, the more they tend to sell. This fails to make the connection between number of visitors and the size of the museum. The economics of why it is worth the British Museum investing so heavily in retail opportunities with its six million annual, consumer-hungry visitors and international tourists is not complex.

Even when not selling actual artefacts, it is important that a museum does not allow commercial expediency to den-igrate its work. There is no point putting across clear well-researched messages in museum galleries if the shop is then selling products that do not meet the same standards. Just as in marketing, there is a potential conflict between the need to maximise sales and the need to project a unified message.

Museums Archaeology Theory

United Kingdom museum theory in the last 20 years has been dominated by the Department of Museum Studies at Leicester University where Susan Pearce developed new ways of analysing the meaning of collections and collecting (e.g., Pearce 1995) and Eileen Hooper-Greenhill has championed the study of museum visitors and communication techniques (e.g., Hooper-Greenhill 1994). This has led to a reappraisal of traditional understandings: "Whether we like it or not, every acquisition (and indeed disposal), every juxtaposition or arrangement of an object or work of art, together with other objects or works of art, within the context of a tem-porary exhibition or museum display means placing a certain construction upon history" (Vergo, 1989, pp. 2–3).

As a discipline, museologists have recognised the fail-ings of a traditional "authorative" approach to displays and interpretations and the value of postmodern and relativist approaches to the past (e.g., Merriman 1999, pp. 2–6; although see Hurst Thomas 2002 for a more cautionary acceptance).

However, as yet, there seems to be a failure intellectually, or in terms of self-confidence, to turn this into a new type of display or interpretation. As Pearce has put it, what the public now mainly comes into contact with is "a mix of orthodox displays and contemporary spurts of deconstruction" (Pearce 1999, p. 14). At its worst, museum archaeological theory thrashes around in the world of postmodernism using relativism, at its worst, in acknowledging no fixed points (e.g., Beard and Henderson 1999). The Museum of National Antiquities of Sweden in Stockholm has turned its recent display of Maya antiquities (*The Maya Game*) into an exercise in postimperialist naval-gazing whose worthiness must bemuse many visitors.

A move away from a purely didactic objective approach to display should be more straightforward (and liberating) for archaeologists than the other data-based subjects, such as geology, natural history, and even social history, because archaeological evidence is so open to interpretation. Innovative and interesting displays have resulted, most particularly involving art and poetry, as, for example, at the National Museum of Scotland and the *London before London* gallery at the Museum of London and the *Living and Dying* gallery at the British Museum (although this is largely anthropological rather than archaeological). The previous prehistoric gallery at the Museum of London also attempted to include relativist ideas in mainstream displays. One-off displays and installations have taken these ideas further, for example, *The Curators Egg* at the Ashmolean Museum and *Mining the Museum* at the Museum of the Maryland Historical Society, Baltimore (see also Chapter 12).

Postmodern archaeological theory has on the whole taken little interest in museums, which is perhaps why the one major exception was greeted with such hostility. Michael Shanks and Christopher Tilley's 1987 book *Re-constructing Archaeology: Theory and Practice* seriously laid into archaeology using the concept of the museum as the disciplines prison: "the past (which others may call the museum, the archive, the library) recedes in an indefinite, perhaps infinite series of galleries. Archaeologists wander the winding and seemingly endless corridors, forever unlocking doors which appear new, armed with different analytical keys, picking over skeletal remains of past societies, scrutinizing shelves of death or gathering 'truths' from self-referencing site reports. . . . But are there new doors? New facts? New Truths? Is there a way through the maze of the past? Or has the archaeologist been condemned to eternal mythical repetition of the present, to forgetfulness? The solution is to demolish the museum, but *destrukuktion*, not *zerstörung* . . . in order to rescue them, reinscribe their meaning" (Shanks and Tilley 1987b, p. 7). But, on the whole, postmodern theory has struggled to make a major difference to museum displays, and many recent archaeological galleries and exhibitions have looked to extend traditional models rather than question them. Saville (1999) provides a rounded attack on the extremes of postmodernism as they have pervaded museum and archaeology thinking, and in particular as he sees it undermining core museuological values.

The other major influence from Leicester has been Eileen Hooper-Greenhill who has developed models for thinking about visitors and how museums communicate to them. Nick Merriman's survey of nonvisitors (Merriman 1991) is associated with this work (see Chapter 11). Hooper-Greenhill has also (1994) provided a detailed analysis of the study of semiology of signification, or the analysis of intentional communication acts in museums.

If postmodernism has been largely characterised by academic thinking, in recent years, practical theory in British museums has been heavily influenced by political agendas. Chris Smith, the first Culture Secretary of the 1996 Labour Government, promoted both the educational role of museums and their potential to act as "engines for social change" and weapons in the war against social exclusion (DCMS 2000). The argument went that museums should play a key part in the education of children, and indeed others through lifelong learning (discussed in more detail in Chapters 11 and 14) but also should play a part in bringing the socially deprived into mainstream society. The result has been a focus of funds and efforts into minority audiences and bringing people who do not normally use museums into them. This mix of theoretical messages, postmodern relativism and a search for new audiences, has led to much internal naval-gazing and some rather mixed external messages, as well as some innovative public programmes, and, perhaps, the breaking down of some traditional museum failings.

The last major area of concerted thought in recent years has been into collections and their role. For archaeologists, this has centred around archives (discussed in Chapter 7, and in Merriman and Swain 1999 and Swain 2005b) and human remains (see Chapter 8 and Swain 2002b). These debates have formed a subset of a wider discussion within museums as to the role of collections. This is founded both in the practicalities of cost and also a more theoretical discussion about relevance (see NMDC 2003 and MA 2005). These subjects, in turn, overlap with debates about cultural property, its ownership, and its occasional return (e.g., Vrdjak 2006).

Postmodernism, or postprocessualism, has also had a powerful effect on archaeological theory, most notably championed by the likes of John Barrett (e.g., Barrett 1994), Michael Shanks and Christopher Tilley (e.g., Shanks and Tilley 1987a and 1987b) and Ian Hodder (e.g., Hodder 2001), and has led to the closely related concept of cognitive archaeology (e.g., Renfrew and Zubrow 1994) and new approaches to the concept of material culture (see Tilley et al. 2006). However, although theory has had a profound effect on academic thinking and writing, as with museums, it is difficult to find too many examples of theory making a profound effect on archaeological practice. Indeed, as Hodder (2001, p. 1 notes), "it has become possible to exist in archaeology largely as a theory specialist." There are exceptions to this, for example the work of Barrett and others at the London Heathrow Terminal 5 Project (e.g., Andrews et al. 2000), and of Ian Hodder at Çatalhöyük in Turkey (e.g., Hodder 2002a). Postmodernism currently dominates archaeological theory but has not pervaded practice as much as some would wish. Again, as with museums, there has also been a rear-guard action, perhaps most famously summed up by Ian Kinnes in his jibe that British archaeology was suffering from "synthesis without documentation" (Kinnes 1992, p. 3).

Both museums and archaeologists have engaged in gender debates as part of the postmodern dialectic. Feminist thought in particular has finally been given a more equitable place (e.g., Jones and Pay 1990). A generation of articulate and assertive, women academic archaeologists have built up a strong literature on the place of women in the "archaeological" past (see, e.g., Gilchrist 1999, Voss 2000, Stig Sørenson 1999, and Jones and Pay 1990). In the United Kingdom, a debate about the visibility of women in museum displays led to the formation of Women, Heritage, and Museums (WHAM) in 1984 (Pirie 1985, Devonshire and Wood 1996). And this has translated into a more positive consideration of the role of women in many galleries, such as the 1994 prehistoric gallery at the Museum of London (Cotton 1997). However, the senior echelons of the museum profession are dominated by males, out of all proportion to the overall gender divide in the profession. More women have made it to senior positions in the archaeological profession, but this hides a profession that is still dominated by men and a very dated concept of male machismo centred on physical labour and drinking!

Some have identified a crisis, or loss of confidence, by museum curators in the face of postmodernism as developed academically and, in some cases, has led to specific criticism of museum archaeology (see above). Although these criticisms should be used as a valuable catalyst for new and imaginative thinking, the museum curator can call upon the largely positive views and responses of the visiting public to build confidence and balance criticism. Not the field archaeologist however, which operates in a world away from a scrutinising public and is driven largely by market forces. They seem impervious to external influence other than those of the market and continue to strive to collect as much "objective" and "scientific" data as possible with the seeming view that there is a direct correlation between the quantity of data recovered and the quantity of new "truths" about the past revealed.

Currently, a popular subject theoretically and in terms of heritage funding is the concept of intangible heritage. This relates to those elements of a culture which are not represented in material objects or writing. It might include customs, practices and oral tradition. As such this poses particular challenges for museums, and even more so for archaeology, in that it has no material manifestation and as such is arguably unrecognisable in the archaeological record.

Museum Archaeology and Politics

The place of museum archaeology within wider society has already been touched on in Chapter 1. In recent years, the place of cultural heritage, museums and archaeology has been a potent sideshow to some of the worlds political and military crisis. The theft and destruction of cultural property can be traced back to the earliest examples of warfare between states (Boylan 2002) and as such is a reflection of the use of such material to symbolise the power and values of one state, or group of people, over another. Since the Napoleonic Wars, the return of cultural property has been a feature of peace treaties, and since the mid-nineteenth-century, attempts have been made to control the damage and theft of cultural property through treaties and conventions relating to the waging of war. It was the Hague Convention of 1954, a reaction to the losses and thefts of World War II, that first gave the concept of cultural property being a shared resource for all humanity. The UK government is only now in the process of ratifying the Hague Convention (see Chapter 4).

Despite the common recognition that museums and archaeological remains and cultural institutions in general should not be destroyed or used as part of armed conflict, they continue to suffer, only emphasising their place in giving material form to ethnic, religious, national and political identity. The National Museum of Lebanon in Beirut was badly damaged during the 1980s civil war (although this was mainly due to its unfortunate location on a front line), most of its treasures were kept safe and its large unmovable statues were famously encased in concrete for protection. The National Museum of Afghanistan in Kabul also suffered during the recent civil war and foreign invasions of that country. The recent Taliban regime also notoriously destroyed ancient Buddhist monuments of Bamiyan. Again in the Middle East the Baghdad National Museum of Iraq was looted during the recent American invasion (Polk and Schuster 2005; Bogdanos with Patrick 2005). Political unrest and war, and the civil unrest and poverty often associated with them often leads to, or encourages, the looting of archaeological sites and the subsequent illicit trade in antiquities. Morag Kersel (in press) has shown how political unrest in the Near East has led Palestinians, desperate for money, to loot archaeological sites. See Bevan (2005) for an overview of cultural destruction and theft through time and a review of some of its more recent manifestations.

Also of political importance have been recent campaigns for the return of cultural property, most famously the Elgin (or Parthenon) Marbles but also including Indigenous "sacred and secret" objects in Australia and North America. All of these events have caused recriminations amongst the archaeological and museum community and acted as sideshows to the main political events.

An example of the political role of museums in times of change is South Africa where with the end of Apartheid a museum system that had used history and archaeology to reinforce white domination was transformed to highlight the cultural continuity and richness of Indigenous peoples. South African museums have been an important part of the battleground for the creation of a new nation (see Mazel and Ritchie 1994 for a discussion of the initial changes, including in Botswana and Zimbabwe). From another region of internal conflict, Hamlin (1997) describes the challenge of presenting history and historic monuments to the people of Northern Ireland where the past has been almost completely propogandersised and where polarised communities have very different mythologies associated with different, and often the same sites. At present, perhaps the most political of all museum archaeological objects are human remains. These are dealt with in detail in Chapter 8.

At a far more mundane level, museums are the regular political pawns of local authority political wrangling over budgets. Here it is difficult to identify a particular political dogma that works for museums. Traditionally, more left-wing parties are considered to be the friend of the arts because they support higher public funding. However, arts and culture often come low down on such party's priority list. Moreover, right-wing parties tend to spend less on public bodies and the arts in general, however tend to come from a more elitist background where such things are given more value. If nothing else this tends to require museums to stay on their toes in continuing to justify their existence.

Archaeology has tended to remain outside mainstream political debate. Occasionally, important discoveries call for government action, sometimes in the face of commercial interest, and occasionally such discoveries have raised popular public support and domestic political controversy. Examples include the Ilisu Dam project in SE Turkey (Kitchen and Ronayne 2001) and the discovery of Shakespeare's Rose Theatre in London in 1988–1989 (Wainright 1989; Schadla-Hall 1989). In the United Kingdom, RESCUE, The British Archaeological Trust has, since the 1970s, tried to keep archaeology on the political agenda (see Mytum and Waugh 1987). The British parliament also has the All-Party Parliamentary Archaeological Group (APPAG) that has published a report on the state of archaeology in the United Kingdom (APPAG 2003).

Museum Archaeology and Popular Culture

If archaeology and museums have some relevance to global politics they also feature in mainstream, popular and mass culture. This is an area that continues to fascinate archaeologists, partly for its entertainment value, partly as it is a way of gauging how the disciplines are perceived by others, and partly because the very "mass" nature of this culture, makes it a powerful medium for communication. It would appear that archaeology in particular and museums to a lesser extent do have a strong presence in this popular culture, from Indiana Jones to Lara Croft to the perennial appearance of mummies and cursed treasure in movies, comics, and even theme parks and a long-standing if sporadic presence on television. (See Holtorf 2005 for a full discussion of the subject; Hall 2002 for a discussion of museum archaeology in film and popular fiction;

Ascherson 2002 and 2004 for a discussion of how archaeology appears in the media; and Russell 2002 for archaeology in science fiction.) The normal response of archaeologists and curators to the portrayal of their subject in mass media is one of amusement tinged with frustration. Factual portrayal tends to be trivialised or sensationalised and fictional portrayals deal in clichés or alter facts to fit stories.

Few archaeological and museological themes appear regularly in mass culture fiction. Egyptology and in particular the discovery of mummies and treasure are perhaps the most regular and almost always have a supernatural, sinister, and perilous element. Other, ancient-treasure-laden civilizations sometimes stand-in for the Egyptians. Human evolution including missing links and "ape men," again often in a supernatural setting, are also popular. It is possible that it is only truly momentous discoveries in "high culture" that make the leap into the world of popular or mass culture, and once the leap has been made ideas take on a life of their own and cross fertilise with other strands of mass culture rather than referring back to their academic origins. So the wonder of Egypt, its many discoveries, and, most important of all, the discovery of Tutankhamen's tomb have found a place in mass culture; but that pharaoh's famous curse is purely a product of popular fiction (see Fagan 2006 for a discussion of the pseudoarchaeology of mass culture).

The importance of popular culture as the place where basic myths are retold and reworked and where most members of the public seek to find entertainment should not be underemphasised. That archaeology and museums are familiar in this world must be good for both disciplines. Cornelius Hortoff has recently argued (Hortoff 2005) that storytelling, not empirical knowledge, is the basis of human culture and we should worry less about how our messages get translated and used. This view remains heretical to most but perhaps there is a need to recognise mass culture for what it is and not be too troubled by how it warps the discipline. That for most the abiding image of museum archaeology is the last scene in the movie *Raiders of the Lost Ark* should be an amusement, a lesson, and a warning to the discipline.

Key Texts

Bevan, R. (2005). *The destruction of memory*. London: Reaktion.

Hooper-Greenhill, E. (1994). *Museums and their visitors*. London: Routledge.

Hodder, I. (Ed.). (2002). *Archaeological theory today*. Cambridge, UK: Polity Press.

Skeates, R. (2000). *Debating the archaeological heritage*. London: Duckworth.

Vergo, P. (Ed.). (1989). *The new museology*. London: Reaktion.

CHAPTER 4
THE LEGAL FRAMEWORK

The extent to which national and international law governs museum archaeological practice including guidance, standards, and codes that support activities.

Introduction

This chapter, more even than the others, due to the sheer complexity of the subject, will keep itself primarily to dealing in general principles, the specific circumstances in the United Kingdom, subjects of particular interest from North America and elsewhere, and international initiatives.

Legislation covering archaeology and museums tends to be divided into several related but more or less self-contained spheres. These can be summarised as follows:

1. Legislation that protects archaeological remains in (or on) the ground, normally identifying sites of importance and stops their disturbance without good justification, and requiring finders of antiquities to report them or hand them over. Such legislation has more recently spread to encompass underwater sites.
2. Legislation that protects portable antiquities or cultural property once it is out of the ground.
3. Legislation that exists to govern correct archaeological practice, although more often this is controlled by codes of conduct, professional standards, and guidance rather than legislation.
4. Legislation relating to museums and museum collections. Again, this is rare; in most cases, museums are governed by professional codes, and are covered by more general laws such as those governing copyright, freedom of information,

and property. In some cases, laws have been enacted to create museums or allow them to be created.

Throughout the world, laws vary depending on how the underlying legislation has developed. The principal difference is between legislation developed from English and Germanic law that puts emphasis on the individual and the rights of the individual to own and control property and land quite independent to the state, and Roman law, such as that developed by Napoleon in France, that gives the state rights over not only what comes from the ground but, in some cases, cultural property in individual ownership (Cleere 1991, p. 30; see Skeates 2000, pp. 19–20 for examples of the later). More recently, the idea of the common ownership of culture by all of humanity (Skeates 2000, p. 20) has muddied these waters further. A large literature exists on the law and archaeology (e.g., Spoerry 1993; Breeze 1993; Cookson 2000). Museum legislation is more rare because, in most cases, it is a subset of other laws relating to property ownership (e.g., Vrdoljak 2006).

The Protection of Archaeological Remains

Most countries have some form of national legislation that protects archaeological sites, monuments, and finds in, or on, the ground, and in national waters, from being disturbed without good reason. National variations depend on the extent of such legislation (that is the range, types, and numbers of sites that are protected), how protected sites are defined, and the mechanisms by which they are protected. In some cases, material can be protected when and if it is discovered, even if it was not specifically protected before.

The protection of archaeology by law and its actual protection in practice can be two very different things. In many countries, poverty, poor infrastructure. and internal conflicts can make protective legislation almost meaningless. Similarly, in some countries the reality of looting of archaeological sites due to poverty have led to pragmatic legal decisions that might otherwise not have been deemed ideal (see Chapter 6 for examples in Israel and Palestine).

The key legal provision for archaeology in the United Kingdom is found in the 1979 Ancient Monuments and Archaeological Areas Act and the 1996 Treasure Act. The 1979 Act allows for monuments to be "scheduled." Once a monument is scheduled, legal authority must be obtained before sites are interfered with in any way (including excavation), and prosecution can follow unauthorised disturbance. In England, the law was administered through the Department of Culture, Media, and Sport (DCMS) with advice from English Heritage (EH). Under new arrangements, the scheme will be managed by EH and the schedule of ancient monuments will be combined with lists of historic buildings, battlefield sites, and historic gardens as part of a major review of heritage protection (English Heritage 2006a).

In 1987, the number of monuments scheduled stood at about 13,000 when it was estimated that this was only about 1 in 50 of known archaeological sites (Darvill et al. 1987, p. 393). This shows that although the Act does provide essential protection to the most important sites, the vast majority of archaeology in England must rely on planning guidance for protection or none at all. During the 1990s, a major project to review and increase the number of sites scheduled also illustrated the need to define more clearly what was meant by an ancient monument as well as the importance of clearly defining monuments through common nomenclatures and descriptions. An ongoing criticism of scheduling is that it is based on the protection of individual sites, not landscapes.

The Archaeological Areas part of the 1979 Act is now all but moribund. It allows for the designation of areas of archaeological importance, and originally had six such areas, all from the centres of historic city-centres such as York. The act demands that anyone planning to disturb a site in one of the areas must give 6 months notice to allow archaeologists to excavate the areas first. Without funding, such a provision is meaningless, as illustrated in the case of the Queen's Hotel site in York where, in 1989, archaeology was destroyed through lack of funds despite the site being vacant and available for excavation (Sheldon 1989). The protection in the 1979 Act for such areas has now been made redundant by PPG16 and the proper inclusion of archaeology within the planning system (see the section on Archaeology Practice in this chapter).

The 1996 Treasure Act replaced the earlier law of Treasure Trove (a law that was developed in the Middle Ages from unknown origins (Cleere 1991, p. 30)). The Treasure Act of 1996 (see DCMS 2002 for full details of the Act and its workings) gave a new wider definition of what qualifies as treasure (now including any metallic object more than 300 years old whose weight is more than 10 percent precious metal, or more than 1 percent if prehistoric, hoards of coins, or objects associated with precious metals). Objects that qualify as treasure need to be reported to the appropriate coroner and if designated treasure they become owned by the Crown. What this means in practice is that it gives museums the opportunity to purchase the find from the finder or landowner at the market price. The Act is largely administered through the Portable Antiquities Scheme at the British Museum (see Chapter 6). The Act simplifies the now archaic Treasure Trove but still reflects an uneasy relationship with the idea of property, the rights of landowners, and what qualifies as an antiquity. In Scotland, where the Crown owns everything recovered from the ground, the situation is at least far more straightforward. Separate legislation exists in England to cover the excavation and movement of human remains (see Church of England and English Heritage 2005 and Chapter 8).

No legislation exists in England to state specifically where archaeological remains will be kept once excavated or recovered. Apart from treasure, landowners retain ownership of items from their land unless they formally hand them over to someone else. This is extremely problematic for archaeological material being deposited in museums because it means that not only is there no formal mechanism as to which museum the material will go, but no formal or legally enforceable mechanism for obtaining ownership (see also the section on cultural property, in this chapter, and Chapter 6).

The main alternative model for protecting archaeology can be found in Southern Europe where any archaeology can be protected by law when and if it is found or disturbed (see, e.g., Skeates 2000, pp. 19–20 for Cyprus and Italy).

Although it, on paper, offers greater protection than the English model, this can lead to major problems for property and other developers.

In the United States, laws to protect antiquities have reflected those of Europe but been given a particular driving force through the empowerment of Native Americans. Davies (2002) provides a brief summary of U.S. legislation. The earliest protection came in 1906 for sites on Federal land, and it is a theme of U.S. legislation that in most cases it only protects material on or from Federal property.

Key legislation in the United States is the Archaeological and Historic Preservation Act (AHPA) of 1974 that calls for the preservation and recording of sites to be destroyed on Federal land; the 1979 Archaeological Resources Protection Act (ARPA) that dealt with the long-term ownership and care of material from sites supports it. A 1984 amendment required consultation with Indian communities that in turn has been replaced by The Native American Graves Protection and Repatriation Act (NAGPRA). In 1988, an amendment to ARPA included a provision that required Federal Land management agencies to establish public education programmes. This in turn was supported by the regulation Curation of Federally Owned and Administered Archaeological Collections (36 CFR Part 79) issued in 1990. This regulation gave guidance to Federal agencies as to how to care for archaeological collections in their care. Federal agencies manage about 33 percent of the land in the United States, and this includes such areas as the National Parks. As such, they are the key leader and manager of the archaeological resource (see McManamon 1994 for a discussion of public archaeology in the United States through Federal sites).

The Native American Graves Protection and Repatriation Act (NAGPRA), enacted in 1990, has changed the face of U.S. archaeology and museum archaeology. It requires the consent of appropriate native peoples for the disturbance of Native graves and the return of all human remains and sacred materials from museums to native peoples if it is wanted. Enactment of the law required U.S. museums to identify exactly what they held in their collections of relevance and, therefore, also had a profound effect on collections management and collections access (Sullivan and Childs 2003, p. 27).

Ownership of archaeological material in the United States is also as confusing and problematic as in the United Kingdom with a myriad of agencies owning material and often a lack of good documentation to clarify this (Sullivan and Childs 2003, pp. 29–31). In the United States, institutions that can act as the repository for archaeological collections include: museums, academic institutions, tribal museums and cultural centres, historic societies, government repositories, and archives.

Maritime Archaeology

Legislation, and the general management of maritime archaeology, has, perhaps understandably, lagged behind land archaeology. In terms of national legislation, maritime archaeology is normally considered to cover the area from high tide out to the edge of territorial waters. As such, it can encompass many types of environments and sites including wrecked ships, coastal defences, and drowned landscapes. Obviously, more problematic are wrecks and other sites that fall in international waters and, therefore, do not fall under the protection of any one state.

Of greatest concern to archaeologists and museums will be historic wrecks and objects from them. Historic shipwrecks can be of immense archaeological value. Not only do they often represent the evidence for important voyages or battles, they also act as wonderful time capsules. Conditions under the water often lead to excellent survival of materials, such as organics, that do not survive on most land sites.

In the United Kingdom, the 1894 Merchant Shipping Act requires finders of objects from wrecks to declare them to the Receiver of Wreck who will publicise them and allow one year for owners to come forward. After this period, material becomes crown property. The Receiver will sell it and give some of the proceeds to the finder. Normal policy is to make historic material available to museums to purchase in the first instance (similar to the Treasure Act for land finds). In addition to this, the 1973 Protection of Wrecks Act allows the Secretary of State for Transport to "designate" certain wrecks within territorial waters as of historical importance. Such sites cannot be disturbed without permission and then only by suitably qualified maritime archaeologists. See McGrail (1991) for a summary of legislation in the United Kingdom and a suggested procedure for how museum curators should deal with maritime finds offered to them.

The Protection of Portable Antiquities and Cultural Property

Once archaeological objects are out of the ground and a direct association with their excavation lost, a new range of legislation comes into play. This is problematic because it runs into property law and the rights of individuals to own and deal in property. In most cases, its aim is to prevent the illegal movement of cultural property across national boundaries. In the United Kingdom, the 2003 Dealing in Cultural Property Act criminalises anyone dealing dishonestly or dealing in unlawfully removed cultural objects from anywhere in the world. In addition, in 2005 DCMS issued guidance (DCMS 2005c) on due diligence for museums dealing with cultural property.

The laws of property, which underpins so much Western legislation, do not relate directly to archaeology and museums but are of obvious high importance. In England, Wales, and Northern Ireland, objects found in the ground, except for those few that qualify as Treasure (see the previous section), are owned by the landowner. So, for the vast majority of material from the vast majority of excavations, the first challenge is to persuade the landowner, normally, but not always, linked to the site developer, to part with their property so that it can be accepted into a museum as part of an archive. A similar situation will exist for stray finds and metal detector finds that will also be owned by the finder, if prearranged through the landowner or by the landowner. In England, the situation for human remains is different, if not less complex (see Chapter 8). According to the law, there is no property in human remains unless they have been altered (normally as part of art), so strictly speaking museums can never own the human remains in their care. Property rights are different in Scotland, where the Crown owns everything recovered from the land.

Many attempts have been made to prevent the theft of antiquities from nations for sale elsewhere as discussed in Chapter 6. There is a massive and very lucrative market in antiquities that generally is based in Western Europe and the United States and involves antiquities from all around the world.

UNESCO and UNIDROIT

It is UNESCO (United Nations Educational, Scientific, and Cultural Organisation) that has been most active internationally in trying to protect cultural property. It has two prime instruments for this. The first is the Hague Convention for the Protection of Cultural Property in the Event of Armed Conflict (see Chapter 3). The Hague Convention has two protocols, the first is the 1954 protocol and the second is the 1999 protocol, which is (not only the second) currently being implemented. The convention prohibits the export of cultural property from an occupied territory and identifies sites and monuments that should not be attacked or damaged in the event of armed conflict.

The second UNESCO instrument is the Convention on the Means of Prohibiting and Preventing the Illicit Import, Export, and Transfer of Ownership of Cultural Property 1970 (ratified by the United Kingdom in 2002). This allows a state to request another state to seize and return cultural objects that have been illegally removed. The 1970 convention deals with public law and therefore the International Institute for the Unification of Private Law (UNIDROIT) has formulated the UNIDROIT Convention on Stolen and Illegally Exported Cultural Objects 1995 to deal with private law. UNESCO also created, in 2001, a Convention on the Protection of the Underwater Cultural Heritage. In addition, UNESCO has published several sets of recommendations covering such areas as archaeological excavation and codes of ethics including one for dealers in antiquities (UNESCO 1999).

Archaeological Practice

The vast majority of archaeological practice around the world is governed by professional guidance, standards, and codes of practice. Because of the international nature of archaeology, such codes tend to be set at national regional and a global level, so an English archaeologist might find themself a member of the Institute of Field Archaeologists (IFA), and the European Association of Archaeologists (EAA), and having to be aware of guidance laid down by the World Archaeological Congress (WAC), the International Council on Monuments and Sites (ICOMOS), and UNESCO.

In England, government guidance laid down in *Planning and Policy Guidance Note 16: Archaeology and Planning* (PPG16, DoE 1990) governs how the vast majority of archaeology takes place within the planning system. It explains the importance of the archaeological heritage, how, ideally, it should be preserved *in situ*, and that if this is unreasonable, it is expected that developers will undertake and fund necessary recording as part of a development and build this into their planning application. The IFA has developed a code of conduct for members and standards documents to measure best practice (IFA 1999).

In the United States, the Society for American Archaeology (SAA) has issued codes of practice, as has the Society of Professional Archaeologists (SOPA) that was replaced in 1998 by the Register of Professional Archaeologists Archaeologists (RPA).

Contract archaeology and the PPG16 model in the United Kingdom are translated as cultural resource management in the United States. In North America, the term is used to relate directly to archaeology that is undertaken by commercial companies in relation to mitigation strategies and recording in advance of development. State-led planning archaeologists, often operating at a city or district level and through the National Historic Preservation Act, identifies appropriate strategies that are undertaken by firms. Detailed circumstances depend on who owns the land (Federal government, private landowner, or tribe) and the nature of the politics within any particular state. Confusingly, the term "cultural resource management" is used in the United Kingdom in a slightly more amorphous way to cover all aspects of the historic landscape.

The Athens Charter (1931) had asserted that the principles guiding the preservation and restoration of ancient buildings should be agreed upon and laid down on an international basis, with each country being responsible for applying the plan within the framework of its own culture and traditions. This was the foundation of what is known as the Venice Charter (1964) that inspired the foundation of the International Council on Monuments and Sites (ICOMOS) in 1965 at Warsaw. This remains a benchmark for the world's conservation community.

Principles for the Recording of Monuments, Groups of Buildings, and Sites (1996) were adopted by ICOMOS at Sofia in response to the requirement of the Charter of Venice (Article 16) that "responsible organisations and individuals record the nature of the cultural heritage." Its five sections cover the reasons for recording, responsibility for recording, planning for recording, the content of records, and their management, dissemination, and sharing. A 1990 Charter covered the management of archaeological sites. In addition, the Burra Charter (1999, revision of 1979) provides guidance for the conservation and management of places of cultural significance and is a product of Australia ICOMOS. It regards conservation as an integral part of the management of places of cultural significance and as an ongoing responsibility. It sets a standard of practice for those who provide advice, make decisions about, or undertake works to places of cultural significance, including owners, managers, and custodians. Its principles are widely applicable and have been generally accepted outside of Australia.

The European Convention on the Protection of the Archaeological Heritage (2001, revision of 1969), also known as the "Valetta Convention," is part of the group of Council of Europe treaties for the protection of cultural heritage. It aims to protect the archaeological heritage as a source of the European collective memory and as an instrument for historical and scientific study. Its eighteen Articles contain provisions for the identification and protection of archaeological heritage, including: the control of excavations and the use of metal detectors; the financing of archaeological research and conservation; the collection and dissemination of scientific information; the promotion of public awareness; and the prevention of illicit circulation of archaeological objects. In addition, The Draft Framework Convention of the Council of Europe on the Value of Cultural Heritage for Society (October 2005) has twenty-three Articles that are a further development of several earlier European documents. It deals, at a high level, with the contribution of a broadly defined cultural heritage to society and human development, and emphasises a shared responsibility for public participation in the care and understanding of cultural heritage.

Museums and Museum Collections

Museums, in general, are often not governed by specific legislation but under a raft of more general laws. The majority of museum practice is governed by nonspecific legislation that covers public bodies (such as freedom of information), laws that govern the control of information (copyright) and property, and professional codes of conduct. Some nations have legislation that provides for museum and heritage protection, in general, under national agencies.

In Britain, the 1845 Museum Act allowed British local authorities to raise money through local taxes to provide museum services. However, this, unlike with libraries, was not compulsory and as such the provision of museum services is not universal and where they do exist they are not immune to closure. Acts of Parliament did create the British national museums including the British Museum (1753, and updated in 1963), the Museum of London (1975), and the National Museum of Scotland (1985). These outline what these institutions shall do, and how they will be run, and any changes require changes to the Acts. The 2004 Human Tissue Act allowed National Museums to deaccession human remains less than 1,000 years old. As there is no property in human remains (see above) it is arguable that this legislation was not needed.

In England, museums are "designated" (now "accredited") through a system administered by the government agency MLA. This requires them to adopt accepted best practice and to put in place policies and guidance (see Chapter 6 in specific relation to collections). It is accepted good museum practice that objects accessioned into collections should be legally owned by the museum. There are several good practical reasons for this that include the avoidance of the bureaucracy of continuing communication with owners and the freedom it gives museums to conserve, loan, display, sample, and, if necessary, dispose of objects or give them to others.

Accredited museums are also required, by law, to care for their visitors. This includes such things as health and safety requirements and, more frequently, provisions for such groups as the disabled.

In the United Kingdom, the Museums Association (MA), and individual and institutional membership organisation, acts as professional regulator. The MA has issued a code of ethics for its members (Museums Association 2002). See Malaro (1998) for a detailed summary of legal issues for museums in the United States.

Key Texts

Cookson, N. (2000). *Archaeological heritage law*. Chichester: Barry Rose Law Publishing Ltd.

Hunter, J., and Ralston, I. (1993). *Archaeological resource management in the UK*. Stroud: Alan Sutton.

Malaro, M. C. (1998). *A legal primer on managing museum collections*. Washington, DC and London: Smithsonian Institution Press.

Vrdoljak, A. F. (2006). *International law, museums, and the return of cultural objects*. Cambridge, UK: Cambridge University Press.

CHAPTER 5
MUSEUM ARCHAEOLOGY: GEOGRAPHIC SCOPE

An overview of museum archaeological provision around the world and its characteristics.

Introduction

There is no doubt that a Eurocentric and Western perspective dominates museums, both in terms of their content and philosophy in the West, and in the approach taken to museums in the non-Western world. This derives from their historical development (as discussed in Chapter 2) and the current world dominance of Western economic power and culture.

Archaeology and perceptions of the past also have a strong Western bias. Chris Scarre (1990, p. 14) notes the imbalance in Western-published archaeological atlases. His survey of six publications shows a distribution by content as follows:

Palaeolithic	10 percent worldwide
Europe	30 percent
The Near East	23 percent (including Egypt)
Far East	10 percent
The Americas	13.5 percent
Africa South of the Sahara	5 percent
India	4.5 percent
Central Asia	2.5 percent
Oceania	2.4 percent.

Books can move with the times and have a much shorter life span than most museum galleries. A similar survey of space given over to different past world cultures in Western museums that purport to cover world civilization would offer an even more biased picture. A visit to most major British regional museums might find a rather out-of-date gallery on local archaeology, a more popular gallery on Egyptology (but with collections all acquired many years before); perhaps a gallery on Assyria; something on classical Greece and Rome; and then, if you are lucky, possibly a "ethnography" gallery with some mixed material from Africa and Australia; and then a "decorative art" gallery with some Far Eastern textiles and ceramics. Even the British Museum, despite recent attempts, has failed to break from this past. Its galleries are still dominated, in location and size, by nineteenth- and early twentieth-century collections of Egyptian, Middle Eastern, Greek, and Roman "masterpieces." World and European prehistory, the Far East, Central America, and now Africa do feature but very much as secondary acts.

Such museums obviously project and maintain a particular picture of the past. But is it unfair to criticise it? As Mike Smith (personal communication) has pointed out for Australia, "However fascinating, complex and relevant early prehistoric archaeology is, there is only so much you can do in a museum display with some partially worked flints and charcoal." Conversely, the archaeology of Pharonic Egypt has produced a vast amount of truly amazing material, a result of an incredibly complex material culture and particular circumstances of preservation. Perhaps, if criticism is warranted, it is for the museum curators and archaeologists who have persisted in researching and excavating certain cultures and persisted in collecting and displaying certain material.

Outside the Western world, where, historically, world archaeology has not been collected, most museums collect and display national and regional material (you would struggle to find a museum in Africa or South America with collections of European archaeology). These museums tend to be hang-overs from the Colonial period (particularly in Africa) where there is yet to be a serious buy-in from local publics, civil servants, or governments; or as symbols of nascent wealth and political identity, for example, in China, the Middle East, and parts of Central and Southern America. They can also be a combination of the above with a desire to attract foreign tourists and their money. Brodie (in Brodie and Walker Tubb 2002, pp. 13–14) gives examples of archaeological museums in Turkey, Cyprus, and Nigeria that have made a material difference to regional tourism and as such local economies.

The remainder of this chapter summarises the characteristics of archaeology in museums as it is found around the world. This obviously can be no more than a brief overview that can mention only a few examples, however, hopefully it provides a background to what follows, compliments the listings in Chapter 16, and illustrates core characteristics in different geographic regions.

United Kingdom

In the United Kingdom, wondrous chaos theory has left a mix of museums and museum archaeology at many differently sized institutions with different organisational and funding basis (see Fisher 2004 for a personal summary of Britain's best museums and galleries). At local and regional levels, a patchwork of local authority and semi-independent museums means that there is something to offer in almost every town. It has been calculated (Wood and Cotton 1999) that more than 500 of the 2,000 museums in Britain have archaeological collections. See, for example, Swain (1997a) for a survey of museum archaeology in the county of Surrey that identified nineteen different museums with some kind of archaeology displays, but with only one, Guildford Museum, of any size and offering a comprehensive account of the regions past; and only one, Haslemere, offering any World archaeology. See also Wood (1997) for a summary of archaeology in small British museums. The majority of smaller museums deal with local archaeology. A few exceptions, such as Haslemere continue to offer an encyclopaedic, universal model with galleries showing material from the Classical World. Another example is the Perth Museum and Art Gallery Scotland, where collections and displays include regional archaeology, Egyptology, and ethnography as well as local history and natural history.

On a larger scale, most British cities have museums that cover regional archaeology as well as the classical civilizations and "ethnography."

There are a number of larger regional museums in key historic towns and cities with important archaeological collections and displays that reflect a long tradition of excavation, research, and display. These include, for example, the large Museum of London, the National Museum of Scotland, and the National Museums and Galleries of Wales, and the smaller Dorchester, Norwich, and Roman Canterbury museums to name but a few. Throughout these museums, the Roman period is emphasised, prehistory is downplayed, and the post-Roman period merges uncomfortably with later history.

University museums often hold key archaeological collections, for example the Ashmolean in Oxford and Fitzwilliam and the Museum of Archaeology and Anthropology in Cambridge. Such institutions, freed of local authority targets and linked to academic institutions, might be models of dynamic and advanced thinking and practice. Unfortunately, the opposite is often true, and they tend to be bastions of conservative views and displays (see, e.g., Phillipson 2003 for a traditional view of museum roles). As MacDonald has stated (2002, p. 9), university museums have "gradually slipped lower on the higher education agenda, at the same time unable through lack of resources to serve a broader audience," although there has been a "belated reawakening" to which the Petrie Museum at University College, London, is a fine example; leading on digital and education access programmes (MacDonald 2002) to engage with the local ethnic minority populations.

Independent archaeology museums are rare in the United Kingdom. An example is the Kilmartin House in Scotland that, despite continued threats to its existence from lack of funding (e.g., Smith 2004), has maintained a high reputation for community work, displays, and its website. At the other extreme is the wonderful and eclectic John Soane Museum in London where the eighteenth-century architect's collection of antiquities remains as he originally displayed them. Some of the best, or at least most interesting, archaeology museums and displays in the United Kingdom are directly linked to archaeological sites and monuments. These include such sites as Segedunum, Tyneside, and the Jorvik Viking Centre in York.

Although many in the sector would like more resources, British museums tend to be well-funded and have good quality displays that work hard to address visitor needs and desires. Since the advent of the Heritage Lottery Fund and other project-based funding sources, many galleries and museum facilities have been renewed. Recent new archaeology galleries include The Corinium Museum in Cirencester, The Collection Lincoln, and the *Medieval London* gallery at the Museum of London. Although these galleries tend to be of a high quality and the envy of much of the world, they also tend to take a similar and quite conservative approach to design and put educational values above emotive ones.

Europe

Archaeology in European museums closely reflects archaeology in Britain with a range of national, local authority, university, and independent museums. The huge variety in size, sophistication, and scope reflects the long history of archaeological and museum development and the incredibly dense and complex mix of cultural, political, national, regional, and community motivations that have, at different times, sponsored museum projects. The majority of the museums are funded by local authorities. Again, as with British museums, these museums are of varying standards, and often suffer from a lack of funds to keep displays and programmes up-to-date. Unlike in Britain, in some European nations a stronger tradition exists for supporting national pasts through museums exists. For example, in France, the Musée des Antiquités Nationales de Saint Germain en Laye and the Musée National de Préhistoire reflect a tradition of national pride in their distant past. National museums that feature national antiquities also exist in Spain, Italy, Sweden, and Denmark, to name only the more prominent. Many of these institutions originated in the nineteenth century with a very direct wish to create national cohesion through a celebration of shared pasts.

Attempts at more general characterisation are difficult. A tradition of Roman archaeology is a powerful influence in Southern and Western Europe. For example, a number of important sites mark the northern boundaries of the Empire, including the famous reconstructions of the frontier at the Saalburg in the Taunus Mountains built in the 1890s, and, more recently (2000), the Varusschlacht Park and museum were opened celebrating a German victory against Roman legions. Oddities include such wonders as the Pompejanum, Bavaria, a state monument and museum, originally built in the 1840s for King Ludwig I of Bavaria, as a copy of the so-called Castor and Pollux house in Pompeii and as a specific exercise in giving German scholars access to Roman culture. It houses some of the state collections of Roman antiquities.

Northern European archaeological museums, minus the Romans, tend to highlight Viking archaeology, for example, at the National Museum of Sweden, National Museum of Denmark and the Stadsmuseum, Gothenburg. France away from the Roman southeast has many important prehistoric museums and sites and also prehistoric "parks" such as the Parc de Préhistoire de Bretagne that has life size open air dioramas of prehistoric human life and dinosaurs and the Prehisto Parc, Tursac, that concentrates on prehistoric peoples. There is even the Parc Asterix an archaeological theme park based on the famous cartoon character.

Eastern Europe is still to catch up with the West but recent times have seen the redevelopment of old museums. An example is the Butrint Museum in Albania. The story of this museum is a story of Albanian twentieth-century history. Excavations in the 1920s by the Italians, under orders from Mussolini, tried to find evidence for the visit of Aeneas on his way to found Rome. The first museum was designed and built by the Italians in the 1930s. It survived until 1943 when it was looted as the area descended into anarchy during World War II. It was restored under the communists but was used to project Illyrian culture over that of the Greeks and Romans. It was looted twice more as communism fell. It was reopened in 2005 after a complete redisplay was funded as a collaborative effort of the Butrint Foundation, the Albabnian Institute of

Archaeology, the Leventis Foundation, and the Packard Humanities Institute (Renton 2006).

Many museums in Europe are sited on the location of major archaeological discoveries. Examples include the Neanderthal Museum in Germany, which features an innovative design and a strong education programme; and the Roskilde Viking Ship Museum in Denmark, with its stunning waterside location and associated traditional shipyard, and Musée de Tautavel, European Center of Prehistory on the site of Palaeolithic discoveries in Southwestern France. These examples illustrate the very varied nature of museum presentation that has developed from common roots.

Across Europe, innovative design and presentations can be found. In the crypt of Geneva Cathedral, a brave, if flawed, attempt has been made to preserve the archaeological stratigraphy and explain through it the complex sequence of occupation. At Neuchatel in Switzerland at the beautiful Laténium Archaeology Park and Museum, modern design has been used to contextualise the artefacts from the local prehistoric lake site, and the museum building itself has been designed to be sympathetic to the local landscape. At the Louvre in Paris, the monumental remains of the medieval castle have been brilliantly preserved within the underground access areas of the museum. In many other places, particularly in Southern Europe, traditional museums based on eclectic or local collections of "classical" antiquities persist, for example, the Archaeological Museum of Palermo in Sicily and the Etruscan Guarnacci Museum in Volterra, Italy.

Southern Europe is dominated by the Classical Mediterranean civilizations, and museums tend to be of the more conservative decorative arts type. See Skeates 2005 for an overview. There are exceptions, the superb Alicante Archaeological Museum was awarded the distinction of *European Museum of the Year* in 2004 and has spectacular displays supporting wonderful collections. Athens has recently seen innovative museum displays built into its new metro stations (Hamilakis 2001).

In many parts of Europe, and unlike in Britain and North America, museums are part of national heritage services that in principle allow for a more orderly management of archaeology. For example, in Greece, museums come under a department of culture that administers them through epherates or regional divisions. Archaeologists also have a strong control over museum displays, possibly hindering their accessibility to wider audiences (Penny Kalligerou, personal communication), however again there are exceptions. The current redisplay of archaeology at the Archaeological Museum of Ioannina, in North West Greece, will use design to sympathise with the 1960s building and maximise the visual impact of its rich prehistoric and later collections.

There are still plenty of examples of private collections of antiquities in Europe, although it is not common to find these in publicly accessible museums. For example, see Mouliou (1997) for an analysis of two Greek museums based on private collections, the Paulos and Alexandra Canellopolos Museum and the Nicholas P. Goulandris Foundation Museum of Cycladic, and Ancient Greek Art.

In Europe, as in Britain, there tends to be a quite clear distinction between ethnography and archaeology; although a less clear distinction between classical archaeology and decorative arts.

Africa

Archaeology, museums, and archaeology museums have still failed to make a major impact on Africa. In the majority of countries, bedevilled by debt, poverty, political instability, and the ethnic and racial instability that was a product of colonial divisions' museums have not been embraced by the population, championed by rulers, or understood by civil servants, other than as a luxury for foreign tourists (see, e.g., from different regions Nzeewunwa 1990, MacKenzie 1990, and Skeates 2005 how museums and archaeology have failed to make an impact). In all of these cases, the archaeology and the museum provision has largely been a legacy of the Colonial period: either put in place by colonial powers, a "parting gift" by well-meaning excolonials, or a product of ill-defined postcolonial aspirations.

In parts of Africa, the looting of antiquities has done untold damage to the evidence of precolonial cultures, before they have been studied by archaeologists in any detail, and now may never be understood. Local people are often involved in the looting, seeing it as one way for making money. Only occasionally are authorities acting to prevent this. In Mali, where destruction of archaeological sites is particularly acute, the government has developed a community-based initiative to protect the vanishing culture. The Culture Bank concept combines a museum and a bank that allows local inhabitants to use their cultural objects as collateral to obtain small business loans (Morag Kersel, personal communication). Looting has also largely stopped in Cameroon, and, generally, there is a feeling that the situation is improving as local communities become more empowered about their own cultural pasts (Andrew Reid, personal communication).

The two exceptions to the norm in Africa, for very different reasons, are South Africa and Egypt. South African museums and archaeology have gone through a painful transformation from being an instrument of Apartheid to a servant of black majority government (e.g., Goodnow 2006). The situation in South Africa is extremely complex, and it is not yet clear what role museums and archaeology will have in the new world order.

The place of Egyptology in Western culture looms large when considering African museum archaeology. It is difficult to consider Egypt and Egyptology other than as a unique case. The number of active archaeologists in Egypt probably represents half the number for the whole continent (Andrew Reid, personal communication). Egyptian museums developed out of the colonial period and live with that legacy but are now seen firmly within the cultural and economic development of that country through the value of tourism. The Grand Museum of Egypt is currently being built at Giza on the outskirts of Cairo to hold the countries collection of Pharonic antiquities including, as a centrepiece, *a museum within a museum* to hold the 5,000 finds from Tutankhamen's tomb. This in turn is the centrepiece of a network of planned new museums for Egypt including the Imhotep Museum at Saqqara and the Crocodile Museum at Kom Ombo. The current Egyptian Museum in Cairo, one of the great archaeology museums of the world, will be renovated and given over to Pharonic art. Other North African countries also draw on the "classic" legacy of their Roman and Phoenician heritage for tourism.

The other great legacy of Africa to human history and archaeology is, of course, to be its cradle. The value of this to Africa is yet to be fully realised. In 1965, Mary and Louis Leakey grandly returned the skull of a *Zinjanthropus boisei* (or *Australopithecus boisei*), found in the Olduvai Gorge in 1959, to the President of Tanzania. At that time, for the new nation to be associated with the origins of humanity were considered something to champion. The skull now rests in the vault of the national museum. Other museums set up by the Leakeys on the sites of important, if visually uninspiring and inaccessible early palaeolithic stone scatters, have been maintained by Kenya but with little enthusiasm. Recent anecdotal reports suggest that Christian fundaementalists may object to stories of evolution being told through these collections. The National Museum of Kenya in Nairobi is currently closed for a 2-year period; however, a travelling exhibition created with the British Museum is being undertaken in 2006 (see Heywood 2006 for a review and Ouma and Abunga 2006 for a critique of this project).

The influences of global tourism have also been problematic in sub-Saharan Africa. World Heritage sites seem to be used as political collecting cards, and there is sometimes conflict between the conservationists who wish to preserve sites and culture "unspoilt," while local people wish to move into the twenty-first century.

The majority of archaeology in Africa is undertaken by local universities, although active fieldwork projects are rare, and by foreign (European and North American) universities. The entire active archaeological population outside Egypt is probably less than four hundred individuals. Very few museums are involved in active work, although the Kenyan National Museum is currently undertaking a research project into slavery funded from the United States.

Things are a little brighter at a local level. Localised communities are more likely to have a direct cultural link to their immediate past, and it is here where external funding can have a real effect. Attempts to stop looting have already been mentioned. Other community centres and museums have also been a success. In Botswana, a travelling museum known as the *Zebra on Wheels* is operated by the National Museum, Monuments, and Art Gallery (NMMAG). It currently has four vehicles operating independently in different parts of the country. In Kenya, a novel way has been found to protect the Gede Ruins National Monument. The so-called Kipepeo project is run by the National Museums of Kenya. The project encourages locals to leave the site undisturbed by paying them for collecting local butterfly pupae that are then sold around the world to collectors.

A tragic but important facet of museum archaeology in Africa is the Genocide Memorial Centre in Kigali in Rwanda that acts as a memorial to the recent atrocities. Archaeology has the potential to do much to break down the regions racial animosity; however, a visit to the precolonial National Museum of Rwanda will find every artefact clearly labelled with an ethnic origin (Andrew Reid, personal communication). Many other memorials in Rwanda simply consist of bodies deliberately being kept exposed by relatives, until the authorities "do something" or to ensure that people never forget.

Museums are also being used as part of the process of coming to terms with tragedy in Kenya and South Africa. In South Africa, Memory Boxes are being created by those suffering from AIDs. In Kenya, community museums have been set up by members of the community to commemorate the Mau Mau period. These have only emerged since the change in President and the recognition that Mau Mau happened. They often involve people's front rooms being used to display passbooks and other material culture that people have retained from that time. These later examples suggest that having largely rejected the European model of museums African people may be finding their own unique way of finding value from combining material culture and places to preserve collective memory.

North America

North America differs from Europe in not having such a well-established network of local authority museums. U.S. museums are run by Federal, state, tribal, local, and private organisations. *American Ancient Treasures* (Folsom and Folsom 1983), although now somewhat dated, still offers the most complete listing of North American sites and museums.

There is also a blurring between ethnography and archaeology as the majority of archaeology in displays is of Native American Indian material. With a clear distinction between contemporary culture, classical European roots and Indigenous cultures, archaeology museums tend to hold collections of classical antiquities displayed as decorative and fine arts (such as at the Museum of Fine Arts in Boston, the Cleveland Museum of Art, and the Field Museum in Chicago) and sometimes Native American archaeology displayed as ethnography (again, examples, include the Field Museum). The more recent phenomena of "historical archaeology" that in the United States means the excavation of postcontact white settlement has not yet made its way into many museums, although it has had a strong influence on site based living history museums, such as Jamestown Settlement, Colonial Williamsburg and Old Sturbridge Village. These sites are a characteristic feature of the eastern United States and include traditional museums mixed with full-scale reconstructions or the redevelopments of historical sites (see Chapter 13).

The United States has examples of Native American run museums that vary in their adherence to traditional models. The Turtle in Niagara Falls, NY, is described as a "Native American Centre for Living Arts under Hodenosaunee management," the building is of a nonorthodox modern design, based on a turtle shell. Similarly, the Huhagam Heritage Centre that acts as a museum and community centre for the Gila River Indian Community is a most beautiful building complex built to sympathise with the peoples it represents. Alternatively, the Six Nations Museum in Onchiota, NY, is a small wooden building dense with objects often displayed for theatrical rather than didactic purposes (Blancke and Slow Turtle 1994, pp. 446–448).

The interpretation of Native American cultures in U.S. museums has changed radically in the last 20 or so years. For example, at the Smithsonian Institution, Native Americans were previously banished to the National Museum of Natural History (Blakey 1990, p. 40), where the layout of galleries appeared to show Native Americans with an evolutionary link to early hominids (Blakey 1990, p. 41). The Mall now boasts the National Museum of the American Indian in a building that finally breaks from the traditional model for history museums (see Chapter 15).

University museums are also very important for archaeology and often reflect the policy of U.S. university archaeologists in the past to have done most of their fieldwork abroad, normally within the "Classical World." Good examples include the Peabody Museum of Archaeology and Ethnology, in Cambridge, MA, and the University of Pennsylvania Museum of Archaeology and Anthropology in Philadelphia. A small subset of this group is the seminary colleges and Christian universities that have undertaken excavation and fieldwork in the Holy Land.

Archaeology is not prominent in Canadian museums. As in the United States, there is an overlap with anthropology and with cultural centres developed by First Nation peoples. The Canadian Museum of Civilization in Quebec and the Museum of Anthropology in Vancouver have collections, programmes, and displays on Indigenous peoples that are primarily ethnographic in nature.

Central and Southern America

Despite not being one of the wealthiest parts of the world, there are some very good museums in Central America. These are mainly built on the sites of, or developed from the cultures of, the Aztec, the Olmec, and the Maya. The archaeology of the region benefits from truly magnificent monuments, often in excellent condition and well researched. Much of the impetus for developing museums has been the attraction of foreign tourism. However, there has also been an attempt to use both archaeology and, more particularly, material culture in museums as a way of developing national and regional identity.

Most of the museums in Mexico are run by INAH (Instituo de Nacional Antropologia y Historia). This organisation is also responsible for the archaeological investigations throughout the country and the display of finds and sites for tourism. Their displays extend to outdoor museums encompassing whole sites (or in the case of one Olmec site, moved to the centre of Villahermosa to allow for the continued exploitation of the original site for oil). Some of the larger sites, such as Teotuhacan, Chechen Itza, La Venta, and Palenque, have on-site museums; these tend not to be as well thought out as the major state museums, of which there is one in each of the state capitals.

There has been central government investment in the state museums as a way of developing regional identity and promoting tourism. As such, previously antiquated displays and labelling are being improved and are now often highly innovative and technologically advanced. Interactive computers in Spanish (and often English) have been incorporated into the larger museums, such as at El Tajin and Palenque. Mexican museums have one eye on foreign tourists but also encourage local use. Of note throughout Central America is Free Sundays. All national residents are able to access museums and sites free on Sundays (tourists still pay). There is also a differential charge for locals during the week.

Elsewhere in Central America, the situation is dominated by a lack of funds and, therefore, the place of museums is well down on the list of government priorities. Belize is planning for a national museum but at present does not have the necessary funds and only has temporary displays. Some of the country's archaeological sites and larger towns have small museums, but they are very limited and variable in their presentation.

Guatemala also has local museums and museums directly associated with its surviving monuments; these, again, are variable, although the one at Tikal represents the material from the site in a sympathetic way and incorporates some of the excavation stories. Much of the most valuable material has been taken to Guate City.

Honduras has the exceptional Copan site and open-air museum. Similarly, El Salvador has Ceren, the Central American equivalent of Pompeii, with an amazing open-air museum, giving aspects of every day life in the Maya world prior to the Spanish arrival.

In South America, ethnic integration means that postcolonial tensions have not been as acute as in the north, although recent events suggest this may change. The Government of Peru is currently claiming for the return of material from Machu Picchu held in the United States, and Indigenous communities have objected to the planned display of mummies at the Museum of High Altitude Archaeology in Argentina. This corresponds to a relatively undeveloped museum archaeology community in much of the continent. The Archaeological Museum of San Pedro de Atacama in Chile is perhaps more the norm. Founded by a Belgian Jesuit priest in 1955, it is now administered by the University of the North and its collections and displays include Andean mummies.

Asia, China, and the Far East

The next generation of museums, including archaeology museums, will not be built in America or Europe. They will be in China and the Middle East. This is where both the money and the will for such projects lie. The ambition of projects, such as the Museum of Islamic Art in Doha, Qatar, leaves Western museum professionals gasping with awe. Designed by I. M. Pei (of Louvre pyramid fame), it holds a wonderful collection of art spanning the Islamic world from Spain to China, and from the seventh to the nineteenth centuries. The building will include 45,000 m^2 of space and will be surrounded by its own created landscape including a lake.

Another major growth area for museums at present is China. The country has a government-led initiative to preserve and promote cultural heritage, a fact that is made palpable in many of the museums themselves, where the visitor is greeted by poster images of the president alongside details of cultural plans for that region (Solicari 2005). Many new museums are being built, and old ones are being renovated or completely rebuilt, including the grand Capital Museum in Beijing, which opened in 2005.

There is still little information on Chinese museums for Western consumption. Websites for these museums are still being developed. Joanna Capon's book offers one of the few overviews of museums in China as a whole (Capon 2002). The scope, range, and number of Chinese archaeology museums are bewildering. Many of its museums are site-based, often on the site of royal or aristocratic tombs. The most famous, of course, is the Museum of Qin Terra-Cotta Warriors and Horses, one of the archaeological wonders of the world (see Rowe 2006 for a recent summary). But there are many more not so well-known outside China, including, for example, The Qianling Tomb in Shanxi Province; and the Hubei Province Museum, Wuhan, that in 1999 opened the Chime-Bells Museum. Here, one tomb contained a collection of musical instruments dating to 400 B.C., and the museum includes a theatre where traditional music concerts are a part of the museum experience.

It is fair to say that by Western standards most Chinese museums are still old-fashioned and poorly designed and interpreted. However, this is changing rapidly under an influx of foreign influence. At present, many museums offer a combination of chronological mixed media displays and traditional art historical displays by object type. Most displays employ an easily recognisable means of highlighting the most important objects. In Shaanxi, this takes the form of a huge photograph of each key object, in front of which the original is displayed. In many other museums, such as the Xinjiang Regional Museum in Dunhuang County and in Turpan, those considered to be the most important artefacts are exhibited on a base of red velvet. Written interpretation is often minimal, although both Dunhuang County Museum and the Shaanxi Provincial Museum have teams of multilingual gallery assistants on-hand to answer questions and interpret the displays, emphasising a strong educational drive. English translation text panels emphasise the feeling of "pride" that the museum's collections hope to inspire. Collections in China are almost exclusively of Chinese objects and are seen as a patriotic resource, emphasising China's role in world culture (Solicari 2005).

Newer museums in Japan and South Korea are a mix of Western and Eastern design, examples include the Seoul Museum of History with spacious galleries and excellent visitor facilities. The Osaka History Museum, Japan, looks like an ultramodern office block and contains preserved archaeological ruins with viewing areas in its basement.

Elsewhere in Asia, archaeology museums are mainly traditional and of the postcolonial type, for example, the Indian Museum in Calcutta. The non-Western take on museums can also be seen in the language used in India to describe them. Translations of local names include: "house of magic," "house of the dead," and "house of strange things" (Momin and Pratrap 1994, p. 290). In India, museums double up as religious shrines because they hold so many images of deities.

Australia and New Zealand

Museum archaeology in Australia and New Zealand is, as might be expected, and as with North America, dominated by its mix of European influences and recent Indigenous empowerment. Either state or commonwealth governments fund the major Australian museums. These museums have traditionally had a strong natural history element that includes a tradition of collecting, displaying, and researching prehistoric archaeology. They are also the legal repository of excavated material. Involvement in archaeology has lessened in recent years as museums have employed fewer archaeologists. Similarly, museums have moved away from research-led projects to public programme-led projects.

The major change in museums in the last 15 years, and one that has defined Australian museum archaeology, is the relationship with Indigenous communities. This obviously has a large overlap with anthropology and ethnography. Because museums have held collections of "secret," "sacred," and "ceremonial" objects and human remains (although most of these

85

have now been repatriated), a special relationship has often developed between museums and individual Aborigine communities with museums often taking on the role of "keeping places" for such objects. In towns, urban Indigenous communities have used old ethnographic collections as a catalyst for cultural renewal and revival of traditional crafts. A good example of the complex process of reconciliation that museums are going through in an attempt to change from colonial institutes to community centres is given by the Strehlow Research Centre in Alice Springs (Galt-Smith, unpublished).

Most displays that feature archaeology in Australian museums deal with Aborigine culture and are primarily ethnographic in nature, using archaeology to support more recent material. Few museums have attempted major exhibitions focussed entirely on archaeology, possibly because "prehistoric archaeology, although featuring complex ideas, relies on unprepossessing collections: a few chipped stone artefacts, small pieces of red ochre, bones and shells (food remains), the rare bone artefact. . . . and the charcoal of old camp fires" (Mike Smith, personal communication). The National Museum of Australia has taken a different approach (Mike Smith, personal communication). It does not feature a major exhibit on archaeology, but, instead, it has used archaeology wherever it complemented the theme of an exhibit.

Aboriginal archaeology is now broadly perceived as being too difficult. It is highly regulated and reliant on long-term relationships with a community. A major trend in Australian archaeological research, at present, is maritime archaeology. Another response has been for Australian archaeologists to develop projects overseas, and to shift to historical, or contact-period, archaeology. Some areas of archaeology (e.g., physical anthropology) are no longer viable given community opposition to research on human remains (see Chapter 8).

Occasional anomalies illustrate how individuals can still influence the nature and distribution of archaeology museums. The Abbey Museum of Art and Archaeology in rural Australia has archaeological collections from the Old World, undertakes medieval tournaments, and is planning a medieval village. Its collections were put together by the Rev. John

Ward in the early twentieth century in north London and witt the somewhat unorthodox community he founded when he came to Australia via Cyprus after World War II (see the Abbey Museum of Art and Archaeology 1989).

New Zealand also has a range of museums, many of which include ethnographic/archaeological collections of Maori material; for example, the Auckland Museum (Auckland War Memorial Museum). The National Museum Te Papa is considered a model of sympathetic ethnic integration.

Key Texts

Capon, J. (2002). *Guide to museums in China.* Hong Kong: Orientations Magazine Ltd.

Folsom, F., and Folsom, M. (1983), *America's ancient treasures.* Albuquerque: University of New Mexico Press.

Gathercole, P., and Lowenthal, D. (Eds.). (1990). *The politics of the past.* London: Unwin.

Fisher, M. (2004). *Britain's Best Museums and Galleries.* London: Penguin.

PART 2

COLLECTIONS

The characteristic smell of the archaeological store, compounded of embalmed oddments, massed ceramic and preserved wood, faintly spicy and faintly dusty, is the sweet stench of mummification, and curators become cemetery-haunting necrophiliacs compelled by a dubious romantic impulse to arrest time and decay.
(Pearce 1997, p. 51)

It could certainly be said, from the archaeological point of view, that to deposit an object in a museum is a lesser evil rather than an aim to be pursued for its own sake.
(Charles-Picard 1972, p. 135)

CHAPTER 6
ARCHAEOLOGICAL COLLECTIONS

Individual items of value, often collected in the past, sometimes by dubious means, and often of limited research value The nature of collections, values and ethics, collections management.

Collections

At the heart of museums are their collections. When a list of all the elements that make up a museum (collections, buildings, staff, public, buildings, researchers, etc.) is made, any one of them can be removed, except the collections, and the concept of a museum would still exist. In essence, a museum is the dynamic relationship between a collection, those who curate it, and the public (as discussed in Chapter 1). But this relationship starts with, and must be characterized, by the collection.

Susan Pearce has led recent studies into the nature of collecting in the European tradition and how it is founded in the individual and individual motivations (Pearce 1995). Whether this can be shown to have a correspondence in museum collecting, is unclear, however, Pearce has shown that collecting appears to perform the basic need to fulfill our human wish to make sense of and control the world around us.

Pearce (1997, p. 49) has divided the archaeological collections likely to be found in a museum into six types:

1. Single pieces or small groups found as chance finds, often with very limited records attached. The majority of these in any given museum collection is likely to be local finds.

2. Large groups formed as private collections, sometimes with substantial records attached. These may be from anywhere in Britain or abroad, but may well include local material. They were mostly acquired before c. 1950.

3. Material from museum-based excavations. These will be local with, of course, excellent records. The material is likely to be of relatively recent accession.

4. Material from excavations conducted by other bodies, including that from all old excavations, and from new excavations where consultation is a possibility.

5. Material from fieldwork projects. This is likely to be of recent and ongoing accession, and the museum should have links with the organisation.

6. To this list must be added material that has been discovered through the use of metal detectors. Here a judgment has to be formed about the value of associated information.

In this book, archaeological collections are very deliberately divided into two main groups: individual objects (discussed in this chapter and covered by Pearce's numbers 1, 2, and 6) and assemblages of objects as parts of archaeological excavation archives (discussed in Chapter 7 and covered by Pearce's numbers 3–5). This is of course a false division. Many individual items now accessioned into museum collections once came from archaeological excavations, and many items from archaeological excavation archives are treated as individual items in many museum processes. Nevertheless, in the ways museums store, catalogue, use, and think about their collections, the division is a valid one.

As archaeology developed as a discipline during the later nineteenth and early twentieth centuries, the concept of the excavation archive grew, and with it the idea that objects received their meaning from their context and association. However, by the time that this occurred many museums were holding large collections of objects that had been largely decontextualised, or had never been given a proper context in the first place.

These collections, of pots, flints, coins, metals, and so forth, dominate archaeology museums, their galleries and stores. They are dominated by complete objects such as pots or flint tools, or objects with a perceived value such as coins and brooches. Thomas (1992, p. 3) has argued for the "Total Collection" where, conceptually, every item in a collection is given equal value whatever it is, its origin, and its use. In actual fact, although most museum professionals would agree with this concept, there is an unspoken hierarchy that sees the display, high-value objects at the top, and the low-value handling collections, or stored collections, at the bottom. Most of these collections have been inherited by the current generation of curators who must live not only with past choices as to what was collected but also as to how it was classified, conserved, and stored. As Pearce has noted, "the key act of power in which the curatorial self is realized is that of classifying" (1999, p. 18). Beaker pots are only beaker pots because curators decided they were. The size and nature of these collections is also sometimes a burden on the modern museum. As was made clear in the seminal report on the cost of collecting (Lord et al. 1989): acquisition is easy, it is caring for something once a museum has it that is difficult, and made more so by the tyranny of antidisposal that persists despite recent reports, such as the Museums Association (2005) and the NMDC (2003), that have accepted the need for selective disposal.

Historic and Private Collections

Much material now in museums originally derived from private collections accumulated in the eighteenth and nineteenth centuries, and, as such, mirrors the predilections of the individual collectors (Plate 1). These were then donated over time, often as bequests, into public museum collections in the later nineteenth and early twentieth centuries. It has been suggested that 42 percent of local authority museums were founded on the collection of a single individual or society (Wood 1997, p. 59). Many key museum's archaeological assemblages originated in such personal collections. Important examples, to name just two, are the Greenwell Collection of British antiquities at the British Museum (Kinnes and Longworth 1985), and the Stourhead Collection at Devizes Museum (Annable and Simpson 1964). In addition, in the late nineteenth and early twentieth centuries, major excavation programmes were funded on the "distribution system" whereby those who funded a dig were given a selection of the finds at the end of the season, thus leading to a diaspora of finds from important excavations to many different destinations.

The reasons behind the accumulation of these original collections and the motivations of the collectors have been much debated (e.g., Pearce 1990, p. 21). Certainly, this period lacked any overarching attempt at objective rigor and was as much about the collectors and their worldview as it was about the material they amassed. Modern curators and archaeologists have tended to distance themselves with this period partly as a means of validating their own methods. However, modern collections and collecting methods continue to be profoundly influenced by these early collections. Many museums are still dominated by material from the Mediterranean, and particularly from Rome, Greece, and Egypt, a direct result of eighteenth-, nineteenth-, and early twentieth-century value sets, and, thus, collecting habits. Romano–British material, which was sought by early collectors as a cheap alternative to material from Italy, has a more prominent place in modern collections than does material from other periods of Britain's past. This is reinforced by the primacy that Rome is given in English education, itself a hangover from this period. Collections also continue to value the individual fine object over the mundane, and museums continue to seek to "complete" collections, where such a concept is, in fact, a creation.

The early collections, although sometimes collected from archaeological contexts, were not archaeological in the sense that they quickly lost their context and associations. They became individual items, often with a very vague provenance, if one at all, and were valued on their individual merits. Most

MR. CHARLES ROACH SMITH'S COLLECTION OF LONDON ANTIQUITIES, LATELY ADDED TO THE BRITISH MUSEUM.

PLATE 1. Interior of number 5 Liverpool Street, c. 1850. The antiquarian collection of Charles Roach Smith, later to find its way to the Museum of London and the British Museum. (Photo: Museum of London.)

museum archaeological collections continue to be dominated by such material and museum staff struggles not to value such individual items over assemblages of more mundane material with good archaeological provenances. This huge body of material has presented its own problems for modern curators trying to distinguish between illicit and legally obtained objects (see below). A vast amount of material originally lost its provenance as grand tour souvenirs, and identifying modern illicit antiquities is often made near impossible by the large number of eighteenth- and nineteenth-century "illicit antiquities" already in circulation and camouflaging new ones. "From an old collection" (Brodie, and Walker Tubb 2002, p. 3) is not an uncommon provenance of a sale item.

Cultural Property, Its Ownership, Value, and Restitution

As with so many other aspects of museum archaeology, the place of objects and collections becomes far more complex and political once it leaves a local scale. This is seen most clearly in the current mass of claims for repatriation and its accompanying debate. The most famous case of archaeological remains being claimed for repatriation are the Elgin (or Parthenon) Marbles held primarily (but not exclusively) at the British Museum (see Skeates 2000, pp. 30–36). They represent the classic example of a battle in a modern political arena for archaeological remains taken during the colonial and imperialist period. This has been called "archaeology's greatest controversy" (King 2005). It is something that everyone is supposed to hold a view on, and the arguments for which are carried on at the highest level (see, e.g., most recently King 2005 for the retention argument, and its rebuff in Flynn 2006b). For this reason, the arguments are also hedged about with diplomatic politeness and subtle use of semantics. The British Committee for the Return of the Marbles has recently renamed itself, "The British Committee for the Reunification of the Parthenon Marbles (BCRPM)," accepting that the previous term repatriation was inappropriate in this case (BCRPM 2005, p. 1).

The debate, and its prominence, is suspiciously Westocentric in nature. As Lowenthal has hinted (1990, p. 310) because Ancient Greece, and indeed the Parthenon, has a very special place in the Western civilization origin myth, the debate over the fate of the marbles receives attention and credibility far out of proportion to other claims for restitution, such as, for example, that for the Benin Bronzes from Nigeria.

Recently, a rash of other claims has joined the battle for the Marbles. In 2004, legal attempts were made (unsuccessfully) to prevent examples of Aboriginal etched birch bark artefacts from the British Museum and Kew Gardens in London, to return to Britain after being loaned to an exhibition in Melbourne Australia (see Morris, 2004a for a summary; the barks were eventually returned after legal hearings in Australia). In 2006, the Peruvian Government, with the support of its first Indigenous president, renewed its claims for the artefacts from Machu Picchu to be returned from Yale University. In addition, the Italian Government has recently made claims for the return of objects from the Getty and the Metropolitan Museum of Art. This debate is not going to go away. It is gaining pace and more and more objects are being claimed back by more and more diverse groups. A point might come when it is a recognised point in the growing maturity of a state when it claims back its missing patrimony from previous colonial and imperial powers.

These arguments also work at local, regional, and national levels. Should a nation's top treasures automatically go to a national museum, where they might become lost amongst other treasures, or should they stay in the area where they were found, maybe being seen by fewer people but contributing to local tourism and local pride? The recent trend has been away from the finest objects automatically going to larger museums. There has also been an encouraging trend towards partnership and loan agreements.

This inevitably begs the question as to whether a world, in which someone could only see an item of cultural heritage in its country or region of origin, would be a better place. The almost unthinkableness of such a notion perhaps only reinforces how culturally programmed "we" are in expecting to encounter world cultures in "our" museums, however incongruous and revalued they may be there. The counter position recently prosecuted so strongly by the British Museum (see MacGregor and Williams 2005), which argued that threatened and diverse cultures benefit by the showcasing of their material culture in London or other Western cities, is also one completely constructed from a Western perspective. There are a few examples of where Indigenous peoples, such as the New Zealand Maori, have identified the benefits to be had from their culture being celebrated thousands of miles away (Lowenthal 1990, p. 309). All these debates centre on fundamental arguments about value and ownership to which as yet no universally agreed principles have emerged.

Trade in Antiquities

If one fault line exists between western museums and countries or communities of origin, another exists between the museum community and private dealers and collectors. It is felt by many museum curators that archaeological objects only have a place in public museums, and private collections, and the trade in antiquities is frowned upon as encouraging looting and keeping important material out of the public domain. This situation, already predicated on a dubious value set, is made the more ironic by the fact that, as already discussed, most museums originally acquired their prime collections during a period where the purchase of antiquities and their acquisition for personal gain was the norm.

Just as Western Europe and the United States remain the heart of the museum world, they are also the home to the widespread collecting of world antiquities by private individuals, and, as such, the trade in such items. Some private collections are finer than those in public museums and occasionally become major independent museum exhibits in their own right or contribute to museum displays (e.g., the Getty collection in the United States and the Sainsbury collection in the United Kingdom). But the dividing line between legitimate trading in antiquities and the trade in stolen items is a thin and movable one. Even organisations, as established as the Getty, have recently been embroiled in controversies over the origins of items in their collection (Gumbel 2006). The modern world is articulated in terms of property and ownership and is where value is most easily expressed in monetary terms. Antiquities are part of this system, and there is a huge international market in them. Much of this market is legal, well-intentioned, and positive. However, the vast amounts of money involved, and the relatively easy way to acquire material at its source, have contributed to a global illicit market in antiquities, focused on theft or exploitation in the developing world, and purchase and huge profits in the West (see Renfrew 2000 and Brodie and Walker Tubb 2002 for a full discussion). This trade has been ranked just behind drugs and arms trafficking in terms of international sales figures. Recently, art and antiquities theft has been estimated as a global business valued at anywhere between US$2 and 6 billion per year (Bernick 1998, pp. 91–116 quoted in Kersel, in preparation)

Museum archaeologists, just like fine arts and decorative arts curators, need to recognise and be familiar with this world. Objects will often need to be given a monetary value, for example, when arranging for museum exhibit exhibition-loans. It is also the case that private collectors and traders are sometimes themselves world experts in their collections and have an expertise that is valuable to curators. Key objects that are wanted for collections may come up for sale and, in some countries, including Britain, opportunities exist for the state to help museums acquire objects from private owners. Again, much of this relationship is positive and unproblematic. The relationship between museums and the seamier side of the antiquities trade has not been unproblematic. Although there is nothing inherently wrong with private collecting, and the trade in objects, it has, along with museum collecting, led to looting, theft, the destruction of archaeological contexts and sites, and the creation of a large number of fakes – many of which are or have been in museum collections and have influenced scholarly research.

In many developing countries, the selling of antiquities is a major source of income for impoverished locals. For some nations with extreme poverty and a rich archaeological her-itage, the combination has been disastrous for contextualised remains. In countries such as Mali (see Togola 2002 and Walker Tubb 2002, pp. 286–287) and Jordan (see Politis 2002), it has been suggested that parts of their ancient past are now almost lost to archaeology through looting. The motivations, methods, and solutions to the looting and subsequent illicit trade in antiquities are particular to particular circumstances. Morag Kersel (in preparation) has looked at three case studies, Israel, Palestine, and Mali. In Mali, a Peace Corps initiative to protect the country's vanishing culture has developed into a community-based museum known as the Culture Bank. The Culture Bank initiative allows local inhabitants to use their cultural objects as collateral to obtain small business loans. In theory, this provides microcredit, protects archaeological and ethnographically significant objects, produces income, and encourages villagers to participate in cultural activities. Israel has a legally sanctioned antiquities market overseen and monitored by the Israel Antiquities Authority (IAA). Under national legislation, it is illegal to excavate archaeological sites without the correct authorization, but it is legal to buy and sell archaeological material from collections predating 1978 (the year the national patrimony law was enacted). In 2000, estimates put the trade of some eighty licensed antiquities dealers at close to US$5 million per year (Sontag 1999 quoted in Kersel in preparation). In Palestine, looting of antiquities has risen drastically since the onset of the *al-Aqsa Intifada* in 2000 that left many Palestinians unemployed. The unrest has also ended Israeli and Palestinian cooperation in antiquities policing efforts. Recognising the magnitude of the looting problem, a nongovernmental Palestinian cultural heritage organization (the Palestinian Association for Cultural Exchange [PACE]) is working with local villagers to act as the protectors and monitors of archaeological sites at risk from looting, development, and neglect.

There are many complex facets to the uneasy relationship among museums and archaeologists, legal trade and collecting, and illicit trade. For example, the relationship between modern art and archaeology has turned Cycladic Greek figures into artistic masterpieces to be sold as art irrespective of provenance and led to the continued looting of archaeological sites (Skeates 2005, p. 312). The digital revolution has also played a part. Monitoring of ebay for antiquities is now a regular part of any curator's job. And illicit items have been identified being traded on it (McFarlane 2005), although maybe its open nature will prevent its wide use. War has also played its part. Looters and traders exploited the anarchy that followed the recent invasion of Iraq. U.S. Colonel Matthew Bogdanos, who investigated thefts from the National Museum of Iraq in

Baghdad during the recent war, has been quoted as saying, "the patina of gentility that we associate with the world of antiquities has always rested atop a sordid core of criminal activity" (quoted in Flynn 2006a). Harsh words indeed.

The control of the trade in illicit antiquities is reliant on international cooperation. The two key international accords that have attempted to prevent international illicit trade are the Convention on the Means of Prohibiting and Preventing the Illicit Import, Export, and Transfer of Ownership of Cultural Property that was adopted by UNESCO in 1970 (and is normally referred to as the UNESCO 1970 Convention), and the Convention on Stolen and Illegally Exported Cultural Objects adopted in 1995 by UNIDROIT 1995 which augments UNESCO 1970 (and is normally referred to as UNIDROIT 1995; see also Chapter 4).

Tubb (2002) provides a summary of UK initiatives dealing with illicit trade in cultural property. It has not been a particularly glorious story. London is one of the key world centres for the trade in antiquities and the pressures on government not to put this lucrative market at risk have been immense. A key moment in the UK story was the publication of *Stealing History* (Brodie, Doole, and Watson 2000). However, as Kathy Walker Tubb (2002) makes clear the legislation that does exist tries to prevent the trade and illicit movement in antiquities. That is it deals with the material once it has left the ground, when most damage is already done by the removal of any archaeological context.

Some have suggested that the trade in illicit antiquities is diminishing. One encouraging sign is the greater recognition of the importance of provenance in dealing with antiquities by collectors (Flynn 2006b). It has been argued (Nørskov 2002) that the curators and dealers are taking more note of the difference between provenanced and unprovenanced objects, leading to a greater demand, and increasing price, for the later. Although for the United States, Davies (2002, pp. 238–239) has suggested that the market is seeing less attribution to provenance. On the downside, Davies (2002, p. 240) has suggested that the introduction of NAGPRA in the United States may have prevented some private collections being donated to public museums and led to them being put onto the market, in the knowledge that under NAGPRA they would have been returned to Indigenous tribes.

One of the most often put arguments by those who trade in antiquities (e.g., Walker Tubb 2002, p. 291) is that many artefacts are not "priceless treasures that should be in museums" and that museums, anyway, have cellars and stores bursting with objects that are underused, undervalued, and often deteriorating. These are accusations that deserve more than a knee-jerk reaction. The first argument has some credibility; there is nothing wrong with individuals or communities owning or possessing archaeological artefacts outside of a museum environment. Indeed, it would be patently ridiculous to suggest otherwise. What is required, though, is the recognition of how important archaeological context is, and how, to the archaeologist, it is those very objects that are not treasures, in their context and with their associations, that are most useful in building up pictures of the past. And what is a tragedy is when objects are taken from these contexts without consideration of the story that is being lost forever.

The argument about bulging museum basements is more problematic. The simple truth is, and as is discussed elsewhere in this book, it is the case that many museums do hold objects that are not properly curated, and, taking into account the argument about context above, there is no need for certain categories of object to have even more representatives in museum collections.

In some parts of the world, the Western model of values is less relevant. In China, the relationship between culture and commerce appears more relaxed. Antiquity shops are present in several of the country's major museums, including Xi'an and Urumqi. On a similarly commercial note, the gift shop of the Terracotta Warrior Museum plays host to the farmer who originally discovered the buried army and who now dutifully signs copies of the guidebook, creating limited-edition souvenirs and promoting the notion of cultural celebrity. Certainly, the issue of cultural value and authenticity is one which arises time and again in relation to China's museums, with many reports stating that undeclared replicas are often displayed in place of the original (Solicari 2005).

Fakes and Forgeries

An obvious by-product in the market for antiquities is the creation of fakes and forgeries. Only recently, police in Turkey have arrested the director and other staff at the Usak Museum when it was discovered that two pieces of the sixth century B.C. "Lydian Hoard" had been stolen and replaced by forgeries. There is a long history of fake antiquities, usually associated with an attempt to make profit but also, at times, linked to academic rivalry.

Forgeries are, of course, not limited to archaeological collections, and in such areas as fine art where prices are far higher, the problem is more acute. However, archaeology is plagued by this problem. Cause celebes such as the so-called Piltdown Man are exceptional, but a stroll through the British Museum would find such objects as a crystal skull once thought to be a masterpiece of precontact Mexico and now thought to be produced in nineteenth-century Europe from Brazilian crystal. Once a prized treasure, although always suspected, it is now a mere curiosity (Jones 1990, pp. 296–297). Doubt still hangs over other iconic objects in major museums such as some of the European Palaeolithic and later "Venus figurines."

The sheer quantity of fakes and the long and protracted arguments over authenticity highlight just how difficult it is to prove authenticity (if such a thing can actually exist), how tenuous some archaeological identifications are and, once again, how important provenance and context are to archaeology. In many cases, it is only a clear archaeological context that will give an object true archaeological value. For the museum archaeologist, the embarrassment of acquiring, maybe purchasing, an object that proves to be a fake is one hazard, surely the danger that research can be undermined through fake objects is even more serious.

Forgeries also have their place in the social history of archaeology and collecting. For example, in London, objects manufactured in the nineteenth century to service the demand for antiquities now have their own place in museum collections.

Portable Antiquities and Metal Detectors

Since the early 1970s, a major source of new objects in museum collections, and a major subject of debate for the profession, has been the growing hobby of metal detecting. Metal detecting became a mass-participation hobby in Britain, the United States, and Western Europe in the 1970s when cheap metal detectors became available. The hobby became more sophisticated with the arrival of high-resolution machines in the 1980s (see Addyman and Brodie 2002 for a review of the subject for Britain).

From the beginning, archaeologists were uneasy with this type of detecting. First, there was the recognition that objects would be removed from their context thus taking away important evidence and damaging the strata. Second, there was also the concern that detecting was being undertaken on vulnerable archaeological sites that deserved to be excavated or properly protected. There is no doubt that "nighthawking" of Scheduled Ancient Monuments did, and does, take place and that valuable archaeological sites have been damaged and important finds collected and traded in a way that meant their original context was lost. However, the exact scale of such detecting, and its exact effect on sites, has never been properly ascertained. It is likely that a professional elitism also affected archaeological opinion. Metal detecting in Britain has traditionally been undertaken by men from nonprofessional backgrounds, and archaeologists have often found it difficult to understand or sympathise with their motivations, even though many detectorists (as they are termed) have often become specialists in object identification and clearly have a passion for understanding the past.

The antagonism between professional archaeologists and detectorists came to a head in the 1979 "STOP" (Stop Taking Our Past) campaign spearheaded by the Council for British Archaeology. This failed to stop detecting and led to a long period of mutual distrust that archaeologists have had to work hard to overcome. It was countered by the DIG campaign (Detector Information Group). Slowly relations between archaeologists and mainstream detectorists did improve through the realisation that a vast number of important archaeological finds were being recovered, and were sometimes making a material contribution to the identification and understanding of the past. The first area where archaeologists started working positively with detectorists was in Norfolk, very much under the personal leadership of museum archaeologist Tony Gregory (see Sussams 2000, pp. 39–34 for a summary of how the close working relationship between detectorists and museum archaeologists developed in Norfolk).

Detectors also begun to be used on excavations, primarily to go through spoil where it was realised they could find objects, particularly small coins, missed by the diggers. One of the places where relations developed in the most positive way was London, where, led by Brian Davison and Geoff Egan at the Museum of London, a formal partnership developed with the Society of Thames Mudlarks. The Mudlarks who detect along the City Thames foreshore under permits issued by the Port of London Authority not only bring all their finds in to the Museum for identification but also provided volunteers to detect on excavations. This relationship has continued and has left the Museum of London with a highly important database of finds (Burdon et al. 2000) and has recently led to the identification of Hindu objects deposited in the Thames. Investigation of these finds by Nicola Burdon at the Museum uncovered a previously unknown practice by a key London community, the use of the Thames as a sacred river by Hindus, and illustrated the value of archaeology and the study of material culture to understanding cultural activity and for making links with modern communities. It was members of the Thames Mudlarks, so familiar with the Thames foreshore, who brought in many of the objects and donated them to the Museum (Burdon 2004).

The growing appreciation of the value of detecting in identifying archaeological finds, and the concern over illicit detectoring, led to a major national survey funded by English Heritage and undertaken by the Council for British Archaeology. The report that resulted (Dobinson and Denison 1995) suggested that as many as 40,000 archaeological finds dating to before 1600 were being uncovered each year. The report led to the creation of the Standing Conference on Portable Antiquities (SCoPA). The Conference, in turn, led to a review of the Treasure Trove law and eventually the introduction of the 1996 Treasure Act (see Chapter 4 and DCMS 2002).

The recognition of the importance of detectored finds also led to the introduction of the Portable Antiquities Scheme. This scheme introduced a voluntary code for the reporting of all finds and the establishment of professional staff, mainly based in museums to record these finds onto a central computerised web-available database. From an initial six English areas covered by the scheme in 1997, and the increase of this to eleven in 1999, it is now national and well-established. The scheme was initially funded by the Heritage Lottery Fund through DCMS and run by a central executive based at the British Museum. It is currently funded directly by the government through the MLA. The portable Antiquities scheme has transformed museum archaeology, not only by bringing a new emphasis to collecting and recording antiquities but also by rejuvenating its staff base. The scheme has also witnessed a major increase in the number of treasure items being declared under the 1996 Treasure Act. Hobbs (2001) provides an introduction to the PAS scheme.

The undoubted success of the PAS is not without concerns. There has been some evidence of objects being sold at inflated prices on the basis of PAS identification and authentication. It is also the case that the scheme is spending a large amount of public money servicing a very small and particular part of the general public (detectorists) and a very particular part of the archaeological heritage (unstratified and often unprovenanced metal finds), while openly condoning a hobby that is still on occasion used to damage archaeological sites. See Jordan (2002) for a view of metal detecting from the point-of-view of the metal detectorists.

TABLE 1. Museum policies relating to archaeological collections

Acquisition policy, including the collecting area
Archive deposition guidance, including legal, copyright, and digital standards
Collections management standards
Loans policy
Disposal policy
Research framework
Human remains policy
Ethical policy
Public identification service

Documentation and Collections Management

A key part of museum archaeological work is the documentation and management of collections (see Fahy 1995 and Thompson 1992 for more comprehensive overviews). As the holders in trust of public property, there is a responsibility on museum staff to know exactly what it is they are caring for and where it is at any one time. A whole series of museum documents and policies will govern collections and ensure they are accountable, and there is clear transparent evidence for why they are in the collection, where they are in the collection, and what they are being used for. Table 1 lists the museum policies that would be expected to be in place, and that would relate, at least in part to archaeological collections.

Normally, every object in a collection is given a unique alphanumeric code that is either marked on the object or kept with it; and a separate index of objects is kept for reference. This is normally referred to as the *accession number*, and this is the term that will be used here. In most museums this index is developed into a detailed database that keeps detailed records of the object. The exception to this rule is for large archaeological excavation or fieldwork assemblages where the sheer number of objects makes individual accessioning impractical. Much bulk archaeological excavation material also only makes sense as an assemblage and as such group documentation is both logical and practical. This material is dealt with in Chapter 7.

Accessioning of museum collections has two prime purposes: (1) to allow for the unique identification of an object and to track its location; and (2) to provide an easily accessible home for associated information that might include such things as conservation records or research material.

Museum documentation has evolved from early handwritten registers to card indexes to computer systems (see Pearce 1990, pp. 113–120 for the development of such systems). It would now be considered unacceptable for a museum collection not to have a computerised index; however, many curators still use familiar card indexes and the completeness and usefulness of computer records vary enormously, particularly in relation to archaeological archives.

Pearce (1997, p. 50) notes how many old museum labels are becoming artefacts in their own rights, not only for their social historical value but also for forming a tangible link between past and present curators. Some museums have even begun to display original labels and packaging as artefacts in their own right. The Canterbury Roman Museum includes such items in a display to make a direct link with the early pioneering excavations in Canterbury after World War II.

A number of specially designed computer packages have been designed for museum collections including, for example, *MODES* developed by the MDA and *Multi Mimsy* used by several national and larger museums. Table 2 lists the range of information that a computer record might hold for an individual object.

The majority of museum documentation systems are designed around identifying, codifying, and holding associated information about individual "high-value" objects. Many core collections, such as those described in this chapter, and

TABLE 2. The range of information that might be held on a computer record for an individual accessioned item

Accession number
Description by type
Description by date
Description by material
Donor
Date accessioned
Storage location
Storage history
Digital image
Dimensions
Cross reference to conservation records
Reference to any publications
Accumulated research information

some objects from archaeological archives (described in Chapter 7) suit this type of system. However, the vast majority of excavated material (as parts of archives) do not. Most archives are made up of a very large number of mundane nonspecial objects and records that only take on value in relation to each other. As such, they need a different kind of documentation system, but one that will allow them to be curated and studied in relation to the individual items and their systems.

What excavation archives require are computer systems that do not cater to individual objects of high value but the relationship between many mundane items. Archaeological excavation site recording (see Chapter 7) is based around identifying individual pieces of fieldwork through a unique site code (normally alphanumeric based on the site location and the year of excavation, for example, MIN86 = Royal Mint

Site starting in 1986; SBH88 = Southwark Bridge House, excavated in 1988). Within the site, identification is by "contexts" or soil layers or "events." It is also important to be able to cross-link between many different types of related data. For a site assemblage this might include plans and drawings, photographs, context descriptions, and finds catalogues. For this range of data, relational databases that allow different types of data to be held separately but combined as needed in any possible relationship become useful.

The problem of course with all labels, indexes, catalogues, and so forth is that they fix a new and created meaning to an object that it is then often difficult to remove and which forms associations and ideas. A documentation system, if designed properly, should act in proxy for the object itself and allow the curator or researcher to have easy access to all the possible information he or she might need about an individual object, and that object in relation to all others in a collection. The use of key words is essential here. There needs to be a common thesaurus of terms that always mean the same thing and that are commonly understood. This disciplined approach is relatively new to museums and archaeology, and it has left a difficult backlog. It is no good trying to find all examples of Roman first-century brooches on a museum database if, in the past, some brooches were documented as fibula or clothes fasteners, and some first-century brooches were originally dated as being second century. There is therefore a need for consistency, a clear and unambiguous nomenclature, and the ability to update and refresh records.

If such inconsistencies might exist in an individual museum's collections, the problem becomes even more acute when studying across different museum collections. It is unlikely that a single museum will hold all examples of a particular type or category of archaeological find. As such, researchers are likely to want to search across several collections. For example, artefacts from Roman London can be found at the Museum of London, the British Museum, and most London local borough museums. Objects from dynastic Egypt will be found in thousands of museums across the world. This makes the need for consistent recording and naming and identifying of objects even more important.

Many attempts have been made to digest and simplify the myriad challenges of providing the necessary documentation for archaeological collections of all kinds. One of the more useful, and more recent, although unfortunately it does not seem to be being used as much as it should is the *Standards in Action* (Longworth and Wood 2000) produced by the MDA.

Digital Data Management

As with so many other aspects of museum work, digital technology already dominates museum collections management and has the potential to continue to change it at a startling pace. Museums have seen the proliferation of data and the means to access it. Indeed, probably the biggest challenge facing the museums, and no doubt others, is not so much how to store digital data but how to manage the vast amount of data available and find ways of making it usable in a practical way.

As discussed in Chapter 7, most primary archaeological data is now being produced in digital form or relies on digital data to give it meaning. Many smaller museums are not equipped to collect, curate, and access this information and new organisations are needed with the expertise to curate digital information. In the United Kingdom, the Archaeological Data Service (ADS) part of the Arts and Humanities Data Service (AHDS), a higher-education service, has been performing a key role in setting standards for digital data collection and management and also for providing a home for data sets. This has provided a somewhat over optimistic picture, because it would be unrealistic to expect the ADS to continue to perform this role unquestioningly, and without limit, forever. However, for the meantime it has taken away some of the concerns held about museums and other institutions not having the expertise to manage and make digital data accessible. See Beagrie (1998) for an introduction to AHDS, Wise 1998 for an introduction to the ADS, and Condron et al. (1999) for the development of strategies for digital data.

Technology has already seen the development of techniques to electronically "tag" or "mark" objects as part of the war against the illicit trade in antiquities (Walker Tubb 2002, p. 284), and bar coding has been introduced by some museums. Such techniques are the logical future for the need of museums to track and hold increasingly complex amounts of information about their collections.

Disposal and Dispersal

The traditional view about the disposal of museum collections, including archaeological objects, was that it didn't happen. This "presumption against disposal" developed at a time when museum collections were still growing and the value of material was not being seriously questioned either at a practical or philosophical level (see Pearce 1990, pp. 74–76 for a summary of this approach). It is based on the idea that all museum objects must by their very nature be valuable, and that no opportunity must be given to museum authorities to sell-off their precious collections for short-term gain. When it has been discussed, disposal of archaeological material normally centres on the vast amount of low-value excavated material that is of no monetary value but that takes up valuable storage space.

In the United Kingdom, the Society of Museum Archaeologists (1993) made the first attempt to seriously address the question of disposal. The approach it took was to deal with finds by category (pottery, building material, etc.). It did this by going to specialists in each field and asking them to comment on retention and disposal policies. Not surprisingly, each specialist emphasised the value of their artefact type, and the resulting document ended up as an argument for retaining almost everything.

More recently, this is a subject that has been addressed in the United Kingdom for museum collections in general (see NMDC 2003 and MA 2005), and a debate has begun about archaeological material specifically. Again, this debate is centred on the fact that museums are spending a lot of money curating many museum collections that are hardly ever used.

This is a debate that mainly centres on archaeological excavation material and is dealt with in more detail in Chapter 7. Most museums continue to shy away from disposal and have policies that enshrine this approach. A less urgent issue, but one that seems to interest archaeologists most, is where material should be disposed of so that it does not "contaminate" the archaeological record for future generations. Many complex methods have been employed for this over the years.

Collecting Areas

There are a whole series of reasons why a particular archaeological object or collection might end up in one museum rather than another. And an equally long list of reasons to explain a particular museum's collecting area. Collecting areas are a key part of museum governance that help it decide what to, or what not to collect, and perhaps more importantly define relationships between museums. The United Kingdom's protracted and muddled history of museum development mean there is a patchwork of collecting areas that has caused some problems for archaeological contractors (see Chapter 7). Green (1991) gives the example of Norfolk and Suffolk, and notes that to find the historical lack of rigidity in collecting policy means that objects can end up where you would not expect them. She also notes other factors that might affect collecting: the buying power of a particular museum; the "shopping" habits of the public (you are likely to bring a find to the museum in the town where you go to do shopping); the absence of a museum in a particular region. Other factors will include the security level in a museum that might make it unsuitable to accept valuable objects; and the expertise and indeed interests of staff. All of this means that anyone undertaking research into a particular area might need to check the collections of many museums before they are content that they have tracked down all possible finds of interest.

Most collecting areas are now defined by local authority boundaries, in effect meaning that museums collect within the region where they obtained funding. For museums that collect abroad, things become more complicated. The fact that collecting areas have evolved through time, thus leaving some museums with objects that no longer correspond to their current areas, also has the potential for problems. Pearce (1990, p. 80) suggests these need to be considered in terms of cultural arguments (where has the museum collected historically, and what area makes sense for it in terms of its audience and collections); management (what area is it practical for it to collect from in terms of its resources); and political (how does its collecting area correspond to the political boundaries of the authority that funds it). This of course brings the role of collections full circle, back to values they are given by different groups, and the very particular values they acquire when entering a museum collection.

Key Texts

Brodie, N. J., Doole, J., and Watson, P. (2000). *Stealing history: The illicit trade in cultural property*. Cambridge, UK: McDonald Institute.

Brodie, N., and Walker Tubb, K. (2002). *Illicit antiquities*. London: Routledge.

Fahy, A. (Ed.). (1995). *Collections management*. London and New York: Routledge.

Longworth, C., and Wood, B. (2000). *Standards in action, working with archaeology* London: SMA/MDA.

Museums Association (2005) *Collections for the future*. London: MA.

Pearce, S. (1995). *On collecting: An investigation into collecting in the European tradition*. London: Routledge.

CHAPTER 7
EXCAVATION ARCHIVES

Archaeological excavation "archives" (the finds and records from a piece of fieldwork), unlike the collections described in Chapter 6, are often not of high value and are characterised by the mundane, fragmentary and broken. Yet, they often offer huge research potential and unique insights into the past. They also present very real challenges for curation, display, and interpretation. Their sheer quantity has also provided many museums with serious resource challenges.

Excavations

Fieldwork in many disciplines produce field notes, records, and data that support and give meaning to the samples and specimens collected. What makes archaeological fieldwork unique is both the complexity and importance of the records that make sense of the fieldwork practice, the level of personal interpretation involved, and that in the vast majority of cases, the records are the result of a destructive process and therefore come to be the only evidence for what has been recorded. Archaeological excavation is destructive. It is only by undertaking excavation that the vast majority of evidence about the past is obtainable; however, at the end of the process the site or monument no longer exists. This has led to the concept of "preservation by record" whereby the records made as part of the excavation, with the artefacts and samples recovered, take on a unique importance.

Indeed, this dogma, the imperative to make a complete and objective record of an excavation that must be then kept forever as a record of what was once there, underlies much of current archaeological and museum archaeological theory. It is perhaps now in need of revision.

Excavation leading to the recognition of stratigraphy and the relationship between different soil layers and their morphology, and the artefacts and samples recovered from layers, give a sequence to a site that, under analysis, can be turned into a narrative of past human activity and behaviour. Again, because the original site has been destroyed these records have a special importance. The only way of corroborating the interpretation made, or indeed reinterpreting it, is through an analysis of the records and finds.

From this, it becomes clear that the proper recording of archaeological remains, the proper ordering and managing of the records made and their long-term secure keeping is of immense importance to the archaeological discipline. Traditionally in England the combined records and finds have been known collectively as archaeological archives and their long-term care and management has been seen as the responsibility of museums.

Archaeological archives (the term will be used throughout this chapter but is explained further below) should represent a prime research and heritage asset; and yet historically they have been underresourced and underused. For many years, UK museums have struggled to find the resources to properly store archives, nevermind maximise their research and educational value (Swain 1998a). This situation has been made worse by the organisation of archaeology in the United Kingdom where the practitioners are now primarily peripatetic commercial organisations quite separate from the museums that are expected to curate archives.

Nomenclature

The term "archive" is not commonly used outside the United Kingdom, and even here some are uncomfortable with it. Traditionally, and for many currently, the term "archive" has very particular associations with documentary records and how they are managed. There is no place for objects in this model. So, for some archaeologists even if the term "archive" is used, it will only refer to the written records associated with an excavation or piece of fieldwork, not the finds. This distinction is sometimes made real by the way fieldwork records and finds are stored and managed separately. In both Scotland and Wales, it is normal practice for the records from excavations to be "archived" and kept by the respective Royal Commissions (RCAHMS the Royal Commission for Ancient and Historic Monuments Scotland and RCAHMW, Royal Commission for ancient and Historic Monuments Wales), but the finds from excavations go to regional or national museums.

This practice of separating finds from records is not unusual elsewhere, and has often been the practice in the past. However, in England, the concept of the unified archive has taken hold and is strongly argued for (e.g., Swain and Merriman 1999).

Other terms are used. The terms "archaeological assemblage," "site assemblage," "site record," and "site collection" are all used. In North America, the term "archeological collection" is often used as meaning the same as "archive" in the United Kingdom (see Sullivan and Childs 2003 for a full discussion of U.S. usage).

The great advantage of the term "archaeological archive" is that it can be used to describe an entity that makes sense in archaeological terms. It is the combination of contextualised objects and records that makes archaeological excavation evidence different from individual noncontextualised finds. The archive is a description of such data for a particular intervention. So, as discussed here, an *archaeological archive* is all the finds, records, and associated evidence from a particular piece of archaeological fieldwork, normally an excavation.

The Archive

Table 3 summaries the possible contents of an archaeological archive. Some sites, for example, evaluations where no archaeology is found, will contain only a very small amount of material, possibly no finds or no environmental samples, and very few of the items listed. However, large, complex urban sites will not only include all of the items listed but large numbers of each element. It is a frightening list, both in terms of its length and the different types of material present, many

TABLE 3. The possible elements of an archaeological archive deposited in a museum. Those marked with an * could be all or partly in digital form.

Bulk finds

Ceramic building material (including tiles and bricks)

Pottery sherds

Vessel and window glass

Flint waste

Mass-produced iron

Repetitive and unworked architectural stone

Mass-produced stone items (e.g., querns)

Mass-produced and waste bone, horn, ivory, shell, antler artefacts

Mass-produced wood items

Leather waste and off-cuts

Unidentified plaster, wattle and daub

Registered finds

Coins

Tokens

Bronze and other nonferrous metals

Special iron objects

Architectural stone

Glass objects

Stone tools and weapons

Gemstones

Individual or special bone, horn, ivory, shell, antler artefacts

Wood artefacts

Leather, textile, basketry and rope objects

Painted or decorated plaster

Wattle and daub with architectural features

Decorated tiles

Complete pots

Human remains

Complete skeletons

Bones and groups of bone

Soft tissue

Samples

Kiln or other industrial debris

Wood samples (including for dendrochronology)

Stone, ceramic

Environmental evidence

Animal bones

Fish bones

Beetles

Snails

Environmental samples

Pollen

Soil

(continued)

Table 3 *(continued)*

Primary context records

Context sheets*

Note books*

Site photographs*

Site plans and sections*

Finds and sample indices and lists*

Project Files

Contract files*

Project designs*

Preexcavation fieldwork archives (field walking, geophysical, aerial photography)*

Research Archives

Archive reports*

Finds reports*

Specialist finds reports*

Draft reports*

Finds and stratigraphic databases*

of which will require different types of conservation, storage, and curation conditions. Other items could be included. These might include drafts of publication text and original artwork used for publication, although there is limited value in archiving these once publication has taken place. Some have also emphasised (Ferguson and Murray 1997; and see the following section) the importance of the social element of archaeology and how this should be an important part of archives.

This might include details of who worked on the site, weather conditions, and so forth.

Managing Archaeological Archives

The challenge of managing this complex and varied collection of material encompasses not only the need for particular methodologies for particular elements (paper records will be managed differently than photographs, potsherds, etc.) but that the relationship between all the different elements is maintained. For museums primarily geared up to manage the acquisition of a few individual objects per year, this can be a daunting task. Gaimster (2001, p. 5) has suggested that curators are "too often bogged down by the tyranny of archive management" to allow them to undertake research. And Merriman (2000) has also argued that too much time is spent by museum archaeologists serving the archaeological process as created by the archaeological community through such activities as archive transfer at the expense of public archaeology. If archive curation is not to overwhelm the museum and prevent research and public archaeology, systems will need to be in place that both allow for the efficient transfer of archives into the museum, and then allow for effective curation once it is there.

Efficient transfer relies on close and clear working relationships between the museum or repository and the archaeologists working in their collecting areas. A vast amount of potential future problems and work will be eliminated if, when an excavation takes place, records and finds are prepared and ordered in such a way as to make the creation of the initial site archive straightforward. This will include such mundane items as correct box sizes and the use of archival materials, to more complex areas such as the completeness of the record being deposited; questions of ownership; storage methods for records; and finally problems associated with computer records (Sullivan and Childs 2003, pp. 36–37). For all of these reasons, clear published guidance and ideally agreed upon standards are needed that can be accessed by the archaeologist. These are becoming more common (e.g., Museum of

London 1998) and common guidance is currently being prepared by the Archaeological Archives Forum for use in the
United Kingdom (see next section). Sullivan and Childs (2003,
p. 68, table 5.1) summarises standards required of repositories
in the United States.

Archaeological Fieldwork and the Creation of Archives in the United Kingdom

The current theory and practices of archaeological excavation
(briefly summarised in Chapter 2) can be traced from antiquarian investigations in the eighteenth and nineteenth centuries through to an attempt at scientific excavation in the
early twentieth century that is still used today albeit within a
commercially driven framework.

The origin of the term "archive" in the sense that it is now understood in England is lost. It certainly goes back to 1975 when
it was used in the so-called Frere report (DoE 1975). The Frere
report (named after its author Sheppard Frere) was an attempt
to find a model for publishing and archiving the material
from excavations. It identified four "levels" of data. The Level 1
Archive was the *site* itself, the physical archaeological remains
that were being examined and that would be destroyed by the
act of excavation. As the site is destroyed by the process of
excavation the next level, the Level 2 Site Archive becomes by
default the primary evidence for the archaeology. The Level
2 Site Archive is made up of all of the *primary material that is
removed from the excavation.* This includes the finds and samples
but also all the drawings, photographs, and recording sheets
that describe the site and how it has been interpreted in the
field. Under the Frere model, the Level 2 Site Archive becomes
the primary evidence and therefore takes on a special significance for the future. It should be sorted and arranged but not
altered. It must be preserved as the closest evidence remaining of the original site. It must also be accessible, as anyone
who might wish to reinterpret the excavation in the future will
come to the Level 2 Site Archive for their evidence.

Under the Frere model, the Level 3 Research Archive was the
research that is undertaken on the Level 2 Site Archive material.

It is a means to an end (the Level 4 Archive) but is still very important as it makes sense of the Level 2 Site Archive and shows how the excavator has come to the conclusions that they will describe in the Level 4 Archive (it is a bit like the workings that are encouraged in a mathematics exam). The Level 3 Research Archive should therefore also become an element of the archive and be kept for posterity.

The Level 4 Archive is the *published report*, the interpretation of the excavation for wider, but primarily peer-group, audiences. Although the Frere report acknowledged the importance of the Level 2 Site Archive and Level 3 Archive reports, it emphasised a process leading to the ultimate goal: the published report or Level 4 Archive. This, therefore, enshrined a previous model, espoused, for example, by Mortimer Wheeler, that the ultimate goal of any archaeological excavation was the publication of the results. Also influential at this stage was the so-called Longworth report (British Museum 1982) and Dimbleby report (DoE 1978) both of which also emphasised the importance of the "archive" and its long-term care and accessibility for research. See also Davies (1986) for a summary of the archive position in the early 1980s.

There is no doubt that dissemination through an accessible and affordable means remains a healthy goal for archaeological endeavour, and it is still the mechanism by which most archaeological data is communicated and used. However, as formulated by the Frere report, and indeed most models since, it underplays the value of the archive and overplays the role of the publication, that will normally only ever seek to communicate one particular view of a particular aspect of the excavation to a limited audience, and at a very high relative cost. The vastly increasing number of excavations that now take place, the vastly increased level of data that comes from these sites, the increasing cost of traditional publication, and the smaller emphasis that is put on initial interpretations being definitive, only emphasises this point.

This increasing level of data, the increasing amount of time taken to archive this, and increasing costs and delays in publication led to a new attempt to deal with postexcavation in 1983. This time it was the so-called Cunliffe report (from the Chair Professor Barry Cunliffe, DoE 1983). In its introduction, the report restated the archaeological gospel: "based on the precepts of Pitt Rivers and Wheeler that all excavation is destruction, that total excavation is total destruction, and that a discovery dates only from the time that a record is made of it, not from the time of its being found in the soil. It has been an unchallenged rule that the archaeologist should publish his results" (DoE 1983, p. 1).

The Cunliffe report kept the four levels of output but relabelled them and gave a different emphasis. The Site Archive remained, containing primary and processed data. Then it introduced the concept of the Research Archive (old Level 3) that now dealt specifically with research into the material that was to be published. The publication (old Level 4) was to be divided into two including a "report digest" that would be volume printed and a microfiche element that would hold additional information. The whole process would be advised by a Research Design that would be prepared after the end of excavation and would identify those parts of the excavation results that were worthy of publication and how this would be done. The Cunliffe report also put emphasis on greater selectivity and efficiency in excavation and postexcavation practices.

In many ways, the Cunliffe report was simply an update of the Frere report. The three areas where it introduced really new concepts were in taking away the assumption that everything dug up would be fully archived, fully researched, and fully published (a concept some archaeologists still struggle with); the idea of a research design that in effect introduced the idea of project planning to postexcavation, an essential step; and finally by suggesting the use of microfiche it begun a debate about using new technology to make the dissemination of archaeological data cheaper and easier. Microfiche never really worked, and specialists hated having their work consigned to it, and it is only now with the internet and digital data that this concept is being realised.

The next attempt in England to further influence the way archaeological projects were managed and, therefore, how archives and publications were created came in 1991 with the publication of *Management of Archaeological Projects* by English Heritage and normally referred to as MAP2 (English Heritage 1991a; there was a previous *Management of Archaeological Projects* [MAP1] that was far less influential). MAP2, largely the brainchild of Gill Andrews, was primarily a guide for organisations receiving funds from English Heritage as to how they would need to run their projects in order to receive funding, but it has become the standard model for carrying out archaeological projects in Britain, regardless of funding.

MAP2 takes the Cunliffe report further by emphasising the need for the development of clear research outputs and the constant review of these by means of assessing the data. It divides the archaeological project into five stages:

1. project planning,
2. fieldwork,
3. assessment of potential for analysis,
4. analysis and report preparation, and
5. dissemination.

From these five phases, a site archive will be produced from the fieldwork, an assessment report from phase 3, a research archive and report text from phase 4 and all of these will combine to form a Project Archive at phase 5, but only if at review stages at each phase it is considered that there is material and data capable of answering research questions.

MAP2 was born out of a desire to cut the large postexcavation backlog that had developed in England. It offered an efficient way to prioritise the expensive process of publication. As such, it was linked to the archive. Hinton (1993, p. 6) argued that the then obsession with archives was simply renaming the "unpublished backlog" and taking away the primacy of final publication. This misses the point of how archives and publications should supplement each other. MAP2 also, by accepting that only some elements of an excavation will warrant publication, puts extra importance on the archive that will not only support the conclusions made in the publication but be the prime repository for those elements that are not published at all.

MAP2 is an intelligent document that if followed should lead to more-focused and speedy postexcavation work. However, possibly due to the innate conservatism of archaeologists it has in many cases led to even more work with the creation of assessment reports that justify research and publication that often end up longer than the reports they seek to justify. It is fair to say that it has made little overall influence on archives other than to make them even bigger and more complex.

The arrival of MAP2 coincided with the full onset of commercial archaeology in the United Kingdom. From the late 1980s the vast majority of archaeological fieldwork, and therefore the vast majority of archives, have been created by projects undertaken by independent peripatetic contracting archaeological organisations funded by property developers. These organisations now operate in competition with each other and compete for work. The system is regulated by a network of local authority planning or "curating" archaeologists who seek to ensure archaeological work takes place on relevant developments by inserting clauses in planning conditions and then monitor the work that takes place. This model has no legal foundation but is underpinned by planning guidance. In the case of England this is *Planning and Policy Guidance Note 16: Archaeology and Planning*, or PPG16 (DoE 1990; see also Chapter 2).

PPG16 puts the onus on developers to make sure they plan for any potential archaeology on a site they wish to develop, and to build this into the planning application they make. It is stated that ideally archaeology should be preserved *in situ*, but recognises that this will not always be possible or desirable and that as an alternative preservation by record is acceptable. Thus, PPG16 perpetuates the model of preservation by record developed in the 1970s. Museums are only mentioned twice in PPG16, in both cases as places to go for information about an areas' known archaeology. Although it identifies the need for an archive and for the dissemination of results, it offers no clear guidance as to how archives are to be created or where these are to be deposited.

PPG16 and the "developer pays" commercial model for archaeology has been a huge success in professionalising archaeology and archaeologists so that they provide minimum disruption to the property and development industries. It has also led to a major expansion in the archaeology "industry" and a major influx of funds to archaeology. Many tens of millions of pounds sterling are now being spent annually on archaeology in England. The industry is also attempting to build up a regulatory framework and professional infrastructure mainly through the efforts of the Institute of Field Archaeologists (IFA). The IFA was founded in 1982 on the basis of individual membership and has issued by-laws, standards, and policy statements to regulate archaeological activity (IFA 1999). In 1995, it introduced a scheme to create Registered Archaeological Organisations (RAOs, see Swain 1995 and Hinton and Swain 1999). This process however, has taken place largely in isolation from museums and without having the archiving process as a priority, although The IFA Finds Specialist Interest Group has tended to act as a champion of archival work (e.g., Brown 2005). On the whole, although archiving requirements are now built into most archaeological documents and many archaeological contracting organisations have archive officers and recognise the requirement, the whole archiving debate is being primarily driven from the museum side. See Hopkins (2000) for a summary of the archive process from the perspective of planning archaeologists and Mepham (2000), Brading (2000), and Rawlings (2005) for a perspective from large and small contractors.

The Frere report, Cunliffe report, and MAP2 were the archaeological solutions to the growing cost and time of carrying out postexcavation and publication. None of them were aimed at dealing with the curation of the archive although all accepted that this was a fundamental part of the process. It was mainly left to the museum and museum archaeology community to think about how the archive produced by fieldwork would be cared for. MAP2 continues in use, however, English Heritage is currently introducing new project-management guidance that will cover all historic environment projects, not just archaeology. This new guidance will take the form of a series of guidance papers under the overall heading *Management of Research Projects in the Historic Environment* or MoRPHE (English Heritage 2006).

The Storage Debate

What did all this mean for museums? Almost all of the discussions over how archaeological data should be analysed and managed was undertaken by field archaeologists concerned with communicating information to other archaeologists. Although there was an implicit understanding that the finds and records from excavations would reside in museums, there was no debate with museum archaeologists and no thought given to the practical implications of this. Museum archaeologists in the meantime failed, on the whole, to engage with the debate about archaeological data and instead continued to think in terms of storing, displaying, and using objects. And it was storage needs that became the driver of museum engagement with the issue.

Although it is often described as a relatively modern phenomena (Swain 1996), archaeologists have for many years recognised the problems involved with digging up ever more material. As long ago as 1904, archaeologists in Britain were expressing a concern about the ability of museums to store and curate the material resulting from archaeological excavations. In that year, Flinders Petrie suggested the provision of a National Repository requiring:

> A square mile of land, within an hours journey from
> London, should be secured; and built over with
> uniform plain brickwork and cement galleries at a rate
> of 20,000 square feet a year, so providing 8 miles of
> galleries 50 feet wide in a century, with room yet for
> several centuries of expansion space.
> (Petrie 1904)

Three elements of this description are worth noting; "within an hours journey from London" implies the need for rapid access. "20,000 square feet a year" implies a large mass of material. "Several centuries of expansion space" implies that the rate of deposition will be continuous. And these three observations remain true for British and, indeed, European and North American archaeology. There is a lot of it, it keeps coming, and there is a belief that ready access should be provided to it.

Although museums had for many years recognised the problems inherent in being asked to acquire ever more material, a vocal debate on the subject did not emerge until the later 1980s. This derived partly from the massive increase in archaeological material from "rescue-" and "developer-" funded work, for the first time producing material of more marginal academic interest. As discussed in this chapter and in Chapters 2 and 3, this period also saw a more complete break in communication and relationship between museums and field archaeologists. In most cases, archaeology was being undertaken by independent practitioners, monitored by archaeologists not linked to museums, and funded by private property developers. Mepham (2000, p. 7) reports that between 1980 and 1998. Wessex Archaeology undertook about 1,600 archaeological projects at an average of 200 per year (some of the total did represent different elements of the same overall project). In 1998, 40 percent of the archives from these sites were still undeposited with 14 percent because the stated museum for deposition had no space to take material. This situation leaves contractors as the default repository even though they normally cannot, or would not, be expected to fulfill the requirements of a museum. Similarly, Rawlings (2005) reports leaving a post at a contractor with only 132 of the 200 projects he had managed safely deposited in a museum.

Museums were completely disenfranchised from this system but were expected passively to accept the products of work. At the time, the image of unidentified lorries arriving at the entrance of a museum unannounced and full of boxes of unsorted finds expecting to find a home became common (e.g., Hinchcliffe and Schadla-Hall 1986, p. 47, fig. 2). The archaeologist Peter Hinton described (although not in print) archives as resembling low-level nuclear waste. In some places, individual museums were able to impose order. Duncan Brown in Southampton has been one of the most tireless champions of a well-ordered, consistent, and rapidly deposited archive (e.g., Brown 2000). Southampton has been one of the places were a well-integrated model for archaeology has been successful.

In 1991, the Society of Antiquaries of London sponsored a working group to study archives; however, this failed to deliver any action. A number of articles were written highlighting the growing crisis in storage of archaeological archives (Swain 1996, 1997b) and occasionally the subject made it into the media, however, as no priceless remains had actually been thrown away or museum explode from being overfull, no direct action ensued. This was made more complex in England by the government agencies overseeing museums and archaeology being quite separate and happy to look to the other for solutions. Archaeology was overseen and funded by English Heritage (EH) that saw the care of archives as a museum responsibility. Museums came under the Museum and Galleries Commission (MGC) who thought the archaeologists should be dealing with the situation. In 1996, these two organisations finally came together to address the problem, possibly prompted by the situation in London (see the next section). A joint English Heritage MGC survey was commissioned into the state of archaeological archives in England (Swain 1998a).

The project involved a questionnaire survey of those English museums considered to hold archives and be actively involved in collecting them as well as visits to some areas and interviews with key individuals. Its results showed that indeed most English museums had no storage space to accept new archaeology, and, yet, large amounts of material was held by archaeological contractors for transfer and new material was being generated all the time. Further to this, the survey showed that in some areas there was confusion over archaeology collecting areas (see the next section and Chapter 6), a lack of qualified curators and conservators (see Chapter 10), and very little active use being made of archives. However, the survey also showed that most museums were spending relatively little money on curating archives and did not predict that this amount would rise sharply. This was probably because those who answered the questionnaire recognised that very little money was available or was likely to be forthcoming for such uses. Perhaps more telling was the responses as to how museums were planning to deal with archive curation in the future.

TABLE 4. How museums were planning to deal with future archive storage needs (Reproduced from Swain 1998a, p. 38.).

Project underway to review problem	18 (19%)
New store planned	16 (16%)
Stop or suspend collecting	10 (10.5%)
Selective disposal of material	9 (9.5%)
Reorganise to maximise existing space	8 (8.5%)
Look for storage elsewhere	6 (6.3%)
"Panic"	6 (6.3%)
Lottery bid planned	5 (5.3%)
Everything OK	4 (4.25%)
No comment	12 (12.75%)
Total comments	94

This information (reproduced as Table 4) made depressing reading.

These responses suggested that museums were considering disposal or the suspension of collecting, not for museological or academic reasons but simply because they could not hold any more material. Others were clearly thinking about, or planning for, increased storage, but without seeing an obvious solution or putting the problem within a wider context of archive value and use.

The 1998 survey had nineteen conclusions and linked these to nine recommendations (Swain 1998a, pp. 6–11). The recommendations are summarised here:

1. More curators and conservators should be found to curate archives.
2. Museum collecting areas should be defined.

3. Core standards for contractors should be provided.
4. A study of resource centres should take place.
5. A study of archives held by contractors should take place.
6. MGC and EH should review the box grant scheme.
7. The use of archives should be studied.
8. Disposal guidance should be reviewed.
9. The challenges of digital archiving should be addressed.

The publication of the 1998 survey coincided with the closing down of the MGC (to be replaced by "Resource," now known as the Museums, Libraries and Archives Council or MLA) and major changes at English Heritage including the retirement of the Chief Archaeologist Geoffrey Wainwright who had overseen the survey. Although some little progress was made on its recommendations, including a more detailed survey of the pros and cons of resource centres (Suenson Taylor and Swain 1999), there was a hiatus in progress until 2002 when the new chief archaeologist at English Heritage David Miles commissioned a new survey of archives as an update of the 1998 survey. This report (Perrin 2002) reaffirmed the findings of Swain (1998a) and perhaps most importantly led to the foundation of the British Archaeological Archives Forum (Swain 2004b). This group with representation from the entire UK archaeological and museum archaeological community has identified a number of projects to try and address the challenges outlined in the 1998 and 2002 reports.

To date, the AAF has overseen the completion of a set of guidance on disaster planning for archaeological contractors holding archives (Aitchison 2004); and is currently undertaking the preparation of guidance on archive preparation, transfer and curation that will hopefully be accepted nationally. Finally, through the Society of Museum Archaeologists, a study and review of museum collecting areas for archaeology is being undertaken (see the section below and Chapter 6). The problem of disposal has for the moment not been directly addressed although it remains a topic of concern within the wider museum profession (see the section below). The challenge of digital curation has to some extent been mitigated by the presence of the Archaeological Data Service (ADS, see Wise 1998 and Chapter 6) that accepts, curates, and makes accessible digital records from archaeological research.

London Archaeology and the LAARC

The first museum to try and put archive theory into practice was the Museum of London. In 1996, the Museum publicly stated that it would no longer accept new fieldwork archives. The Museum has calculated that at that time it was spending about £250,000 per year on storing archaeological material, money that it considered could be better spent elsewhere. It also noted that it had no control over the amount or type of archaeological material that was being generated in London, and that was being funded by developers as part of a market-led process (Swain 1997b). Ironically, most of the archaeology in London was at that time being undertaken by the Museum's own archaeological unit, the Museum of London Archaeology Service (MoLAS).

In London, in the past 30 years, this situation had become acute. The unprecedented level of excavation in the historic urban core has resulted in the largest body of archaeological records and finds of its kind. This is an immense research resource, making London one of the best-understood historical cities in Europe (MoLAS 2000). However, it has brought with it huge logistical problems for the Museum of London which takes and cares for the archives from excavations.

In 1998, under new leadership, the value of this resource was recognized, and the Museum set out to create the London Archaeological Archive and Research Centre (LAARC), not only to house the archive but also to ensure it was properly curated and made accessible (Plate 2). The LAARC is housed in the Museum's Mortimer Wheeler House resource centre, about 2 miles from the main Museum building and its galleries. It shares the building with the offices of the Museum's archaeology service and much of the Museum's social and working history collections. A grant from the Heritage Lottery Fund and funding from central government, The Getty Grant

Program and many other organisations, archaeological societies, and individuals, financed its creation. Two new large storage areas have been created as well as a visitor centre and two study rooms. State-of-the-art roller storage has been installed and a computerised index and access system (the latter available over the web) have been developed. The LAARC project, which included not only building and equipping the new spaces but also designing the computer systems and undertaking a minimum standards programme on the archive, cost about £2.5 million. Funding for the six-person team who manage the LAARC is found primarily from the Museum's recurrent costs.

The London archive is by far the largest in Britain. It currently includes about 150,000 individual boxes of finds stored on 10,000m of shelving. And includes finds and records from about 5,200 individual excavations from throughout Greater London. And, of course, this figure is growing every year. Therefore, about 20 years expansion space has been built into the plans. This will be achieved partly through current spare space but also by the rationalisation of existing material.

The Museum has prepared rigorous standards for the preparation of new archives resulting from excavations (Museum of London 1998) and expects the archives from all excavations in Greater London to be deposited in the LAARC. It has taken a while for the twenty or so archaeological contractors that regularly operate in London to become accustomed to this new disciplined approach, but the will does seem to be there and material is now being deposited at an increased rate.

Meanwhile, the Museum has also turned its attention to that material already in its care. This has been generated over about 100 years by many different archaeologists working for many different organisations. Material is not compatible and often not easily accessible. A huge effort is being made to bring all this material up to an acceptable level of care and accessibility. A key part of this work was the Getty Projects-funded Minimum Standards Project. This involved a team of curators and conservators checking through the archive and ensuring that the basic records and storage conditions will

Plate 2. Archaeological finds as part of excavation archives at the Museum of London's London Archaeological Archive and Research Centre. (Photo: Museum of London.)

allow for the long-term health of the objects and that they are accessible for research.

Research has been spearheaded by the publication of a London archaeological research framework (McAdam et al. 2002) and a series of partnerships with London's archaeologists. A key partnership is with the Institute of Archaeology, which now offers an MA degree in London Archaeology, its students doing placements at the LAARC and writing their dissertations on material held there. The HEFCE Archive Archaeology project (see the next section) is part of this partnership.

Another key part of the London archaeological community is its local societies and again the Museum is working with these groups to encourage research and use of the LAARC. Several societies were actively involved in the planning of the LAARC and even donated funds for its creation. It is hoped that society projects either researching London's past or helping with collections management in the LAARC will allow local society members to feel actively involved in London's archaeology – something that has been very difficult in the last 10 years as more and more archaeology has been funded commercially by developers. Another initiative is for the LAARC to host a central London Young Archaeologists Club (see Chapter 14).

Curation Costs and Charging

For sometime in the United Kingdom, some institutions have charged for accepting and curating archives. This originated in the 1981 "box grant" scheme operated by English Heritage, whereby a grant of £12.69 per 0.017 cubic metres (in effect £13 per box) was made available to certain museums to store the archives from excavations they had funded. When the scheme was set up, museums had to meet specific criteria that acted as a benchmark for archaeological curating before they would qualify for the scheme (MGC 1986). The box grant scheme has now all but died, mainly because English Heritage funds so few excavations. However, the principle has been taken over by many museums for developer-funded excavations, and the 1998 survey found a large number of museums charging to accept archives (Swain 1998a, p. 36).

It is unclear whether these amounts would really support the costs of storing archives in the long-term. As a theoretical accounting exercise that saw the money invested and used purely for this purpose it probably would. However, in reality this would never happen. Small amounts of sporadic income are eaten up within museum finances and storage space that cannot be purchased by the square meter as needed. Nowhere has money levied for archive deposition been able to fully fund archive curation. Generally planning archaeologists are against the idea of charging (e.g., Hopkins 2000, pp. 4–5). This is based on the fact that that they are already asking for developers to pay for excavation and postexcavation costs, and for landowners to donate finds, to ask them to pay for storage as well may be asking too much. Because it is not compulsory, or within any legal framework, it also allows the possibility of landowners choosing a cheaper option: an alternative noncharging museum maybe, or to store the finds themselves. This somewhat random method for charging for archive deposition is mirrored by the situation in the United States (see Sullivan and Childs 2003, pp. 113–118 and Table 8.3 for costs used in United States). Elsewhere it is normally expected that public funds will fund long-term curation.

Sampling and Disposal

One of the issues touched upon again and again in the debate over archive storage and curation is whether museums should be disposing of material, and whether archaeologists should be keeping all that they recover. This has already been covered in its wider context in Chapter 6, but it has a particular relevance to archives because of the sheer bulk and the mundane nature of so many of the objects.

This is a complex issue that works at both a theoretical level: what is a sample, what is the true value of material and can that value be predicted for the future? And at a practical level based round the capacity of museum stores, and their ability to buy, equip, and curate new ones. It is therefore essential that any debate about disposal is taken for the greater good of the archaeology, not on short-term financial grounds.

All archaeologists can probably point to stored archive material that has never been accessed for research or any other purpose. Most would also be able to give examples of breakthroughs in research that were only possible because material had been kept even though its value had not been recognised at the time. Sometimes objects only get recognised as what they actually are years after excavation when more complete pieces are found.

As intimated, archaeology and the preservation of archaeological collections are based on two premises. The first is that archaeological excavation is an unrepeatable experiment and that there is a duty to preserve the results of this experiment "by record." The aim is to create an objective record of what has been excavated that can be continually reexamined and reinterpreted for infinity. The record acts *in-proxy* for the site that has been destroyed.

This model (see section above and Chapter 2) remains a basic tenet of archaeological practice. But in a postmodern age, most would now accept that there is no such thing as objectivity or absolute truths that can be revealed by excavation and the reexamination of records. Similarly, as Hinton (1991, p. 9) has noted, *preservation by record* is "a reflection of retention and recording policy already exercised on site, coloured by the research objectives and methods of the day." Nevertheless, archaeologists cling on to the "preservation by record" orthodoxy.

The second premise is that museums have a duty to preserve their collections forever. Curators must not let collections deteriorate, and they must not dispose of them (see Chapter 6). For archaeology, this is made more difficult because museums do not choose what they are expected to collect – they cannot decide how much archaeology comes out of the ground, it is in the hands of others, the cultural resource managers, the developers, the state archaeologists. So, theoretically, museums are making a commitment to the endless curation of an endless supply of archaeological material.

Yet, even though it is essential to preserve and record everything, and then keep everything, the majority of the members of the archaeological profession do not seem to be prepared to find the resources for proper curation, or make use of this resource by continual reexamination and research (see section below). The archives from key sites do get reworked and reanalysed. In Britain, the Mesolithic hunting camp at Star Carr, Yorkshire (Clark 1954), is a good example of this. But this is only a tiny drop in the ocean compared with the vast amount of material that is not being actively worked on.

Is there still a strong argument for keeping all the archaeological collections that exist and all the material that comes from new excavations? The question of disposal goes back to those two gospels of archaeology and museums: *preservation by record* and *keeping things forever*. This is a subject that is now being addressed in the United Kingdom for museum collections in general (see Chapter 6), and a debate has begun about archaeological material specifically. Similarly, in the United States, the National Park Service is currently considering a deaccessioning policy (Terry Childs, personal communication). The debate is centred on the fact that we are spending a lot of money curating many museum collections that are hardly ever used. If the profession can, for a moment, put aside the preservation by record ethos, just what is the evidence that material is worth keeping? A model based on asking what samples are really required for future research should underpin archiving. This idea has been discussed for the United States by Sullivan and Childs (2003, pp. 108–111).

Some categories of archaeological material are highly researched and have the potential to reveal new information in the future as scientific techniques improve and the knowledge base increases. Human remains are one such category (see Chapter 7). It is also the case that the archives from major sites, type-series, and important objects will always be in demand. Strong assemblages from good contexts on representative sites will also always have an important part to play in research, display, and education.

However, unstratified material; uncontextualised material; residual fragmentary material; mass, mundane, and repetitive bulk finds; and very small assemblages from evaluations have a very limited research potential. Also, releasing this material from archives allows a more imaginative use of the material for teaching and other uses (see Chapter 14).

Archive Use

Of course, any discussion about disposal must be linked to an understanding of what is being used and how. In 2003, a 3-year "Archive Archaeology" project was set up, funded by the Higher Education Funding Council for England (or HEFCE). It was undertaken by Bristol University, Durham University, and University College London in partnership with the Museum of London's LAARC. The project is seeking to encourage English universities to take the use of archives seriously as a teaching and research resource for undergraduate and graduate study. The project started with a survey; the results of which are summarised in Table 5.

The findings of this survey make predictable if depressing reading. They show clearly the importance put on excavation as an essential archaeological tool but the failure to recognise the archives, collections, and records that result from excavation as an equally important and linked resource. It is easy to make a direct correlation between these findings and the lack of use of archives and museum collections by archaeologists, and the resulting lack of value these resources are given by the majority of the profession.

As early as 1991, Peter Hinton (1993, p. 8) was concerned at the apparent underuse of archives at the very time when their importance was being championed. The 1998 Swain survey also suggested that archives were underused. The report showed that 29 percent of archive repositories had received no enquiries or visitors at all in the previous year and that usage overall was low and dominated by research for displays. Ironically, if predictably, the survey also showed that the archives that were most in demand were those from excavations that had been most fully published and disseminated. The classic example of this is the archive for the Danebury Iron Age Hillfort, which was excavated between 1969 and 1988 by Barry Cunliffe and very fully published in a series of synthesised discussions and through a series of major monographs (e.g., Cunliffe 1984). The site is internationally known and is often referred to in major overviews of archaeology (e.g., Times Books 1988, p. 167). The archive is held at Hampshire Museum service and is regularly used by research projects from around the world (Dave Allen, personal communication). It also provides the content for the Museum of the Iron Age, Andover. The site is arguably a victim of its own success, and professor Cunliffe's energy, in being taken too readily as a type site for the Iron Age, but must be seen as a model for the speedy

Table 5. How students at the twenty-four English Universities that teach archaeology use fieldwork, and archives, and museums in their teaching. (From unpublished interim report of the HEFCE Archive Archaeology project)

Questions	Yes, compulsory	Yes, optional	No
Is fieldwork an element of degree?	24	0	0
Does this include postexcavation element?	23	1	0
Are there dedicated training excavations?	24	0	0
Is there a dedicated postexcavation training?	1	0	23
Do students visit excavations?	24	0	0
Do students visit SMRs/HERs?	2	19	3
Do students visit museum galleries?	5	18	1
Do students visit museum collections?	0	17	7
Do students visit an archive centre?	5	3	15

postexcavation analysis, dissemination, and full archiving that should be the norm. The other potential uses of archives in museums, for example, for public programmes, are dealt with in detail in Chapter 14.

Collecting Areas

Museum collecting areas for archaeology in general has already been discussed in Chapter 6. Collecting areas for archives do though have a particular importance. This is because of the way that archaeological archives are generated by fieldwork quite independent of museum concerns. Under the PPG16 model, archaeological fieldwork will take place wherever and whenever a decision is made in advance of development that preservation by-record is preferable to preservation *in situ* (see the section above). The fieldwork will then generate an archive and that archive will need to be curated in an appropriate regional repository, normally expected to be a museum. However, nothing in this system ensures that such a museum is available. As noted, there is no legislation to insist that local authorities provide museum services, and in some parts of the United Kingdom, no services exist, and some of those that do, have neither the capacity, nor the staff expertise to accept and then curate archives. Occasional large excavations in areas otherwise not known for rich archaeology can exacerbate this situation. In the late 1980s, a large Romano–British town was discovered and excavated in advance of house building at Heybridge in Essex. No local museum existed that could accept the archive, let alone one with archaeological curatorial expertise. The archive, along with many others remains were left in the care of the archaeological contractors who carried out the excavation. In England, several attempts have been made to map museum collecting areas for archaeology under the auspices of the SMA and AAF. The most recent survey, undertaken in 2006, hopes to provide a definitive map of collecting areas and where provision is needed or overlaps.

Although it might be hoped that important finds will cross local authority boundaries in order to find a suitable museum home, the expense of curating archives, and the way museums are normally closely linked to specific local authorities covering specific areas means there is normally a reluctance for museums to take on material from another area. Indeed, there have been examples of museums deaccessioning material that they collected historically and now falls outside their funding area. This happened in London with the (now closed) Passmore Edwards Museum that, at one time, collected through historic "West Essex" or east London but then sought to deaccession all material that did not originate from the London Borough of Newham where the museum was located and from where it was funded.

This situation is not confined to the United Kingdom and will exist wherever the contract, developer-led archaeology model has been developed independently of a museum system. A similar situation exists in the United States, even though there is not the close linkage between archives and museums (see Sullivan and Childs 2003, pp. 112–113 for discussion about identifying collecting areas in United States).

Archives and the Social History of Archaeology

As the discipline of archaeology ages the value of archives in telling the story of archaeology's development is also being realised. In the United Kingdom, it was Diana Murray who first argued for using archives in this way, and for the need for the creation of archives to record those involved, not just what they were recording. Archives are being used more and more as historical resources (see, e.g., Lapourtas 1997 for a discussion of Arthur Evans excavations and reconstructions at Knossos, drawing upon the Evans archives in the Ashmolean Museum). The plans from excavations at Maiden Castle at Dorchester Museum, written in Mortimer Wheeler's own hand, have taken on a greater significance than their role simply to record archaeological events. The Canterbury Roman Museum actually displays some of the early boxes, packaging, and labelling of its early finds as artefacts in their own right.

Outside the United Kingdom

This chapter has dealt almost entirely with the very specific circumstances of archives in United Kingdom, primarily English, museums. This is not because it is a purely English situation but because it is the United Kingdom where the development of market-led planning-related archaeology is very advanced and has highlighted the flaws in the traditional model that sees archives as an essential result of excavation that is deemed worthy of long-term curation and reuse. Most particularly, it is an outcome of the great increase in the archaeological material that has come from well-regulated planning-led contract archaeology. The other part of the World where this system is as well-established is the United States. Indeed, as discussed briefly in Chapter 2, in the United States a problem arose with large amounts of archaeological finds and records without a sustainable future before it did in Europe. By the 1970s, many repositories were filling up without resources for curation (Sullivan and Childs 2003, p. 19). A number of surveys have identified a similar ongoing "crisis" to that in the United Kingdom (see Childs 1995 and Sullivan and Childs 2003, pp. 42–43 for a summary). A 1986 government report revealed, for example, that a large number of excavation archives for sites dug prior to 1975 were lost or destroyed. It also estimated that US$50 million would be required to catalogue the backlog of finds held by the National Parks Service (Jameson 2004, p. 41). In the United States, arguments have been made (with similar pros and cons) for regional repositories (Sullivan and Childs 2003, p. 43).

For an up-to-date and detailed analysis of the archive situation in the United States, see Sullivan and Childs 2003. They paint a picture very similar to the one in the United Kingdom, although they put a different emphasis on causes and effects. They talk about a crisis in curation of archaeological collections (2003, p. 1) that has primarily developed out of a failure of archaeologists to accept that curation is not something that is only thought about at the end of the fieldwork and research process. They note The U.S. Government Accounting Office report *Cultural Resources – Problems Protecting and Preserving Federal Archaeological Resources* (GAO 1987) that stated, "repositories were understaffed, overstuffed, and under funded" (Sullivan and Childs 2003, p. 25).

There was a move in the United States towards standards for the care of archives in the 1980s due to the great increase in excavations, and this was reinforced by Federal legislation

(Sullivan and Childs 2003, pp. 32–33). Sullivan and Childs (2003, p. 34) suggest the solution to the "curation crisis" lies with education and training of more curation staff, and better communication and interaction between curators and field archaeologists.

Many archaeological repositories do exist in the United States, often run by major universities, national organisations, private organisations, or through state funding that meets the very highest standards of curation and care. Examples include the State Archaeological Repository and Conservation facility for Maryland, and the APVA resource at Jamestown. Some of these centres are truly excellent. A further example is the Smithsonian resource centre at Suitland, MD, for the National Museum of the American Indian that not only includes excellent curatorial and research facilities but has been built in sympathy with Native American wishes over such things as materials, orientations, colours, and even dedicated spaces for ceremonies.

Elsewhere in the world, plenty of examples can be found of archaeological collections poorly stored, underused, and inaccessible. However, so far few other places have sought to confront this situation directly, although debate has begun in Europe. On a global scale, there are still far too many examples of foreign university projects that take archives out of their country of origin making them often inaccessible for future research, and, obviously, unusable within communities. Surveys are needed to discover just how serious the problem is internationally.

Overall, the picture painted for the situation in the United States by Sullivan and Childs (2003) and others, although differing in detail, is incredibly similar to the situation in the United Kingdom and elsewhere in Europe, suggesting there are problems fundamental to archaeological practice at its core rather than particular circumstances in particular places.

Key Texts

Merriman, N., and Swain, H. (1999). Archaeological archives: Serving the public interest? *European Journal of Archaeology*, 2(2), 249–267.

Perrin, K. (2002). *Archaeological archives: Documentation, access and deposition*. London: English Heritage.

Sullivan, L. P., and Childs, T. S. (2003). *Curating archaeological collections*. Walnut Creek: AltaMira Press.

Swain, H (1997). Archaeological archive transfer, theory and practice. In G. T. Denford (Ed.), *Representing Archaeology in Museums, The Museum Archaeologist*, 22, pp. 122–144.

Swain, H. (1998). *A Survey of Archaeological Archives in England*. London: Museums and Galleries Commission.

CHAPTER 8
HUMAN REMAINS

Once dealt with simply as another type of artefact, for a number of reasons human remains, normally skeletons but also examples of "soft tissue," are now thought of quite separately and are currently a major subject of debate that includes such issues as repatriation and reburial. They also have the potential to be hugely important as scientific evidence and controversial subjects for display.

Background

Fifteen years ago, human remains would not have merited their own chapter in this book. For most museums, and for most archaeologists, they were dealt with in the same way as any other type of artefact, or at the best as scientific samples. In recent years, they have taken on a far more prominent place in collections. Most would now accept they have a unique status that requires a unique treatment. This change has its origin in the political empowerment of Indigenous communities in Australia and North America and claims for the restitution and reburial of ancestral dead held in museum ethnographical, archaeological, and medical collections (see, e.g., Fine-Dare 2002 for a discussion of United States, Fforde 2004 for a detailed discussion, particularly in regard to Australia, and Fforde et al. 2002 for a wider discussion of issues). This, in turn, has led to a debate about the role of all human remains in museums (see Swain 2002b for a discussion of display in Britain, Legassick and Rassool 2000 for a discussion of remains in South African museums, and Lohman and Goodnow 2006 for further examples). Against this is a background where most archaeology museums hold human remains of some kind, normally skeletons, and archaeologists continue to regularly excavate remains and argue for the immense importance of human remains as evidence for the lives of past peoples. It is also normal to see human remains on display in museums. These include Egyptian mummies and skeletons as parts of grave assemblages from many later periods. These sometimes include remains with surviving soft tissue of some form. Occasionally, remains are displayed as examples of palaeopathology, sometimes to show specific cultural practices, and sometimes simply as props (see Cassman, Odegaard, and Powell 2007 for a guide to museum use in the United States). It has been estimated that the remains of, at the least, 61,000 human individuals are held in 132 English museums (Weeks and Bott 2003, p. 11).

The study of human remains can contribute to a large range of research topics. Ancient human remains, and their context, are an important source of direct evidence about the past, including: the study of "human evolution and adaptation, and genetic relationships; population relationships through genetics and morphology; past demography and health; diet, growth and activity patterns; disease and causes of death; history of disease and of medicine; burial practices, beliefs and attitudes; and the diversity of cultural practices in which the body and its parts are used" (DCMS 2005a, p. 8). The study of human remains also contributes to the treatment of disease and to the development of forensic science, which assists in the identification of human remains and in crime detection. Ironically, this means that of all categories of archaeological material, human remains are the ones that most curators would least like to see lost. The majority of the museum-going public also feel comfortable about seeing skeletons and other human remains on display in museums (see the next section), and it has been suggested that the presence of human remains in displays is one way of bringing the public into direct contact with past people and "humanising" displays and interpretations. Indeed, many look forward to seeing human remains in museums, and there is no doubt that there is an element of voyeurism, or at the least morbid titillation about viewing remains. Popular culture is dominated by the supernatural and the recently dead and long dead are a potent part of this.

The use of mummies and other ghosts from museum displays in popular culture shows how, within Western culture, human remains have been divorced from the sacred. They are not inherently sacred; they only acquire this label by association. This is not the case for many other cultures. Many archaeological, ethnographical, and medical collections hold the human remains of cultures for which the treatment of the dead is sacred. Many remains were also taken from societies who were, and are politically, disempowered and to whom the holding of ancestor's remains by others perpetuates wrongs done. It is through this morale maze that the museum archaeologist needs to tread. Is it acceptable to display skeletons in Western museums for school children to feign horror at? Is it acceptable to return or rebury human remains that have the potential to answer key questions about humanities past? And the hardest question to answer of all: do the dead have rights? Who is best placed to speak for them when they cannot speak for themselves?

Human Remains and Archaeology

Human remains are of particular importance to archaeologists, not only because they offer our only physical evidence for ancient people themselves, but also because in the vast majority of cases they are found as they were deposited and therefore offer evidence of the beliefs and practices of past peoples; they are not the rubbish and discard that characterise most archaeological finds. There is a large literature on the study of human remains in archaeology (May 1998; Spencer Larsen 2000).

Human bone will survive in the majority of soil conditions. The older the remains, the less likely their survival; but bones have to be many thousands of years old before they fail to survive. Their contribution falls into three main areas. First, large cemetery assemblages, with good archaeological records, providing date and context, offer a cross section of past populations and can be used to help understand their nature (average life expectancy, health, demography, etc.) and how they were affected by their environments. Second, human remains from

149

graves can contribute to an understanding of the beliefs and practices of past societies. Third, very early remains, sometimes fossilised, and examples from around the world, help us understand human evolution and how the human race has spread itself around the world and adapted to different environments. New scientific techniques, such as the study of DNA and isotopes, have the potential to identify the origins of skeletons and the health and living conditions of the dead.

The Excavation of Human Remains, Law, and Guidance in the United Kingdom

In the United Kingdom the legal basis for the excavation of human remains is very clear (see also Chapter 4). There is the legislation and planning advice concerned with archaeology in its widest sense. This includes the 1979 Ancient Monuments and Archaeological Areas Act and Planning and Policy Guidance Note 16: Archaeology and Planning (PPG16). When it comes to human burial, the law is not designed purely for the purpose of archaeology. Under the 1857 Burial Act, it is illegal to disinter a body without lawful authority. This authority comes in the form of a licence from the Secretary of State for Constitutional Affairs (until 2004, the licences came from the Home Office). Other legislation exists that covers the development of disused burial grounds and the removal of cemetery furniture, such as tombstones. Permission to disturb bodies buried in consecrated ground must come from the church (see Church of England/English Heritage 2005 for a full summary of English law protecting burials).

Therefore, in effect, cemetery excavations in England occur when a developer seeks to build over a disused burial ground. The local authority decides whether the development can go ahead, and if it does, the archaeologist concerned obtains a licence from the government to remove the burials. The licences will normally state that the excavation will be for the purpose of the scientific study of the burials and that reburial will take place at an appropriate time after study has been completed. Often, they will also state that remains of high scientific value can remain archived rather than being reburied.

The licences do not make any stipulations or offer any guidance about the museum use of human remains. So, guidance must be sought from elsewhere on such issues as display and handling. A large and detailed literature on the ethics of excavating, curating, and displaying human remains has developed. However, this has dealt almost entirely with foreign cultures and religions (see Skeates 2000 for a general discussion and Cox 1998). Concerns about the ethics of excavating earlier generations of Britons, beyond those who may have living close relatives, has until recently been less clear-cut. A good early summary of the issues was published in 1995 by Mike Parker Pearson. Pearson (1995) notes that in Britain there is a history of controversy but that it has not settled on a consensus viewpoint: "British attitudes to dead bodies are ambivalent, contradictory and volatile" and that, as such, there is still latitude in the way human remains are treated. One reason for this is that the Christian faith does not have strong views on the sanctity of the dead body once the soul has departed. Indeed, excavation shows it was very normal in the past for the church itself to disturb burials. It is normal to find burials and indeed extensions to churches cutting earlier burials, and to find charnel pits of disturbed bones where areas of cemeteries have been cleared.

Parker Pearson concluded with a code of ethics for human remains (1995, p. 18). This makes a useful addition to museum codes of conduct with relation to human remains produced by the Museums Association and International Council of Museums (MA 1999; ICOM 1996). However, as already mentioned, most of these codes refer to the treatment of human remains from particular ethnic, cultural, or religious groups which hold strong beliefs as to the treatment of the dead, and to the treatment of human remains where existing relatives might still be alive. Once these have been discounted, the main call is for suitable respect and the kind of professional treatment that would be visited on any archaeological remains. This rather vague situation has changed radically within the last few years, and there is now clear guidance on both the excavation and curation of remains in British museums.

Human Remains within Museum Collections

The whole landscape for the acquisition, study, display, and curation of human remains in British museums is changing rapidly. This is due to a number of separate but not unrelated initiatives. These include the passing of the Human Tissue Act that regulates the rights of those dealing with human tissue less than 100 years old (Department of Health 2005); the publication of the 2003 DCMS "Palmer report" (DCMS 2003) into the use of human remains in museums, and the subsequent guidance for museums published in 2005 (DCMS 2005b); and, finally, the 2005 report by the Church of England and English Heritage into the excavation and study of human remains from Church of England sites (Church of England/English Heritage 2005). These initiatives cover England, Northern Ireland, and Wales, but not Scotland. Guidance already exists there for the excavation of human remains (Historic Scotland 1997), and a working group is currently convened to cover the same areas as the DCMS guidance.

The 2005 DCMS *Guidance for the Care of Human Remains in Museums* along with the Human Tissue Act and Church of England/English Heritage report, provides, for the first time, clear guidance and regulation for dealing with almost all aspects of human remains as they have an impact on archaeology and museums in England. The catalyst for these changes can be found in three places. First, the Alder Hey scandal of the 1990s (for background, see The Royal Liverpool Children's Inquiry 2001), where it was discovered that the organs of children who had died in hospital had been retained without the consent of parents. This led to a widespread analysis of how and where human remains were held by public institutions and under what circumstances. Second, the disquiet felt by many over the traveling exhibition *Body Worlds* that used "plastinated" human remains to illustrate anatomy and other aspects of human physiognomy. Third, there have been a growing number of claims for the repatriation of human remains from Indigenous peoples, and the changes in legislation in the United States, and policy in Australia that facilitated return in those countries. British museums and universities acquired large collections of human remains in the nineteenth and early twentieth century from Indigenous peoples, normally without the consent of those peoples, and, in most cases, for the purpose of proving modals of racial superiority that are now disproved and discredited. A number of remains have been repatriated, normally from nonnational museums with ethnographic collections. As yet, no returns have taken place from institutions with large collections of human remains held primarily as scientific collections (see Fforde 2004 for a complete review of the repatriation issue as it relates to Aborigines and British museums).

Britain will be affected in its future action by its particular historical past. Enlightenment values and the Church of England, neither of which put any particular sacred significance on remains, have heavily shaped domestic attitudes to human remains. Nondomestically, Britain must deal with its colonial past and the attitudes of Empire that came with it. A particular driver for relations with Indigenous people has been the claims for repatriation from Australian Aborigines and the support Australian domestic and foreign government policy have given their claims. In July 2000, the British Prime Minister Tony Blair and his Australian counterpart John Howard made a joint commitment to improve communication between British museums and Aborigine communities and to facilitate better methods for dealing with claims for return. This, and the Alder Hey scandal, led eventually to the Human Tissue Act and the forming of the British Government Working Group on Human Remains. This group reported in 2003 (DCMS 2003) with a consultation paper following in 2004 (DCMS 2004). From this work came the 2005 DCMS drafting group that delivered guidance for museums holding remains (DECMS 2005b).

A final factor in this debate was a growing concern over the increasing number of human remains that were being disturbed from cemetery sites in Britain by redevelopment and the wish to regulate this activity in terms of archaeological value. This led to the formation, in 2001, of a joint English Heritage–Church of England working group that published its work in 2005 (Church of England/English Heritage 2005).

All of the above may not have a particularly profound immediate effect on many museums and how they deal with remains. Although, the spring of 2006 saw the British Museum agree to return two cremation bundles to Tasmania (Morris 2006). However, this is almost certainly the start of a process that will see human remains dealt with differently and lead, in time, to a new philosophy to their acquisition, care, and use. What is notable is that most pressure for change is coming from within the profession or from external influences, not from museum visitors. There is no evidence that members of the public do not visit museums because human remains are on display – if anything, the opposite is true. Similarly, there appears, on the basis of what evidence there is, to be a string support for the excavation, study, and display of human remains from archaeological sites in the United Kingdom (see the next section).

As noted in this chapter, human remains form an important and prominent part of museum archaeological collections in many parts of the world and often feature in displays. A walk round the galleries of the British Museum reveals rooms of Egyptian mummies, some in their sarcophaguses, some outside them, some partly unwrapped. There are also examples of early natural mummification, including the predynastic burial known as "Ginger" which has good soft tissue preservation. Other galleries include skeletons from other cultures and "Peat Marsh" the late Iron Age "bog body" from Cheshire that also has complete soft-tissue preservation. At the Museum of London, prehistoric skeletons can be viewed as well as skulls recovered from the Wallbrook stream and River Thames. At the Kulturen I Lund in Sweden, unassociated skulls from plague cemeteries are displayed in the medieval gallery along the tops of other displays along with the names of known victims – although there is no direct link between the names and associated skulls. Also in Sweden, both the Gotland Fornsal Museum and the Drotten Archaeological Museum Lund include osteological displays, as does the National Museum of Denmark in Copenhagen. A trip to the South Tyrol Museum of Archaeology in Balzano, Italy, will find the body and equipment of the "Ice Man" known as "Ötzi." (It is interesting that it is the soft-tissue remains that have been given nicknames.) The National Museum of Greenland in Nuuk displays the bodies of a fifteenth-century family preserved in frozen conditions. The Xinjiang Regional Museum in China displays the famous mummies of Urumqi. At the Archaeological Museum of San Pedro de Atacama in Chile, Andean mummies are displayed. These are just a few examples of the thousands of human remains that can be seen on public display. And the public flock to see these displays, and no one calls for their removal.

However, there are no human remains on display at the National Museum of the American Indian in Washington, DC, and generally throughout North America the remains of Indigenous Americans are no longer displayed. Similarly, the remains of Aboriginal people are not displayed in Australian museums. For the 1998 permanent exhibition at the Australian Museum in Sydney, the curators failed to persuade Aboriginal communities to display skeletons, casts, or images of aboriginal human remains. For key parts of the exhibitions story, "outline shapes" were displayed (Specht and MacLulich 2000, p. 47). Recently, Peruvian Indigenous cultural organisations demanded that the Imka mummies on display be removed because they symbolise genocide and should not be used to attract visitors to a museum (Cassman and Odegaard 2004, p. 272). Similarly, the plans to display 500-year-old, incredibly well-preserved, mummies of children from the Andes in the Museum of High Altitude Archaeology in Salta province, Argentina, has led to objections from Indigenous groups who have called this an "insult to their ancestors" (Goñi 2005, p. 22). A leader of indigenous groups is reported to have said that the planned display was "a violation of our loved ones" and that "they should not put our children on exhibition as if in a circus." The Director of Argentina's national museum Americo Castilla added to the debate by stating, "today it is no longer considered ethical to put human remains on display" (Goñi 2005, p. 22).

Policy in Australia means that wherever possible Aboriginal remains have been returned to tribes, normally to be reburied, or put in a keeping place in the National Museum where access is given only to Indigenous people, not Western scientists. The majority of these remains would not be considered of high archaeological importance but there are exceptions. Australian Aboriginal people do not accept Western concepts of time and lineage. *Place* is far more important so any remains from tribal land, however ancient, are considered ancestors. Occasionally this has led to disputes. The most famous example of this is the so-called Lake Mungo Woman. These remains, discovered in 1968, are the oldest known cremation in the world at more than 30,000 years old and as such of huge scientific value as well as being considered of immense spiritual significance to the local and national Aboriginal community. To recognize this shared value, a compromise was arrived at whereby the remains were returned to Aboriginal communities but held in a keeping place whereby they would not be lost completely to future study (Fforde 2004 pp. 114–115).

A more recent, and better-known example of controversy over ancient human remains, has been the case of so-called Kennewick Man in the United States. These remains were discovered in 1996 on Federal U.S. Army land in the state of Washington. They date to about 9,000 years ago. Five Native American tribes claimed the bones under the provision of NAGPRA (see Chapter 4) with the intention of reburial without scientific analysis. A group of physical anthropologists sued the Federal government to release the remains for study and a series of acrimonious and very public debates have ensued, while the remains have been kept at the Burke Museum in Seattle. In 2004, 8 years after the lawsuit begun, judges finally agreed that the remains should be made available for scientific study.

The Native American Graves Protection and Repatriation Act (NAGPRA) enacted in the United States in 1990 (see Chapter 4) calls on all museums holding Indigenous human remains (and other material) from Federal land to publicly list their holdings and proactively seek to repatriate their holdings to appropriate tribes. It has had a profound effect on U.S. museums both in terms of forcing them to research their collections and also for the process of repatriation and the links the museums have had to build with Indigenous communities. As an example, the Smithsonian National Museum of Natural History (SMNH) has repatriated about 3,300 of its 18,000 native Indian human remains under the terms of NAGPRA (Steel, 2004, p. 23). There are mixed views in the United States over the effects of NAG-PRA. Although some have been dismayed at the loss of collections, many have seen the process as positive in the way it has made the museum and archaeological community build links with Indian communities. See Steel (2004) for a discussion of the traditional pro and con arguments to breaking up collections through repatriation, and Peers (2004) for a discussion of how experience in North America (in this case, Canada) has shown that consultation over remains with Indigenous communities can lead to improved and productive relationships for anthropologists.

Public Responses

So, should museums continue to collect, store, display, and research human remains? As already noted the situation in North America, Australia, and New Zealand is very different to that with human remains from noncontested origins in Europe. A small survey of the public who visited archaeological events and museums in Cambridgeshire, United Kingdom, showed that of 220 responses 85 percent were aware that archaeologists frequently kept skeletons after excavation; 70 percent thought they should be reburied, but of these 71 percent thought this should only be when all scientific potential had been exhausted; 88 percent thought it was appropriate to keep human remains for future scientific study; 56 percent thought the dead person's previous religious beliefs should be a factor in the treatment of remains; 79 percent expected to see human remains on display in museums; 73 percent thought this was appropriate; 71 percent expected to see remains at "one-off public events hosted by archaeologists," and 69 percent thought this was appropriate (see Carroll 2005, pp. 10–12). Similar support was found in a survey of visitors to displays of Ancient Egyptian remains in UK museums where 82.5 percent of respondents supported display although 14.2 percent supported a "more appropriate and respectful environment" (Kilmister 2003). When the Museum of London staged the *London Bodies* exhibition in 1998–1999 (see the Display of Human Remains section below), the exhibition was a success with visitors. Figures suggest about 15,600 people came to the Museum specifically to see the exhibition. Since detailed records started in 1992, *London Bodies* registered the highest proportion of visitors going round and the highest average daily visitor figures of any of its temporary exhibitions (the figures have since been surpassed by other exhibitions).

Twenty-eight comments on the exhibition were left in the visitor comments box and 134 comments were made as part of market research surveys. Of these, 110 were positive, and 62 were negative (figures will not exactly correlate as some individuals gave more than one view). Of the negative comments, only one visitor was unhappy about the ethics of displaying human remains. This compares with seventeen who were unhappy with captions and displays being too high; one visitor who was hoping the exhibition would be "more shocking"; and one visitor who wanted to see more skeletons. Hopefully these figures justify the museum's belief that the general public is happy to see skeletons displayed under the correct circumstances. Ironically, during the run of *London Bodies*, the Museum had to deal with far more complaints about a small exhibition on Oliver Cromwell that had neglected to comment on his actions in Ireland (see Museum of London 1999, pp. 16–17 for a summary and illustrations of the exhibitions).

One year after *London Bodies*, Museum of London archaeologists unearthed a late Roman stone sarcophagus containing a lead coffin at Spitalfields close to the city. Clearly a very rich burial with possible good levels of survival within the lead coffin, it was brought unopened back to the Museum and put on display. Media interest was very high, and this, in turn, led to a high level of public interest. The coffin was opened one evening after the Museum had closed and the skeleton was immediately put on public display, and it remained there for 1 month. This discovery led to an extra 10,000 visitors coming to the Museum. Some queued for 1.5 hours to see the skeleton and other finds. Again, there was no negative response from anyone (see Chapter 14, Roberts and Swain 2001, and Swain 2000).

The *London Bodies* and Spitalfields experiences show clearly that not only are the vast majority of the public comfortable seeing skeletons in museums, on occasions they can be a special draw. The Museum has continued to use skeletons in its permanent galleries. This includes that of a child with rickets in the *World City* gallery that covers the period 1789–1914 (although this has now been taken off display), and two complete skeletons and several skulls in the *London before London* exhibition that covers the Greater London area in prehistory (see Swain 2003 and Chapters 12 and 13). Again, there has been no negative response.

The Museum has also continued to carry out visitor surveys about the use of human remains. These have taken place as part of research for the development of the new *Medieval London* gallery and related to public events using the skeletons from excavations. These surveys, normally including about one hundred respondents, always produce a figure of more than 85 percent (normally more than 95 percent) in support of the Museum holding, studying, and displaying human remains. Admittedly, these surveys have always drawn their respondents from a very particular group: those already choosing to visit the museum or from a group with an interest in history and archaeology.

All of this would suggest a clear division between the views of the Western museum-going public who remain comfortable with human remains in all their forms in museums (no doubt for various reasons) and peoples of other cultures who object to remains being on display and in collections for religious, cultural, or political reasons. The question is whether these different views will affect each other. There are some examples of Native American Indians taking an interest in the study of their ancestor's remains. It is also the case that the "Indigenous view" has led to some soul searching amongst the Western museum community about human remains, and this is beginning to have an effect on some displays and policies. Indeed, the DCMS (2005a) document might be seen as evidence of this.

The Value and Use of Collections

As I have already noted, many museums with archaeological collections hold human remains. In many cases, these might be only a few examples, maybe just skulls, often from anti-quarian collections. Such collections seldom have any archae-ological value, and in many cases it might be difficult to justify them being kept in the collection. More significant are the large archaeological collections that have often come from ceme-tery excavations and that have the potential to contribute to research. The largest collections in the United Kingdom are the Duckworth Collection at the University of Cambridge that is not part of a museum collection, and the collection of the Natural History Museum. Both of these institutions hold about 19,000 human remains each. They include large archaeological assemblages but also individual skeletons and smaller assem-blages from all around the world, and their value is primar-ily for offering examples for physical anthropological study. The Museum of London currently holds about 17,000 human skeletons. Apart from a few skeletons and parts of skeletons in the core collections – mainly skulls, normally derived from antiquarian collections – the vast majority are held as part of archaeological excavation archives in the London Archaeolog-ical Archive and Research Centre (see Chapter 7). These have been recovered as parts of controlled excavations on sites due for redevelopment in Greater London over the last 30 years. All are associated with archaeological records that give infor-mation about the context and circumstances of their burial. The majority come from large assemblages (the largest group of about 10,000 from the medieval hospital of St Mary Spi-tal [Thomas 2004], which make them statistically viable for scientific research.

The Museum is currently undertaking a project funded by the Wellcome Trust to produce an online database of 5,000 of the skeletons to promote research. A further 5,000 of the skeletons from St Mary Spital are being added to this. Recent projects have identified the presence of congenital syphilis in medieval skeletons – the disease was previously thought to have been introduced to Europe by Columbus's expedition to Central America. Another project identified major differences between the health of medieval monks and their hospital charges (in both cases from the medieval hospital of St Mary Spital, see Thomas 2004), and an ongoing project is trying to identify evidence of a known medieval famine in an assemblage of skeletons from victims of the Black Death (from excavations at the Royal Mint site in East Smithfield).

Traditionally, the skeletons have been treated in the same way as other "bulk" archaeological finds: kept in plastic bags, within cardboard boxes on shelves amongst other archaeological finds in one of our off-site stores. The Museum of London has recently reviewed the status of the collections and divided the human remains into three categories: those of no possible future scientific value that can be reburied (about 1,000 of which have indeed been reburied); those of limited research value because of the small sample size that can be stored with limited access (about 1,000); and those of high and continuing research value (about 15,000). Although the above figures would suggest that the vast majority of the London remains will remain within the museum's collections, the important principle is to continually review their status and remember that all remains are in temporary care and are not part of the permanent collections.

All of the skeletons are kept in a dedicated store away from other material. A summary of the remains is available from the Museum's website that will in time be joined by the full database of all remains. Skeletons that are reburied, all of which are from Christian burials, have been reburied in a mass grave at a London cemetery. In the meantime, it is hoped that a long-term store in a disused church or church crypt might be found for the remaining skeletons, where they would be on consecrated ground but still available for researchers. A similar solution has already been found for medieval skeletons excavated from Barton-on-Humber in North Lincolnshire, where following study the skeletons will be stored in the organ loft of a local redundant church. The Church of England/English Heritage (2005) report has identified the need for such stores.

The Museum of London is at one extreme of the range of human remains held by museums. Perhaps a more typical example is Perth Museum and Art Gallery in Scotland. Perth's human remains collections include a full skeleton used as a biological specimen as part of the Museum's Natural Science collection. It was purchased for 45 florins, in 1893, from V. Fric in Prague, suppliers of biological specimens and preparations. It is part of the Museum's much-reduced osteological collection, largely put together in the nineteenth century and presently also comprising five teeth and seven skulls. The museum also holds Scottish archaeological material, all of it of local provenance; ethnography collections including a small volume of human remains, namely a pair of heads from New Zealand and a pair of heads from South America; finally there are Egyptology collections, a mummy and sarcophagus and several mummified body parts.

Prior to the 1970s, the mummy was on permanent display, and there is a strong collective memory in Perth of seeing it on display and expecting it to be on display. As part of its education service, tours are given to see the mummy. The mummy is also used in the occasional exhibition or special event (Mark Hall, personal communication). The museum has had no complaints about the use of the mummy; indeed, given the choice most visitors would like to see it on permanent display. Of its Scottish remains, Perth holds archaeology collections that comprises prehistoric cremated remains, a complete early medieval skeleton, and skeletons, skulls, and fragments from medieval burials in Perth (primarily around St John's parish church) and from the nearby Elcho nunnery. Perth has repatriated its New Zealand material. This was met by a level of misunderstanding and naïve reporting in the local media and complaints by New Zealand white supremacists (Mark Hall, personal communication).

The Display of Human Remains

At present, human remains are displayed in museums as if they were any other type of artefact: normally within glass cases in amongst other displays. Often, attempts are made to reconstruct graves as archaeologists found them. So it is normal to see skeletons with grave goods and sometimes surrounded by real or fake rocks or soil. Soft-tissue remains sometimes require particular environmental conditions, and these can affect display conditions. For many museums, such displays remain an acceptable and even an ideal way to attract visitors. The recent redisplay of the exhibition section of the Jorvik Viking Centre in York (see Chapters 12 and 13) put emphasis on the skeletons from excavations because these were seen as a powerful way of making a direct link between visitors and the people of the past. However, in response to the reconsideration of the place of human remains in museum collections already discussed, some museums have begun to approach display in a new way.

An early attempt to consider the ethics of human remains display was made for the redisplay of the Alexander Keiller Museum in Avebury, Wiltshire (Stone 1994, p. 200, see also Chapter 11). Human remains are still displayed but careful consideration was made of visitor views before a decision was made. For its *Digging for Dreams* exhibition, the Petrie Museum put human remains from ancient Egypt on display but behind a shroud that visitors only lifted at their own choice (Mac-Donald 2002, p. 16). At the Egyptian exhibition at New Walk Museum in Leicester, parts of a mummy are displayed but specifically to challenge the visitor to question the ethical correctness of this approach.

The Turin Egyptian Museum has recently redisplayed an Egyptian mummy not a lot unlike "Ginger" at the British Museum. Here, the skeleton itself has been placed in a large case with blanked in sides so it can only be seen from above. This gives both "privacy" to the remains and also makes the decision to view it a conscious one by the visitor. The accompanying displays make the body the centre of a shrine-like display that gives it a special place that invites contemplation and respect. A similar approach has been taken at the Laténium Museum in Switzerland, where skeletons are displayed in a small room within the overall display.

China has a more ambivalent approach to display. In the Turpan Museum, human remains are displayed in a separate room are clearly marked, "Exhibition of Turpan Ancient Dried Bodies." The remains are incredibly well-preserved natural mummies and include a pregnant woman with a baby still in her womb and a man whose face is contorted with pain. The remains are displayed with a velvet case lining and, interestingly, the groin area is covered with similar fabric for modesty! (Solicari 2005). At the Silk Road Cultural Relics Museum, remains are exhibited in a circular antechamber and have their heads facing Mecca, according to Muslim custom. This is despite the fact that these bodies predate the spread of Islam in the area (Solicari 2005).

Occasionally, new technology is allowing for human remains to be displayed in different ways. Some museums use x-ray photographs to show the inside of unwrapped mummies. The British Museum's *Mummy, the Inside Story* focused on a single mummy and a three-dimensional film of its investigation using medical body-scanning technology to investigate it without having to unwrap it.

Between 27 October 1998 and 21 February 1999, the Museum of London staged the exhibition *London Bodies* (Werner 1998; Swain and Werner 1998; Museum of London 1999; Ganiaris 2001; Plate 3). The exhibition traced how the appearance of Londoners has changed since prehistoric times, with the central feature a series of skeletons presented below perspex covers, laid out in marble dust on mortuary trolleys. The exhibition showed how archaeological evidence from human burials could supplement historical evidence and tell the story of peoples' changing shapes through time. It drew upon the very large collection of human skeletons within the Museum's archaeological archive, and on the detailed analysis that is currently taking place on this material by Museum of London specialists. Apart from the complete skeletons, a number of other human bones were featured to illustrate specific medical conditions, including the pelvis bones from a medieval woman and those of her unborn child, both who had died during the birth.

The museum gave careful thought to its motivations for the exhibition, how the right balance would be achieved between a suitable respect for the human remains and the maximum public access to the stories they told. A defining moment came with the press launch for the exhibition. There was a need to

PLATE 3. The *London Bodies* exhibition (1998) at the Museum of London. (Photo: Museum of London.)

"hook" the press to obtain the publicity the exhibition needed. A themed breakfast was arranged involving "long bone toast" and bloody (strawberry) fruit juice. Journalists were issued torches and led into the subterranean store. There, specialists in white coats gave a presentation under spotlight in the otherwise darkened basement. But the showmanship was only allowed to go so far. A request from the PR consultants that all museum staff should wear surgical masks was refused. It was clearly explained why the museum had the care of these skeletons, the legal foundation for this care, and the reasons behind excavation and analysis. During all dealings with the press and media, only the osteologists and conservators handled bones. Only photographs taken or supervised by the Museum were permitted. Only material from archaeological specimens was used.

In undertaking the exhibition, the museum was conscious that some might be disturbed or upset by it content, or simply not wish to see it. For this reason, it was carefully shielded from the rest of the museum with clear panels explaining its content. Unaccompanied children and school parties were not allowed to enter. The museum prepared a statement on the context of the use of remains for use with external enquiries.

The museum has since prepared guidelines for the future display of remains. The guiding principle in this states: "Human skeletons are an important part of the Museum of London's archaeological collections and provide important evidence about the past lives of Londoners. If dealt with in a responsible and sensitive way they have the ability to act as a powerful method of interpretation for the Museum."

It will be interesting to see whether there continues to be a place for major exhibitions and displays featuring human remains. The Smithsonian National Museum of Natural History is currently planning a major exhibition *Written in the Bone* that will tell the story of the very first European settlers on the American Atlantic Seaboard using their skeletons as recovered from archaeological excavations. It is also interesting that at the very time that museums are questioning the use of remains in other spheres, the place of human remains is being given a new dimension. Gunther von Hagens' touring *Body Worlds* exhibition has met with controversy but also large and enthusiastic visitor numbers. The exhibition features "plastinated" and dissected human bodies. Von Hagens has also carried out public autopsies and anatomy classes, some of which have been transmitted on British terrestrial television. A second touring exhibition *Bodies, the Exhibition* has used similar material.

Another popular aspect of the display of human remains in recent years has been the reconstruction of faces using forensic techniques. This allows for the reconstruction of the possible appearances of people from their skulls by building up muscle and flesh based on known averages. So popular has this technique become that most museums in Britain with archaeological displays also have an example of one of these heads (many were produced for the BBC television series *Meet the Ancestors*). Unfortunately, for the very reason that these reconstructions are based on averages, and are not given expressions, they all tend to end up looking the same and then rely on artistic interpretation put on things, such as a hairstyle, to give them an identity.

The Human Remains of Archaeologists

I finish this chapter with an example that perhaps illustrates the contradictions inherent in the human remains debate. In 1943, on his death, the great archaeologist Flinders Petrie left his skull to the Royal College of Surgeons London as an example of a typical European type, hoping it would be of use in comparative studies of human skulls and, thus, races. Petrie died in Palestine and his head was duly removed, preserved in fluid, and sent to London. For reasons that are unclear, the head was never defleshed but instead it was left in its preserving fluid and consigned to a cupboard where it was largely forgotten.

In recent years, staff at the Royal College of Surgeons and others, including staff of the Petrie Museum, University College London once more became aware of the great man's head. Some initial consternation, and the question of identity over the head's dark brown hair (Petrie died in old age with white hair), was overcome with analysis that showed the preserving fluid had dyed the hair and beard. Other than this, the head is perfectly preserved, but what were they to do with it? There would appear to be three options. The head could still be defleshed thus fulfilling Petrie's stated desire. But there would be no scientific use for such a skull in the way Petrie had hoped. The head could be kept as it is, but again it is difficult to find any use other than curiosity, and Petrie's wish was clearly for his skull to be kept, not the complete head. Finally, the head could be buried or cremated and thus be "laid to rest." As I write, this later option seems the most likely. Personally, I am ambivalent as to what should be done and certainly grateful that the choice is not my responsibility. Whatever, Flinders Petrie remains the only one of the great early archaeologists I have been able to look in the face. And I am grateful for this opportunity!

Key Texts

Cassman, V., Odegaard, N., and Powell, J. (2007). *Human Remains, Guide for Museums and Academic Institutions.* Lanham MD: Altimira.

Church of England and English Heritage (2005). *Guidance for best practice for treatment of human remains excavated from Christian Burial grounds in England.* London: Church of England and English Heritage.

Department for Culture, Media, and Sport (2003). *The Report of the Working Group on Human Remains.* London: DCMS. (The Palmer report.)

Department for Culture, Media, and Sport (2005). *Guidance in the care of human remains in museums.* London: DCMS.

Fforde, C., Hubert, J., and Turnbull, P. (2002). *The Dead and their possessions, Repatriation in principle, policy, and practice.* London: Routledge.

Fforde, C. (2004). *Collecting the dead.* London: Duckworth.

Lohman, J., and Goodnow, K. (Eds.), (2006). *Human remains and Museum Practice.* Paris: UNESCO.

May, S. (1998). *The archaeology of human bones.* London: Routledge.

CHAPTER 9
RESEARCH

For many museums, pure research is becoming more and more of a luxury. However, much past archaeological research has taken place within museums or is based directly on museum collections. This chapter deals with the types of research museum archaeological collections can support, how this can be achieved and worked into wider programmes, and how it can relate to other research establishments such as universities.

Introduction

In considering archaeological research in its widest sense, museum archaeology is normally considered the poor sibling. University archaeologists deliver new theory, field archaeologists deliver new data. Museum archaeologists simply keep the stuff in boxes and put things inside glass cases and possibly write catalogues. This is a perception delivered by the archaeological hegemony that has placed fieldwork and theory as supreme. However, much archaeological research in the past has been undertaken by museum archaeologists and has used museum collections. In recent decades, as theory has been divorced from real things, and fieldwork has been driven by development rather than research, museums and curators have been even more marginalised from the process of new knowledge generation. But they remain key players.

One of the prime reasons that archaeological material is collected, curated, and managed is so that research can take place and new knowledge and ideas about the past developed. Inevitably, archaeological research undertaken in museums will primarily be collections and object based, although much other research, including fieldwork, has taken place from a museum base. Discussions about archaeological research in museums normally revolves around staff not having the time or resources to undertake it, and not enough other archaeologists choosing to do it – preferring instead to undertake yet another excavation (e.g., Saville 1999). Excavation has always been the prime means by which archaeologists have gone about accumulating new data. Although this might have been justified in the past, for a long time now, for many places and periods, even without the arguments about excavation being destructive, excavation is being undertaken for a diminishing return of new data while vast amounts of unrecorded data sit in museum archives (see Schofield 2006, British Archaeology 2006, and Swain 2005b for the beginnings of a discussion about this imbalance).

Similarly, it is suggested that university academics shy away from the research of collections while archaeology becomes more and more theory based. As I already noted in Chapter 3, many academics exist primarily in a theoretical world divorced from real things (Hodder 2001, p. 1). Museum curators are also spending more and more time writing about museology, and its history rather than actually studying their collections (this volume adding to that trend). But, this is simplifying the situation. There is a long tradition of highly important primary research into archaeological museum collections that draw on the advantages of having large catalogued, contextualised, and provenanced collections in one place. For example, Wise (2001) notes the role of the early curator/scholar/digger, such as Rex Hillin Colchester, for laying the foundations to the archaeological knowledge we now use. Much current archaeological knowledge, particularly about artefacts, was based on museum collections or collections that are now in museums (see, e.g., Gerrard 2003, pp. 194–196 for the contribution of artefact studies to recent medieval archaeological research). Although it has been observed that, archaeologists in general, and museum curators in particular, have stopped cataloguing and publishing major corpora of collections that would then facilitate new research (Saville 1999, p. 199). (See Wise

2001 for review of current British museum archaeology and research).

Archaeology has also continued to suffer from a division of expertise whereby few archaeologists regularly excavate sites *and* undertake artefact studies. It is a depressing observation that there has always been and continues to be a gender and a philosophical divide between the male site supervisors and diggers and female finds workers, specialists, and conservators.

How essential is new research to the curatorial process? Must curators be experts with that expertise founded on research, or can they be custodians facilitating the research of others? Is it enough just to know what is held and what its significance is? The normal stated view from within museums (e.g., Gaimster 2001, p. 3) is that research into collections is essential, should be fundamental to curatorial practice, and must come from within an institution. If it is accepted that knowledge about collections for a museum is essential, then research becomes essential as knowledge is not static and timeless, but is dynamic and changing. It could be argued that the research could be done "off-site" and accumulated as knowledge for on-site use. But the staff that are called on to make use of the knowledge and research must be confident in its use.

This overall situation is not helped by a traditional idea of the role and methods of research held by many museum authorities. It is seen as the personal preserve of scholars and has some form of tangential relationship to the overall purpose and running of an institution. As such, research tends to be seen as marginal and wasteful. Curators go to the grave, or at least retire, with their accumulated knowledge rather than embedding it in the knowledge base of their institutions. Or, colleagues and peer groups wait impatiently for the definitive publication that will finally share research with a wider world.

Museum archaeological research can be summarised under a number of headings: research undertaken by museum staff as part of, or a by-product of, other work such as exhibitions or collections management; research by museum staff for its own sake; and research by nonmuseum archaeologists into museum collections.

Research Frameworks

In the United Kingdom, a by-product of the commercialisation of archaeology and the peripatetic nature of archaeological organisation was the development of national and regional research frameworks. These were born out of a concern that commercial archaeology was not being driven by research questions (e.g., Morris 1993). The idea behind research frameworks is that they will be dynamic documents that summarise current knowledge, identify relevant research questions that can be answered by directed work, and lay out strategies for this to be undertaken. Swain (2001) gives a summary of the research agenda process as pursued in London including the research agenda process as developed by English Heritage (1991b, 1997, 2005). On the whole, and with London as the exception, research frameworks have largely bypassed museums and museum collections and their potential as research resources. However, they are useful summaries of archaeological knowledge and do accept the importance of research within mainstream archaeology.

Reference Collections

An area where museum collections have, and continue to make a major contribution to archaeological research, is through the creation and management of reference or type collections of finds. These were often developed historically by individuals for research or by field units to help them, for example, date sites, but are now often maintained by museums.

For example, a ceramic repository for the eastern United States was developed at the Museum of Anthropology at the University of Michigan in 1927, and detailed ceramic reference collections for London were first developed to support fieldwork in the 1970s. At different times, attempts have been made to unify reference collections at a regional, national, or even international level (see, e.g., Nieuwhof and Lange 2003 and Lange 2004 for discussions in The Netherlands).

Research as a By-Product of Other Work

The majority of research undertaken in museums probably occurs as a by-product of other activities, most often
the preparation of exhibitions and galleries. This process
inevitably leads to the reevaluation of a subject and the development of new questions that need to be answered in order
to present a coherent and logical story to the public. Just as
in other museum subjects, occasionally museum exhibitions
have completely changed the way a subject is thought about
in the wider discipline. A classic example was *Symbols of Power at
the Time of Stonehenge* held at the National Museum of Antiquities
of Scotland in Edinburgh in 1985 (Clarke et al. 1985). The exhibition, and the accompanying publication, drew from then
current archaeological theory but summarised and illustrated
it brilliantly, and this has effected the way this period of prehistory has been considered since. Similarly, *23°, S Archaeology
and Environmental History of the Southern Deserts* held in 2005 at
the National Museum of Australia is an example of innovative research thinking that was born out of a conference and
delivered a major book (Smith and Hesse 2005).

Other exhibitions, such as *Archaeology in Britain since 1945: New
Views of the Past*, held at the British Museum in 1986, *Capital Gains!
Archaeology in London 1970–86* held at the Museum of London in
the same year, and *I Celti* held at the Palazzo Grassi in Venice in
1991, perhaps do not offer new primary research but do lead
to a synthesis and presentation of existing data.

If exhibitions are one type of museum work that gen-
erates research, another is collections documentation. This
often starts before an object is even acquired by the museum.
The essential process of identifying and provenancing objects
leads to new information about them. This process continues as an object is developed within a collection. As noted
elsewhere (Chapter 10), conservation work on objects, including cleaning, has the potential to provide new information.

Answering public enquiries about collections also has the potential to deliver new research. For all of this new technology and, in particular, digital technology has the potential to revolutionise the speed of research, its nature, and how it is held for future use.

Research by Museum Curators

Although, as mentioned in this chapter, almost all museum activity leads to research of one kind or another, it is the case that pure research by museum staff into collections is now rare. Some institutions such as university museums still exist largely to allow their staff to undertake research. The large national museums also still preserve the role of the curator scholar. Using the British Museum as an example, Gaimster (2001, p. 4) shows how the curators are the creators of new research. In 1996, the British Museum staff produced 68 monographs and 184 referenced papers in addition to exhibition catalogues, and gave 518 lectures to learned societies, institutes, and the public. Gaimster (2001, p. 5) has suggested that curators are "too often bogged down by the tyranny of archive management" to allow them to undertake research. However, even to consider such a luxury is beyond many. At the other extreme, small museums with only single generalist curators not only will not find research a practical possibility it will be outside their job description. For example, it is estimated that there is Egyptian material in 200 museums in United Kingdom, but only about 10–12 specialist Egyptology curators (Margaret Serpico, personal communication). This is not a situation particular to archaeology. In its *Renaissance in the Regions* report (Resource 2001), and subsequent establishment of Subject Specialist Networks (SSNs), the United Kingdom MLA has acknowledged the need for specialist curators and the need for museums to work together to support specialist collections.

An area where museum archaeologists have traditionally contributed to wider museum research is in the creation and publication of object catalogues. Saville (1999, pp. 104–105) argues persuasively for the value of museum collections catalogues, not only as a key output of research but as a fundamental building block of synthetic research by archaeologists; and a *sine qua non* of basic museum identification and documentation (Saville 1999, p. 105). Many catalogues of objects from museum collections have been created over the years and often remain standard works used by field archaeologists, curators, university researchers, and even dealers and metal detector users. For example, the London Museum's Medieval Catologue first published in 1940 (London Museum 1940) has remained in demand as a standard work and was republished in 1993 (Anglia Publishing 1993). Many catalogues to specific exhibitions become standard works for identifying objects (e.g., the catalogue *Les Vikings* [Roesdahl et al. 1992] that accompanied the travelling exhibition *Les Vikings... Les Scandinaves et l'Europe 800–1200*, to name just one of thousands).

An example of field archaeologists and museum archaeologists working together to produce catalogues of archaeological finds, supported by museum collections, is that in London where the seven volumes of Medieval finds (see Egan 2001 for a review) uses the large collections of stratified objects from Thames waterfront excavations that are often found in fragmentary form but can be identified and supplemented by unstratified, but complete objects from core primarily antiquarian collections.

The internet and applications of digital data have obviously had a major influence on how collections catalogues can be created and disseminated. Museums have perhaps been slow to fully grasp this opportunity and there is a sense that many still prefer the idea of printed and bound volumes. However, in the last few years, major catalogues of museum collections have begun to appear in a digital form often housed on museum websites. Sometimes there is a conflict as to who the audience is for these and many have aimed at a wider audience than the pure research community. Examples that try to be exhaustive and are primarily aimed at researchers include the Museum of London's *Ceramics and Glass Collections* (www.museumoflondon.org.uk/ceramics/), and the

Ashmolean Museum's *Potweb* that catalogues its ceramics collections (http://potweb.ashmol.ox.ac.uk/) to name just two of thousands available. The British Museum's *Compass* and *Children's Compass* (www.britishmuseum.ac.uk/compass) is an example of a more selective site that tries to engage a wider audience.

One of the problems with the research of collections is not knowing exactly what is in them. This goes for large museum collections that are simply too big to be exhaustively studied and even more so for the small dispersed collections that do not have expert curators and need to be compared with other collections to reveal their potential. The haphazard and peripatetic way in which museum collections were accumulated in the nineteenth and twentieth century has exacerbated this. The proposed SSN initiative is aimed at combating this situation. One of its pilot projects is already allowing the diaspora of Flinders Petrie's Egyptian collections across English museums to be summarised collectively on a single database (Margaret Serpico, personal communication). For many years, a similar initiative has been undertaken by the West Midlands Archaeological Collections Research Unit (WEMACRU) that brings together archaeologists from a number of museums to identify common and shared collections.

Research By Nonmuseum Archaeologists

What museum collections should offer researchers are well catalogued, accessible collections of objects, hopefully with detailed contextual information, or at the very least information about what is known of collections. Such seminal works as Stuart Piggott's identification of the so-called Wessex Culture (Piggott 1938) or David Clarke's encyclopaedic study of British Beakers (Clarke 1970) are based on museum collections that were put together mainly under the antiquarian tradition. Such primary research has led to continual reassessment, for example, Renfrew of Piggott (1968) and Lanting and van der Waals' of Clarke (1972), that has helped to develop and to evolve archaeological thought; that the research of material culture becomes a product of "created" classificatory systems is a challenge for archaeologists to overcome rather than an inherent failing of the system.

Of course, museums also remain in the vast majority of cases the holding place for archaeological archives (as discussed in Chapter 7). As such the ongoing reexamination of key excavations and sites becomes a museum archaeology discipline. It is the case that the very best and most widely published sites are often these that continue to be most researched. So, the Star Carr archive from Clark's 1949–1951 excavations (Clark 1954), held at amongst other places the Museum of Archaeology and Anthropology, University of Cambridge, is still perceived as fundamental in understanding the Mesolithic, as does Barry Cunliffe's archive for the excavations at Danebury Hillfort, held by Hampshire Museum Service, for understanding the Southern British Iron Age (e.g., Cunliffe 1984). Indeed, the way a relatively few well-known and well-recorded and published sites continues to dominate thinking may be to the detriment of the subject. The sheer mass of new data from developer funded excavations and the fact that much primary evidence is not easily accessible makes its study problematic (see Chapter 7). A recent study of British prehistory using this very material by Richard Bradley is a test as to how accepted theories might be overturned by the analysis of the new evidence available, and just how difficult this process will be (*British Archaeology* 2006).

The biggest challenge is persuading archaeologists to use museums and museum collections, especially archives, for research. The current HEFCE funded Archive Archaeology project in England is aimed at encouraging university archaeology undergraduate courses to include an element in archive study, in the same way as they include fieldwork (see Chapter 7).

It has been suggested that research into U.S. archaeological collections has increased in recent years (in 1990, 16 percent of Ph.D. dissertations were on museum collections, and this had risen to 30 percent in 1994–1995; see Sullivan and Childs 2003, p. 108). It has been suggested that this may be as a result of NAGPRA and the renewed interest into Native American collections that it has fostered.

Fieldwork as Research

The most obvious type of archaeological research is that carried out through fieldwork, normally excavation. Yet, it is something very few museums now actively undertake. Where fieldwork still occurs, it tends to be from large well resourced museums such as the British Museum, for example, excavations in the 1980s of the High Lodge Palaeolithic site (Ashton et al. 1992) and the Runnymede later prehistoric site (Needham 1991), or by field units attached to museums, as is still the case with, for example, the Museum of London Archaeology Service or Norfolk Museums Service field unit. Elsewhere, museum based fieldwork is undertaken primarily as part of community outreach and for training, for example, the Shoreditch Park project at the Museum of London or the fieldwalking teams operating at Leicestershire Museums (see Chapter 14).

Key Text

Wise, P. J. (Ed.). (2001). *Indulgence or Necessity? Research in Museum Archaeology, The Museum Archaeologist, 26*, Society of Museum Archaeologists.

Chapter 10
Conservation and Collections Care

Archaeological evidence, often very ancient and recovered in a vulnerable condition, offers very particular challenges for conservation ranging from the preservation of entire 16th-century warships, such as the Mary Rose, to the stable storage of rusting Roman nails. The great quantity of objects recovered and their myriad materials offer particular challenges for the care of archaeological collections.

Introduction

This book is not the place for a detailed survey of conservation or even a detailed study of archaeological conservation. Conservation and the care of collections is a massive and complex subject that has its own literature, training, career structure, and standards. Cronyn's (1990) standard work summarises archaeological conservation and its methodologies. Other books are available that summarise archaeological conservation on site (e.g., Watkinson and Neal 1998), conservation practice in museums (e.g., Pye 2001; Knell 1994), and archaeological conservation within the wider sphere of heritage management (e.g., Agnew and Bridgland 2006; Suenson-Taylor et al. 2006). This chapter very briefly discusses the types of work undertaken by archaeological conservators on behalf of museums within the museum context, and how conservation fits into some of the wider issues discussed in this book.

Conservation is a discipline in its own right. Conservators tend to subdivide themselves by subject type, so archaeological conservators see themselves as related to, but distinct from, fine art conservators and social history conservators, and so forth. Distinct training is available for archaeological conservation and most conservators tend to work in museums or as independent consultants; only a few are linked directly to archaeological field units. Conservation plays a key part in field archaeology, research, and curation, however, there are occasional tensions, particularly when conservationists are working on excavations. Cassman and Odegaard (2004, p. 274) note a lack of confidence amongst conservators as to what their role should be: as the champions of preservation, as providers of "technical expertise," or as integrated members of a team. Tensions in the museum are less obvious where the role of conservation perhaps fits better with the ethos of the museum.

Most things that are buried in the ground for any length of time will deteriorate physically. Metals oxidise, and organics are eaten by living organisms (biodeterioration). A few materials do not decay as readily because of their stable nature, such as stone and ceramics. The archaeological record and, therefore, museum showcases are dominated by stone tools and pots because these are the most resistant to deterioration in the ground. However, even objects of stone and pottery seldom survive in the ground in an identical form to that when they were in use.

It is the conservator's prime job to limit or reduce the further decay of objects once the objects have been retrieved. The philosophy and practice of the conservator has changed over time. There was a time when a conservator's prime role was to "restore." This involved trying to return the object to its original form. There are some instances when this is possible and to be desired. For example, when all parts of a broken pot are found it can be put back together, and by so doing both researchers and the public will get a better understanding of its original use. However, philosophically and practically, true restoration is impossible and, in any case, may not be desired. Objects that have been overrestored, to the extent where it is impossible to tell what is original artefact and what is modern addition, blight many modern museum collections.

This is both deceptive to the visitor, in the simple sense that they are given an incorrect picture of how an object survived and looked, but it can also be even worse in that many early restorations sought aesthetic beauty rather than any attempt at accuracy. Overrestoration also prevents meaningful study and can easily damage the original artefact, or what remains of it.

The role of the conservator as someone who restores an object for display has changed over time to one of minimising further deterioration. Cronyn (1990, pp. 1–4) describes the role of the modern archaeological conservator as "the preservation and elucidation of artefacts from excavations. Conservation basically aims to prevent objects disintegrating once they have been exposed to the atmosphere and to discover the true nature of the original artefact." From this definition, it follows that conservation is a fundamental part of both archaeological and museum practice. To this definition, we can add some key concepts to the role of conservation (Stanley Price 1990, p. 285):

1. *Reversibility.* The ability to reverse any conservation treatment, or not prevent any new treatment.
2. *Minimum intervention.* The look and composition of the item must be altered as little as possible to achieve the conservator's aims.
3. *Compatibility of materials.* Any new material introduced should be as close as possible to the original material.

So, modern conservation is about doing the minimum possible to an object to stop it deteriorating further, hopefully, by stabilising it. In addition, the conservator's intimate study of an object often allows the conservator to contribute valuable information about the nature of an object, including exactly what it is made from, and how it was made. This information, in turn, can often lead to evidence about provenance and technology.

Variations on this theme can be found in other interpretations of the modern conservator's role. The American Institute of Conservation of Historic and Artistic Works states that the "primary goal of conservation is preservation of cultural prop-erty." Chris Caple (personal communication) has suggested that conservation is all about revelation, investigation, and preservation and that there is a clear conceptual difference between something looking new and "good" and stabilisation and conservation. Cassman and Odegaard (2004, pp. 272–273) also debate the importance of aesthetics and physical integrity to conservators.

But this is not always as straightforward as it should be. The story of the Bush Barrow Gold perhaps exemplifies some of the contradictions at the heart of conservation. The sheet gold "lozenge" from Bush Barrow in Wiltshire is possibly the most iconic object from British prehistory. The lozenge was exca-vated by the antiquarians Cunnington and Colt Hoare at the turn of the nineteenth century, along with an assemblage of other objects that showed the barrow to be the finest exam-ple of the rich single-inhumation barrow burials from the late third millennium in southern England. This was dubbed the Wessex Culture (Piggott 1938; Annable and Simpson 1964) and is associated with the later stages of construction at Stone-henge. The lozenge, along with other finds from this barrow, found its way, eventually, at the turn of the twentieth century, into the collection of the Wiltshire Archaeological and Natural History Society at Devizes Museum (see Chapter 2).

Because of the importance of the Bush Barrow assemblage, it was placed on permanent loan at the British Museum, where, with the exception of the War years (1939–1945), it was seen by the millions visiting the museum. In 1985, the group of artifacts from Bush Barrow was loaned to the Museum of Antiquities in Edinburgh for the highly influential *Symbols of Power* exhibition (see Chapter 2 and Clarke et al. 1985). The lozenge's delicate nature had always been recognised. An early attempt to write an accession number on its reverse had marked through onto its front. When it was removed from the British Museum display, the lozenge was taken to the conservation department to have a new mount made for it. Once there, and under close inspection, conservators sur-mised that its slightly "crinkled" appearance could be because it was originally slightly domed or convex. The British Museum conservators then undertook restoration to *reshape* the object before sending it on to Edinburgh.

While it was on display in *Symbols of Power*, the lozenge was first seen in its new condition by the curator of Devizes Museum. A highly publicised and very acrimonious debate ensued between the British Museum and Devizes Museum (Kinnes et al. 1988; Shell and Robinson 1988; Corfield 1988). The British Museum argued for the correctness of their interpretation, and the Devizes Museum complained that they had not been asked, or even consulted, on the restoration of *their* object. As a result, the lozenge was returned to Devizes Museum, where, because of security arrangements, it is now kept locked away, and a replica is on display.

For those not directly involved, the whole episode may have injected a degree of interest to an otherwise dull subject. But the story of the Bush Barrow lozenge and its restoration highlight a series of pertinent questions about the nature of conservation, authenticity, consent, and ownership. If there is a scholarly dispute over what this, of all objects, looked like when first made and used, is it possible to ever think of any archaeological object, site, or interpretation as authentic or real in any sense of the word?

Buried Environments and Types of Material

The types of conservation that are needed vary depending on the specific environment in which something was buried and the type of material with which an artefact has been made. Generalisations can be made about types of environment and the conservation interventions at both a macrolevel and microlevel. For example, extremes of acidity or alkalinity in the soil can have profound effects on particular types of material, such as bone, that do not survive in acidic soils. Water, often known as "the great catalyst," can have the greatest effect on the deterioration of artefacts by encouraging chemical reactions. Those environments where water is almost absent – deserts and frozen regions – often provide the most startling archaeological preservation (e.g., materials from ancient Egypt and from Greenland). In most other cases, the presence of water leads to, or encourages, the decay of objects. Another exception is where water saturates soil leading to low-oxygen conditions, here again organic preservation can be exceptional, although it makes conservation problematic. Examples include timbers and other organic objects from the Thames waterfront in London. Other very particular circumstances can lead to unusual levels of preservation. For example, the bog bodies and associated organic material from peat bogs such as those in the National Museum of Denmark, Copenhagen, and in the British Museum, survive through a combination of anaerobic conditions and the natural tanning of the remains. The Viking ships at Roskilde, the English sixteenth century warship the *Mary Rose*, and the Swedish seventeenth century warship the *Vasa* were all preserved in seabed silts.

Preservation of organic material through anaerobic, waterlogged conditions offers a particular challenge to conservators. Such items, by nature, are rare and offer wonderful insights into the past not possible on other types of sites. As such, there is often a demand for not only preservation but also display. To keep remains stable, such material needs to *remain* waterlogged. Because water would have replaced much of the structure of the object, drying will destroy or, at the very least, change the size and shape of the object. Conservation techniques for such objects are now well-established, but are lengthy and relatively expensive. Conservation of waterlogged objects requires that the conservator slowly replaces the water with an alternative material, usually polyethylene glycol (commonly known as PEG) – a wax resin – and when this process is complete, freeze-drying. These techniques become hugely more complex as the size of objects increases. This is because, ideally, objects need to be fully immersed in PEG, and then put inside a freeze dryer. Sometimes, as with the Dover Bronze Age Boat, objects can be broken in to smaller pieces and then reconstructed, but this is sometimes impossible. The *Mary Rose* is still undergoing conservation more than 20 years after its removal from the sea. It is slowly being impregnated with PEG, while remaining wet in a sealed chamber – and while it is on display to the public. The conservation process, in this case, will not include freeze drying. Other organic material, such as textiles, rarely survive in buried environments, again making a textile find all the more precious when it does survive.

Nonorganic materials are normally less problematic. Stone and ceramics have already been mentioned. Their physical robustness and stable chemical composition means that pottery and stone artefacts often survive well. Pottery is delicate and can abrade and, of course, break. Stone can also abrade and can be patinated by chemicals in its buried environment. As such, even with these materials, the archaeological artefact may be a long way from the original object as made and used.

Another common category is metals, and in particular copper alloys and iron. Iron is extremely unstable and oxidises, or rusts, in most environments. The oxidising process often destroys the original surface of the artefact so that, even if desired, it could not be returned to its original form. Normal archaeological procedure is to take x-rays of iron items. These often show an object's original form and sometimes reveal complex details about an object's composition. X-rays, or images taken from them, have occasionally been used in museum displays. Iron corrosion can normally be minimalised by storing or displaying the object in carefully controlled environments.

Copper alloy (in many cases more familiarly called *bronze*) also deteriorates in different environments. It is more likely to keep its original shape and form than iron, but in most environments copper alloy corrodes to green from its original bronze or gold-like colour. This is why museum visitors are normally confronted with green artefacts in museum displays. Because the objects on display may *look* extremely sound, and otherwise uncorroded, it is difficult not to imagine prehistoric and later warriors bedecked in green weapons. Again, copper alloy can normally be stabilised for storage and display.

Precious metals, gold, and silver have a very particular allure for archaeologists and a special place in the mythology of lost treasure. In their pure state, they do not corrode and, therefore, are often found exactly as they were lost, giving a wonderful immediacy and adding to their aesthetic and monetary value. However, both silver and gold were often alloyed with copper to harden them, and the copper will decay in the ground. This means that silver objects, in particular, are often excavated looking less than pristine.

As already noted, the very particular circumstances of preservation and the methods available to conservators explicitly and implicitly affect the way museum audiences regard archaeological objects. Organics go from being mundane to precious because of the rarity of preservation and complexity of conservation: iron is always rusty, bronze is always green, and pots and stone tools predominate.

On-Site "First-Aid" Conservation

Archaeological objects are at most risk when they are first excavated. However, as unsuitable as their buried environments might be, they have almost certainly reached some level of stability within it. An object is upset in a traumatic manner when it is moved, sometimes for the first time in thousands of years, and when it comes into contact with the atmosphere. The more extreme the change in environment, the more risk to the object, so, for example, conservation of marine finds often requires the most immediate intervention. The standard UK work on how to deal with archaeological material *immediately after excavation* remains *First Aid for Finds* (Watkinson and Neal 1998) that, through several incarnations, has been used by field conservators for more than 30 years. It deals with the techniques for immediate lifting, protection, and stabilisation of objects and then their subsequent packaging and transport.

Laboratory Conservation, Analysis, and Stabilisation

Most detailed conservation takes place in the controlled conditions of the laboratory. It is here that a detailed stabilisation occurs and an analysis of how an object has been made and used takes place. This can sometimes be a long and painstaking process. Often, particularly delicate finds, are "block-lifted" in soil from the excavation to allow precise uncovering in laboratory conditions. Here the conservator will not only be making decisions as to how to reveal the object but also how to ensure its long-term preservation. Close proximity and study will also allow input into research questions. It is also here that detailed records are made of the object – its condition and the conservation work that has been undertaken. These records form an essential part of the documentation for the object in its later life and should be carefully integrated with archives or object documentation (see Chapters 6 and 7). Different storage materials and storage environments are available for different types of finds. From the laboratory, objects normally go into storage or on to display and, depending on what has been achieved in the lab, advice will be given about the conditions that must be maintained in order to prevent their deterioration.

Conservation for Display and as Part of a Display

Traditionally, conservation of an object to make it "presentable" was the most important part of the conservator's role, and this is probably why, historically, most archaeological conservators tend to be based in museums rather than in field units. Such work is still fundamental, but now it will be more geared towards ensuring that the object is stable in its display environment than trying to make it look as it once was.

Reconstruction happens at many scales and with many materials. Arthur Evans's use of reinforced concrete at Knossos, at the time, cutting-edge technology, was suited to the climate and conditions of the site (including threats from earthquakes), and allowed Evans to show the palace as "it once was" (Lapourtas 1997). His efforts are now largely seen as unacceptable. Similarly, museums are full of pots that have been reconstructed; some were originally restored hundreds of years ago. Sometimes this has been a matter of gluing back all the pieces, more often it is a case of using modern materials to fill gaps in order to create a pot that looks complete. Certainly, a complete pot will help a visitor understand its original shape and purpose more than a pile of broken sherds, but there is a delicate balance to be struck. Close inspection will show that many pots on display in museums are almost entirely modern in origin (see Burden 2006 for a project to conserve Bronze Age pots originally excavated and restored in the nineteenth century).

At the very least, conservators advise curators about the conditions under which objects can be displayed. Conservators will normally call for stable environments with relative humidity, temperature, and light levels that will greatly slow down and, overall, reduce the deterioration of the object. Occasionally, other materials within a case, such as the paint or material that has been used to line or mount a case will contain chemicals that might adversely react with the artefact.

Some objects demand particular conservation treatments that, through their very nature, become part of the objects display and interpretation, especially when there is an impatience to put an object on display, or when it is recognised that it will be many years before conservation is complete. A classic example of this is the Tudor warship the *Mary Rose*. The *Mary Rose* has been on display since soon after its excavation in 1982, and it is still being actively conserved. The mummies that were frozen in the high Andes 500 years ago, and are now held in the Museum of High Altitude Archaeology, will require very particular environmental conditions for display. To maintain their stable frozen condition, they will be, in effect, displayed in portable refrigerated cases. The inside of the cases will be kept at 20° below zero Celsius (or minus 4° Fahrenheit). The bodies will be surrounded by xenon or argon gas to prevent deterioration and a pressurised atmosphere will help avoid freezer burn. The bodies will rest on scales designed to detect changes in moisture and weight. Technology, in principle, will allow for their preservation forever, however, only at a cost. A $600,000 loan from the Inter-American Development Bank is helping to fund the project (information from Bloomberg.com).

There is, at times, a perceived or actual conflict between the needs of long-term preservation and those of display and interpretation. In fact, more and more museums are waking up to the concept that the process of conservation is often fascinating to the visiting public, and conservators are themselves becoming part of, or materially contributing to, displays and public programmes. The Conservation Centre, National Museums of Liverpool, provides the conservation support for the museum service but is also a museum in its own right that has exhibitions, displays, and programmes of events. Others, such as the Museum of London, have occasionally had conservators working front-of-house on particular projects. This can slow work rates enormously because questions need to be answered, and conditions are rarely perfect, but it provides for wonderful educational opportunities. A more straightforward alternative is to build elements about the conservation of artefacts into temporary or permanent displays. The display of the Bronze Age Dover Boat includes a mass of information about how it was conserved. All-in-all, not using conservators as parts of public programmes and displays is a huge missed opportunity. It may pose interpretation challenges due to the complexity of conservation work, but there is a real appeal to visitors, and it is an important method for communicating archaeological processes.

Long-Term Collections Care and Management

It is now recognised that one of the most important roles of conservation is to ensure the long-term stability of the collections. It is this area of conservation that has seen most investment in recent years, and it is where most advances have been made. Conservators recognise that there is no point in rescuing an object from a site and conserving it in the laboratory if, after a number of years it is going to crumble to nothing while it is in unsuitable museum storage and packaging. This problem is not unique to archaeology. What is particular, for archaeology, is the huge number of objects that need to be stored, and the large percentage of them that will be potentially fragile.

Ideally, all materials will be stored in an environment that suits their stability, and which, therefore, will need very little, if any, active conservation work, and will require minimal later monitoring. The challenges here are largely logistic and economic. There is a need to find the right kind of storage conditions for different kinds of material. Traditionally, archaeological stores (see also Chapter 7) are divided into general stores where stable material such as ceramics, stone, and animal bone can be stored within generous ranges of temperature and relative humidity, and separate specialist stores for organics and metals. Alternatively, storage microclimates can be constructed using specific packing materials and materials, such as silica gel to protect particular objects within general stores.

Although humidity and temperature, and fluctuations in them, are normally considered the most important factors in ensuring the long-term life of objects, other factors are important as well. Light levels will be most important for some materials, such as textiles and pigments. Pests, such as beetles and rodents, can also attack objects and, perhaps more commonly, the packaging in which they are stored. Objects can also do damage to each other. How artefacts are packed and stored in relation to each other is important. How often an object will be viewed or handled is a major factor in deciding storage and packaging needs. A careful compromise is needed between accessibility and protection. Although, as a general rule, wrapping an object up so that it is invisible and needs complex unpacking every time it is required is not the best solution. Methods of "open storage" have been developed, for example, at the Oxfordshire Museum Centre at Standlake, whereby an object can be clearly seen while it is protected. Occasionally, traumatic events, such as fires or floods, can do dreadful damage. Recent natural disasters, such as Hurricane Katrina in Louisiana, United States (Bob Sonderman, personal communication), have illustrated just how unprepared many museum facilities are to protect their collections from such disasters. These considerations, matched with finite budgets, have meant that risk assessment and risk management have become an important part of conservation work.

The most important factor in controlling the long-term environment of artefacts is the building in which they are stored. It is, therefore, a depressing observation that many museums, for economic reasons, are forced to use unsuitable buildings with inherently poor environments, and then spend money trying to correct the environment and improve its conditions. In the last 20 years, a number of museums and museum services have recognised this failing and have invested in good museum stores which often also have the added benefit of being suitable for public visits. Examples include the Museum of London's London Archaeological Archive and Research Centre (LAARC), (see also Chapter 7), Oxfordshire Museum Services Standlake facility (this is a wonderful building but has not been without environmental and visitor access problems), and the Norfolk Museum Service Cressinghall Centre. Other such facilities are planned in the United Kingdom, and it is likely that purposely built, or at least, purposely converted, storage facilities will become the norm for larger museum services with large archaeological collections. The original model for these facilities can probably be found in the United States, where storage facilities were developed in the 1970s and 1980s. However, for now, it remains the case that the vast majority of archaeological collections held by smaller museums are stored in unsuitable conditions where they will be deteriorating, or are taking up a disproportionably large cost as the museums seek to correct their inherently bad storage environments.

As noted, the particular problem of archaeological collections is their quantity and the range of potentially vulnerable materials. The need to assess the state of conditions in an economically feasible way has led to the development of a range of techniques mainly pioneered at the Museum of London in the 1980s. *Collection Condition Audits* (see Keene 1994 for the background and details of such surveys) are methods of rapidly surveying and amassing data about large diverse collections in order to obtain the right information to make decisions about collections management. On the whole, standards and guidelines are now in place for archaeological objects to enter collections in a stable condition and to be maintained in environmentally monitored storage. A challenge that remains is for collections that were amassed in the past and for which no funds or resources are available to bring them up to these standards. The Getty Minimum Standards Project at the LAARC (see Chapter 7) did allow a large backlog of material to be assessed and repackaged. The programme also used volunteer- and work-experience teams to do much of the work thereby turning it into a community-focussed project.

Key Texts

Agnew, N., and Bridgland, J. (Eds.). (2006). *Of the past, for the future: Integrating archaeology and conservation.* Los Angeles: Getty Conservation Institute.

Cronyn, J. M. (1990). *The elements of archaeological conservation.* London: Routledge.

Knell, S. (Ed.). (1994). *Care of collections.* London: Routledge.

Pye, E. (2001). *Caring for the past, issues in conservation for archaeology and museums.* London: James & James.

Watkinson, D., and Neal, V. (1998). *First aid for finds.* London: RESCUE and UKIC and Museum of London.

PART 3

INTERPRETATION

*Then, just before you went inside the auditorium, right near the
doors, you passed this Eskimo. He was sitting over a hole in the icy
lake, and he was fishing through it. He had about two fish right
next to the hole, that he'd already caught. Boy, that museum was
full of glass cases. There were even more upstairs. . . . The best
thing, though, in that museum, was that everything always stayed
right where it was. Nobody'd move. You could go there a hundred
thousand times, and that Eskimo would still be just finished
catching those two fish. . . . The only thing that would be different
would be you.*
J. D. Salinger from *The Catcher in the Rye* (1951)

CHAPTER 11
THE VISITING PUBLIC

*Who is museum archaeology for? How have different types of
public been identified and characterised? What do we know about
those interested, and not interested in museums and archaeology.
How have they been specifically catered for?*

Introduction

As I discussed (Chapter 1), the public are one of the three elements, with collections and staff that make up the dynamic
relationship that encapsulates what museums are. How do
we define the types of public that go to museums, and perhaps more importantly, those that don't? The types of public
that museums try to attract vary around the world. In some
places, attracting tourists for income generation, or providing a service to scholars, is still the primary motivation for
museum governors and curators. So far, it is only in Western Europe and North America that museums have seriously
engaged with the concept of attracting far wider audiences and
studying how this can be achieved. Although an attempt to
relate directly to particular communities has been attempted
elsewhere, for example, in parts of Africa (see Chapter 5). Similarly, for much of the world, archaeology is primarily a scholarly activity which may have no direct interface with the public. However, both museums and archaeology are ultimately
founded on contributing to the public good. As such, it is in
the interests of museum archaeology to engage with and be
valued by as wide a cross section of the public as possible.

As with other subjects dealt with in this book, there is a
wide literature on the public and museums that is quite separate from the specifics of museum archaeology. What will be

summarised here is a discussion of the public in relation to their understanding of and interest in the past and how museums need to recognise and harness this to maximise the number who do use museums and engage with archaeology.

Museum staff have to take the public more seriously than archaeologists because it is the main way by which museums are judged: how many visitors they have. Like it or not, numbers of users will always be a crude but effective measure of success. This, in turn, will be used in terms of market forces as a measure of sustainability. There needs to be a rough relationship between the number of people actually and potentially visiting a site and the cost of running it. Independent museums, such as the Kilmartin House in Argyll, however excellent in terms of the product they deliver, will always struggle to survive if they are in a location that will simply not generate enough users. Kilmartin received about 30,000 visitors a year to its isolated location in western Scotland but works hard to bolster these with web users.

This basic measure of "how many" is now often more complex as museums are pressured to attract certain types of visitor. In England, current visitor targets for publicly funded national museums include specific targets for school children, visitors from "lower" social groups and from the "socially excluded," and from ethnic minorities. Although museum staff continually complain about such targets being a very crude method of measuring success, there is no doubt that by at least forcing museums to work towards such targets makes them outward looking in a way that archaeology is not. Apart from meeting targets, knowing who your users are, as Hooper-Greenhill (1994, p. 54) states, provides information that justifies the continuation of a public service; it demonstrates professionalism through an understanding of audiences and allows the development of knowledge that will lead to an improvement of performance. Museums also need to grapple with the realisation that however democratic they wish to be as organisations, analysis has shown that broad sections of the population are excluding themselves from this offer (Hooper-Greenhill 1994, p. 20).

The most recent trend is to move beyond the mere number of users or visitors, or even their background, to try and measure the public value of heritage to society. However, this too at heart is all about justifying public expenditure (e.g., Clark 2006).

Museums are also used to evaluate the effectiveness of their programmes and displays. Evaluation is now widespread and relatively sophisticated in its methods, although the extent to which evaluators are asking the right questions of the right people is another matter, as is the extent to which the findings of evaluation are taken on board and used in developing the museum experience.

Evaluation is most commonly used as part of the development and review of new projects such as gallery renewals; it is normally divided into three types.

Front-end Evaluation takes place early on in a project to identify public perceptions.

Formative Evaluation takes place during the development of a project and tests communication and interpretation methods to see if they are effective.

Summative Evaluation takes place at the end of a project and tests whether assumptions made were correct.

Types of Public

Pearce (1990, p. 133) has suggested that the public for museum archaeology represents everyone who was not a professional archaeologist and should be divided into three groups: those with "no regular commitment to the past," "those who do take an informed interest in the past," and children. As a start this is fine, it identifies the public who have already been attracted and, therefore, assumedly find something right in what museums are doing and those who don't (see Black 2006 for a more detailed discussion of the types of museum visitor). To take this further, Figure 1 presents a hypothetical model for the potential different audiences for museum archaeology. It is presented as a pyramid where each "slice" represents a proportionate number of people. All but the bottom two groups

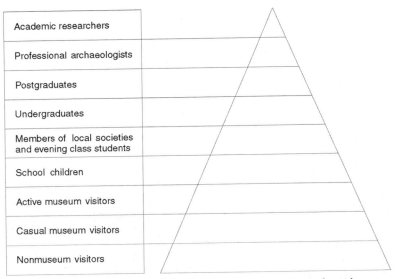

FIGURE 1. The potential audiences for museum archaeology expressed as a pyramid.

fall into Pearce's later group, and the top four represent her "professionals."

What this figure tries to illustrate is the relative size of these different audiences. What it also does is show that there is an inverse relationship between the amount of effort that will be required to attract, provide for, engage, and satisfy each audience and the size of that audience. So, for example, it might be argued that the museum will need to do nothing active at all, save to make its collections available, to attract researchers. These people will be fully motivated, will seek out the service, and will require no mediation: they will already be fully conversant in how to use the collections they need. However, this group is extremely small (e.g., in somewhere such as Greater London with a total population of 7,500,000, only 50–100 individuals will be in this category). The nonmuseum visitors, however, will need the largest investment in order for them to benefit from museum archaeology and are also by far the largest group, again using the London example, numbering several million. This observation illustrates a huge challenge for museums with their limited resources and targets to engage with new audiences. It is also perhaps honest, if not fashionable, to admit that some members of the public will never be that interested in museums or the past, and what is more they have every right to that position.

The Museum-Going Public and Nonmuseum-Going Public, What Is Known

At a superficial level, surveys again and again show a high level of low-level benign support for history and heritage (e.g., English Heritage 2000). Similar results have come from surveys in North America (Ramos and Duganne 2000). However, turning this into active support for, and more importantly, use, of museums is another matter. The traditional view of museums as "temples of learning and preservation, rather than places of social interaction, distanced from the public by unchanging exhibitions, unapproachable staff, limited educational resources, and inconvenient opening hours" (Skeates 2005, p. 314) persists in many places. Similarly, the motivations of those who do regularly use museums can be complex and unexpected, as shown, for example, by the work of Fyfe and Ross in Stoke-on-Trent, England (1996).

It would appear obvious, and is borne out by figures, that museums are, on the whole, visited by well-educated adults often with children (Hooper-Greenhill 1994, pp. 60–68), although it is also the case that they reach a wider social audience than other "high culture" venues such as the theatre and concerts (Hooper-Greenhill 1994, p. 65). Recent surveys show that this class-based divide is persisting despite efforts in the United Kingdom to widen appeal through such policies as no longer charging for entry to National Museums (Morris 2004a).

The most important analysis of the relationship between museums, the past and the public, remains that undertaken by Nick Merriman (1989 and 1991 for a summary), that vitally also looked at the nonmuseum-going public and their attitudes. Merriman carried out a detailed survey of about 1,000 members of the general public chosen at random. His survey was undertaken in 1985. He found that about 50 percent of the British public visit a museum at least once a year and that about 82 percent have visited one at some stage in their lives, 18–23 percent of the population were considered nonvisitors in that they had never gone, or were unlikely to go again. He divided the population up into: frequent visitors (17 percent), regular visitors (37 percent), occasional visitors (14 percent), rare visitors (14 percent), and nonvisitors (18 percent). He noted that some key groups fell outside his work: school children, responsible for about 25–33 percent of visits to national and local authority museums, and foreign tourists representing 22 percent of visits.

Merriman's analysis showed that the well-off and well-educated are most likely to visit museums regularly, whereas the old, poorly educated, and the less-well-off are least likely to visit. He noted that a key reason why the elderly are less likely to visit museums would have been because they were unfamiliar to them when they were growing up. This key group is likely to become more important to museums with time. Although traditionally a smaller audience according to statistics, it is growing, and in the West, it is becoming more demanding and wealthy (Hooper-Greenhill 1994, p. 18). Also, audiences with special needs due to disabilities require special consideration, and it is to museums credit that more and more provision is being made, often backed up be legislation.

Merriman found that people who go to museums do so for a wide range of reasons but most important was for a general or specific interest or as part of social action. He found that the more often people visited the more specific their reason would be. Frequent visitors identified museums as relevant to their daily lives. Infrequent visitors linked museums to traditional unwelcoming ideas, seeing them as unfriendly, and as "monuments to the dead." Gender did not appear to be a factor for museum going. Overall, 90 percent of the survey saw the past as worth knowing about, those who did not were from the nonvisitors.

Merriman sought to explain his findings largely through the ideas of Pierre Boudieu linked to the acquisition and use of cultural capital. Boudieu's model sees the dominant class in society developing a code of values that legitimises their own position and that is created through an established education system (see Merriman 1989, for a critique of Bordieu and other models for understanding museum visitor motivations).

The work of Merriman has had a powerful influence on museum thinking, if not action, when considering museum visitors and views of the past. It states that there is a better-off and better-educated class who feel comfortable in museums, and they use them to further legitimise their own position in society. There is a second group of less-well-off, less-well-educated people who feel uncomfortable in museums and do not regularly visit them. Merriman's work is now more than 20 years old, and that of Boudieu even older, however, they continue to exert a strong influence. New work is needed to meet the challenges to museums within multicultural and multiethnic communities that are now becoming the norm in Western, particularly urban societies. Taking up the challenge of making museums relevant and of value to audiences that may not have historic links to where they now live has often meant engaging with contemporary history and culture, and actually working with and collecting from communities. It is less obvious how archaeology can fit into this model, and, as a result, archaeology is looking a little marginalised in some museum services.

Merriman's work was based in the United Kingdom; however, it would appear to be applicable to other Western countries and as a model for museum going across the world. A broad-brush survey would suggest that perhaps not unpredictably, it is in the wealthy Western countries, where people are generally better educated, have more leisure time, and put more value on social and cultural capital that museums are more used and valued. As discussed in Chapter 5, museums have largely failed to engage populations in poorer parts of the world such as Africa. Even in Mediterranean areas rich in archaeology, museum going is not necessarily a popular pastime. A recent survey showed that 70.2 percent of the population never visited museums in Malta (Skeates 2005, p. 314).

On the world stage, the concept of cultural tourism becomes important (Richards 2000). This is defined as "the movement of persons to cultural attractions away from their normal places of residence, with the intention to gather new information and experiences to satisfy their cultural needs" (Richards 2000, p. 3). In his analysis of this phenomena, Greg Richards emphasises the immense economic importance of this phenomena, but also the difficulty in tying down the nature and motivations of its participants. Cultural tourism is important on a global scale as it has the ability to attract money to otherwise poor areas, but, of course, it also has the potential to harm cultural remains. Richards notes (2000, p. 1) that cultural tourism accounts for 37 percent of world tourism, with a growth rate of 15 percent per year. In the United Kingdom, it is estimated that cultural tourism accounts for 27 percent of all tourist earnings and in 1997 accounted for more than 400 million visits to tourist attractions. As might be predicted, cultural tourists are mainly "upmarket," well-educated, and tend to be highly motivated by culture (Richards 2000, p. 8).

Museums and archaeological sites obviously act as a key component of the cultural tourism market. Where this becomes more complicated is in identifying the exact motivations of tourists to consume culture. Richards (2000, p. 6) identifies the "culturally motivated" the "culturally inspired," and the "culturally attracted" to differentiate between those who are primarily driven by cultural attractions and those who see it as an optional add-on to other motivations. He also notes the difference between recognising the value of education and wishing for entertainment thus creating the need for museums to provide "edutainment." Richards also notes the growth in "creative tourism" (2003, p. 9) whereby tourists wish to acquire knowledge and experience in a proactive practical way. He suggests that museums will need to respond to this and become less passive if they are to take full advantage of growing tourist numbers.

Hooper-Greenhill (1994, pp. 56–70) provides a brief survey of visitor studies for museums in the United States, Canada, Europe, and the United Kingdom. Surveys in North America show a very similar pattern of public awareness as in the United Kingdom with the number actively involved in archaeology dwarfed by a larger passive audience, who value archaeology and heritage but are not actively involved (McManamon 1994).

So, only certain parts of the population regularly engage with archaeology in museums. What do those who do go know about the past? An analysis of the visitor use of the Alexander Keiller Museum in Avebury, Wiltshire, showed that during the 1990s, of the 500,000 members of the public who visited the Avebury Neolithic site every year only 40,000 visited the museum (Stone 1994, p. 195). Of these only about 14,000 actually paid to enter (the rest were made up by about 11,000 school children and 15,000 visits by members of the National Trust and English Heritage). The surveys at Avebury also sought to find out what the public thought about prehistory. Similar surveys were also undertaken by the Museum of London when developing its 1994 prehistoric gallery (Cotton 1997, pp. 7–8), and to find out what visitors thought about the Middle Ages for its new *Medieval London* gallery (Grey et al. 2006). These surveys all found a low level of detailed understanding of these periods distorted by misunderstandings and generalisations.

Amateurs and Volunteers and Local Societies

Local archaeological societies and "amateur" archaeologists are a key component of the wider archaeological community. Most of North America and Europe has local societies, many founded many years ago, that give nonprofessionals the opportunity to become actively involved in archaeology. Indeed, many of these organisations provided the foundations for modern archaeological provision, undertook the first regionally based excavations, research and publication, and, in many cases, collecting and opening and running museums. It is, therefore, even more of a shame that the present relationship between the amateur and professional sectors is sometimes strained.

As both archaeologists and museum staff strive for professional status, both with professional membership organisations, and for the pay, reward, and respect that go with it, the amateurs pose a problem. As museums and archaeology are for the public good, it would be wrong to want to prevent the public from being involved. Within museums, a voluntary staff is often essential to carry out core duties. The museum staff knows that their support of these volunteers is a key part of their job. Within archaeology, a huge discretionary effort is still relied on to support the discipline, and large numbers of the public (estimated at about 6,000 in Greater London) join and become actively involved in archaeological societies that publish journals, hold lectures, and often undertake field-work. Yet, the professionals often undervalue these amateur archaeologists, and there is sometimes an uneasy relationship between the two groups. However, local society members and amateurs also represent an "easy hit" for museums seeking to increase their user numbers. As a result, many community-based programmes have been set up to provide a service for such groups.

Peter Liddle in Leicestershire was the first to put into practice a true model for community involvement in archaeology. Since the early 1980s, he has been forming groups, normally by parish, to undertake fieldwalking and the monitoring of planning applications that might cause archaeological destruction. Peter's dictum is that the public have a right to know about and take ownership of its past. These kinds of programmes are dealt with in more detail in Chapter 14.

Children and Family Audiences

Museums in the United Kingdom have been slow to recognise the needs of the growing family audience (as opposed to the quite different audience of school children; see Hooper-Greenhill 1994, p. 15). This is the need to cater for adults and children acting dynamically together. Moussouri (1998) in a review of family motivations identifies: the exhibition or museum itself; family profile (age, background, gender, etc.); sociocultural patterns (what will the museum offer); personal context (expectations); and social context as combining to deliver a particular *family agenda*. Moussouri (1998, p. 28) that the public expect museums to be educational and appreciate it if the museum also makes the visit and the educational experience enjoyable. The combination of education and enjoyment seem to be a major draw. She also notes that many family visits are pursuing or adding to a previously developed interest (1998, p. 29). Family "negotiations" play a key role in how successful a visit will be (1998, p. 29). From all the above, it can be realised how complex the circumstances are by which any one social group will enjoy a museum visit and, therefore, how difficult it is for the museum to deliver a worthwhile experience to a large number of visitors.

Children, without their parents and guardians, and not as part of a school group, are not thought of as a major audience group. However, archaeologists are aware of the potential of getting converts young. The Young Archaeologists Clubs (YACs) that are a key part of many museums programmes recognise this. YACs were the creation of the CBA, although starting as Young RESCUE, and now run as completely autonomous or semiautonomous bodies around the country reliant on the good will and enthusiasm of adult volunteers, although some have been criticised for being little more than Saturday morning crèches for the children of the middle classes. This is unfair, but more does need to be done to make them accessible to a wider social range of children. The Central London Young Archaeologists Club based at the Museum of London's London Archaeological Archive and Research Centre (see Chapter 7), but founded and run by a group of independent volunteers, has gone out of its way to try and attract a wider cross section of children by finding sponsorship so it does not need to charge for membership, only taking children from inner London boroughs, and actively advertising itself in local inner-London schools. The quality of event received by the children is phenomenal. A recent event included one session learning about Palaeolithic cave painting and putting together "authentic" painting kits including natural dyes, charcoal, chalk, and leather pouches; and a second session where a room was turned into a dark cave and the children undertook their own paintings on a prepared wall.

In the modern world, the precautions that need to be taken by adult volunteers taking responsibility for children without parents and guardians are daunting but necessary. But procedures and training are available from organisations like the CBA and host museums, and the rewards are massive.

The "Indigenous" Public

The current drafting of the declaration of the Rights of Indigenous Peoples by UNESCO illustrates how in recent years such groups have successfully started the process of empowering themselves within the world of heritage and culture. Any museum that holds collections from living Indigenous groups now needs to take note of their views. It is to museums' shame that it has taken so long for this to happen. As Francis McManamon (1994, p. 72) has stated: "It is ironic that the segment of the public most directly connected to the past societies that most American archaeologists study, modern American Indians, has not been a primary audience for archaeological public education and outreach."

This is changing. Native Americans have made strong claims for their rights to have control over their ancestors remains and material culture, with archaeologists wishing to engage with Native Americans, and, in some cases, Indians taking an interest in the archaeology and its potential (McManamon 1994, p. 74). The last 20 or so years have seen First Nation Canadians, Native American Indians, Australian Aborigines, and New Zealand Maoris all become involved in debates over the white Western study of their ancestors. And in those locations, legislation such as NAGPRA in the United States (see Chapter 8), government policy and belatedly dialogue and engagement between Indigenous communities and museum staff have transformed how museums collect, display, interpret, and research material. The opening of the National Museum of the American Indian, as part of the Smithsonian in 2005 (see Chapter 15), sees this process maturing. But as discussed in Chapters 3, 5, and 8, there is some way to go. Specht and MacLulich (2000, p. 52) make a distinction between a museums' "community stakeholders," those who pay for the museum through their taxes, and the "cultural stakeholders" who have interests and rights in the collections. A "them and us" divide still pervades most museum and archaeological thinking. And where progress has been made it is often been through conflict. Devine (1994) describes how First Nation Canadians reacted against Western archaeologists trying to study their past. And Hooper-Greenhill (1994, pp. 20–21) describes how in Canada First Nation unhappiness with *The Spirit Sings* exhibition at Glenbow Museum Calgary, linked to the 1988 Winter Olympics, led to the Task Force on Museums and First Peoples, that helped develop a constructive dialogue between people of the First Nation and museum authorities.

The "Divergent" Public

Another section of the public is fascinated by archaeology and the past but choose to engage with it through approaches at variance with traditional archaeological and museological orthodoxies. These are a growing and diverse number of people, including those, for example, who buy the many books that profess archaeological pasts at variance with the mass of accepted evidence. The books of Graham Hancock and others (e.g., Hancock 1995) contain theories and methods that are largely dismissed by the majority of archaeologists and yet sell, and one would, therefore, assume are read and accepted, by millions (Hancock's own website claims five million book sales in twenty-seven languages). The fans of Hancock are largely armchair archaeologists. Should "orthodox" museum archaeologists be pleased that these readers are taking an interest in the past and that they are content that they have a right to believe what they wish? Or frustrated and annoyed that they are taking in theories that it is believed can be comfortably refuted by evidence? See Schadla-Hall (2000, p. 56) and Fagan (2006) for discussions of some of these "alternative" popular accounts of the far past.

Another divergent group is more active. A growing number of people actively follow "pagan" beliefs and philosophies that they link directly to pre-Christian peoples, beliefs, and religions. Often grouped in the United Kingdom as Druids, an analysis shows there to be many groups with many beliefs.

The pagan groups are beginning to have an influence on mainstream heritage management. They actively use prehistoric sites, including, for example, an annual festival at the summer solstice at Stonehenge. They expect to be involved in management plans for sites and can become militant when not consulted. An example was the stand-offs that occurred between English Heritage archaeologists, locals, and pagans over the so-called Seahenge site in Norfolk (Pryor 2001). A federation of pagan groups has formed the group HAD (Honouring the Ancient Dead) to take a particular interest in pagan human remains in museum collections (see Restall Orr 2004 and Restall Orr and Bienkowski 2006).

Modern pagans offer an interesting challenge for archaeologists and those who communicate the past and interface with the public. They have perplexed the archaeological mainstream, particularly in its current postmodern relativistic incarnation. Should pagans be dismissed as part of the "loony fringe" or embraced as people who truly value the ancient past and have a right to engage with it on their own terms? In her travelling exhibition on Stonehenge, Barbara Bender included the views of pagans (1997, p. 57 and Chapter 10) but struggled to come to terms with their world view observing that: ". . . in 'invented traditions' each event [that is used to create a narrative] may be accurate and documented. It is only the intercalation and subsumation that is spurious."

If archaeologists are going to embrace a relativist world view, there needs to be an accommodation of pagan groups and the acceptance that they are a community that deserves to be respected and listened to. But so do many other groups, some of whom are much larger in number.

Key Texts

Black, G. (2006). *The engaging museum, developing museums for visitor involvement.* London and New York: Routledge.

Clark, K. (Ed.). (2006). *Capturing the public value of heritage, the Proceedings of the London Conference, 25–26 January 2006.* Swindon: English Heritage.

Hooper-Greenhill, E. (1994). *Museums and their visitors.* London: Routledge.

Merriman, N. (1991). *Beyond the glass case, the heritage and the public in Britain.* Leicester: LUP.

Chapter 12
Displaying Archaeology: Methods

Museum exhibitions and displays remain the way most users engage with real objects and the ideas associated with them. This chapter explores the different methods used by museums to interpret collections and ideas through displays.

Introduction

Chapter 13 looks at examples of display and exhibition, and Chapter 14 discusses education and public programmes in their widest sense. This chapter deals with the methods of exhibition design with reference to archaeological material: how the different methods available to museums are combined in different ways to create different types of communication for different purposes and for different audiences.

Inevitably, there is much that is common to museum design for all subject areas rather than being specific to archaeology. Most museum and gallery designers will work across subjects and periods. Indeed, there is probably not a display type that is particular to archaeology and archaeological collections. Displays of objects by typology or series might be considered characteristic of archaeology but are also found in such subjects as natural history. Display by context is also important for archaeology but, again, is equally important for natural history and social history.

A visit to the museums of the world will find thousands of examples of gallery displays and exhibits where attempts are made to communicate past histories and prehistories. What is surprising, and perhaps a little depressing, is not that there are so many, but perhaps how similar they are, and how, in the fundamentals, they have not changed radically over time. Most museums still put partially conserved and reconstructed objects in glass cases, interpreted by written words and supported by pictures and occasionally models and reconstructions.

If many exhibitions have the same component parts, they also tend to be conceived and delivered in similar ways. Normally, exhibitions are in what are known as *temporary exhibitions* (that are planned to be short-term, and often react to a particular new discovery, piece of research, or simply an anniversary) and *permanent galleries* (that are meant to be unchanging and that tell core stories, although in actual fact if only for practical reasons they are never permanent, and as stories and design methods evolve, no one would want them to be). Exhibitions also tend to be expensive in terms of the resources museums have available. This has led to them being long running, conservative, and consensual. It has been suggested that this is exactly what museums and archaeology displays should not be and that shorter, more questioning exhibitions should be put beside permanent galleries (Bender 1997, p. 55).

Museums, more-or-less by definition, use real things as their main method of communication. This is after all their greatest strength and unique selling point over other types of communication (books, films, etc.). However, what it also does is put at an immediate disadvantage those things and ideas that cannot be easily communicated visually against those that can. So, it is easier to understand Stonehenge than a Mesolithic campsite; it is easier to understand a complete Attic red and black vase than a single sherd of prehistoric pot. This presents two challenges: first, how to avoid giving different periods or objects a more prominent place just because they survive better, or are more visually understandable; and second, how to interpret those subjects which are not visually arresting?

These challenges are particularly acute for archaeology because so much evidence does deteriorate and because so many archaeological sites are so difficult to understand visually. The prominence held by the Roman period in British archaeology is partly due to historical and cultural reasons, but this must have been reinforced by the durability and visibility of Roman remains and objects. There is nothing like a mosaic pavement or stone defensive wall to focus the mind.

As discussed in Chapters 2 and 3, approaches to museum communication have been shaped in the past and continue to fall into a number of distinct categories depending on the type of material, the type of institution, the perceived or target audience, and the views of the group or individual within the museum making the decisions. Displays tend to be of the decorative, fine art type, the didactic contextualised social history type, or the emotive reconstruction type (see Pearce 1990, pp. 153–154 on the difference between didactic and emotive displays). Each type has its own vocabulary and set of rules that are seldom deviated from (examples are discussed in more detail in Chapter 13).

Museums must also match their chosen messages to their audience (see Chapter 11) in the knowledge that they have many audiences with many very different needs. Should they make the message an easy one or a complex one? If the message is a complex one, should it be confronted, avoided, or simplified? The displays dealing with the early Colonial period at the Museum of Sydney, despite being considered academically excellent, were later changed because they were thought to be "too cerebral" (Mike Smith, personal communication). Other museum galleries remain dense and scholarly, offering little to general audiences (e.g., the recently closed antiquities galleries at the Ashmolean Museum in Oxford), while others perhaps go too far the other way and do not offer enough of substance (perhaps the Stonehenge Gallery at the South Wiltshire Museum in Salisbury). However, in truth those galleries that are worst at communicating their subject are normally those that have not been updated or redisplayed for many years.

The Nature of Communication in Museums

Museums must be good communicators. Hooper-Greenhill (1994), Black (2006), and others have developed theoretical models for communication in museums, emphasising that this is the fundamental role of a museum gallery or exhibition.

Communication is the process by which one person imparts information to a second. Mass communication is where one person finds a way to pass on information to many. Television is the obvious example of mass communication. Although occasionally one-to-one communication takes place in museums, mass communication is the norm. Mass communication is by its nature one-way, indirect, impossible to nuance or modify in reaction to responses, and takes place in the absence of the communicator, and as such is unequal (Hooper-Greenhill 1994, p. 36). This is obviously far from ideal. Perhaps in time new technology will overcome some of these problems but for now museums must work with them.

Evaluation allows museums to make communication a two-way process by receiving feedback from audiences, but it is only scratching the surface of the complexity of this process (see Chapter 11 for a wider discussion of how public reactions have been captured). It is made most complex by the three-dimensional, multilayered nature of displays. Museums set out to put across many messages to many audiences using many methods. Those audiences, in their turn, have many motivations. Even if a museum can recognise when it is being successful or failing, it is difficult to pick out and measure exactly why.

Authenticity

Discussions of authenticity permeate every part of this book, and are pertinent to discussions of museums in general not just those concerned with archaeology. Museum design needs to confront what is meant by authenticity, by the museum curator and by the visiting public. Authenticity along with value and truth are now seen primarily in relativist terms. For archaeology the question "of authenticity" can be asked at a series of different levels. There is the question of whether artefacts are "authentic," whether interpretations of primary data are authentic, and whether the museum interpretations give an authentic window into the past. The first of these two questions are discussed in Chapters 3, 6, and 10; the question of the authenticity of displays and interpretations is discussed here.

It is not enough to accept that just as there is no such thing as truth, there is nothing that is authentic. Visitors come to museums and expect to be told the truth and to see authentic things. And, yet, by their very nature, museum galleries are false and unreal. They aim to communicate a real event that happened in a real place at a real time, but do this in a different place and different time with some of the objects that were once "real." Many museums see no need to address this issue and feel confident about giving visitors unambiguous authenticity, or, at least, do not feel a need to question the authenticity of their offer. So, Victorian and modern museum buildings contain prehistoric round houses and Roman shops. This approach is now often seen as unsatisfactory.

At the Alexander Keiller Museum in Avebury, Wiltshire, there was a specific desire to acknowledge the role the curator plays in creating the past and the limited nature of the archaeological evidence. A life-size figure of a Neolithic man (Stone 1994, pp. 198–199) was created and dressed with two quite different sets of clothes, hairstyles, and so forth – one on either side of his body. One side (that which first greets visitors when they enter the museum, is dressed in very "primitive" clothes in earthy brown colours, while the other side is more imaginative and includes tattoos and dyed cloth. This is an imaginative idea for dealing with the ambiguities of the past and of archaeological interpretation, although the figure himself comes across as a rather badly dressed 1980s shop dummy. Similarly, at the previous prehistoric gallery at the Museum of London (Wood and Cotton 1999), the curators specifically told the visitors that they would be giving them their personal view of the past and asked the audience if they wished to believe them. For the Museum of London's *High Street Londinium* exhibition (Swain 2004a, and Chapter 13), visitors were often confused as to which were "real" artefacts, and which were modern reconstructions. At Dennis Severs House in London's Spitalfields, visitors are presented with an eighteenth-century house as if its owners "had just left the room," hardly anything is authentic in any sense of the way museum curators would accept it, but visitors, again mainly through confusion, treat much of it as genuine and with genuine reverence, and possibly encounter a feeling of the authentic that could never be achieved with "real" objects in a museum setting.

Presenting Theory

This questioning of authenticity has clearly developed out of postmodern thought. Although postmodernism, or post-processualism, has dominated archaeological theory for the last 20 years (see Chapter 3), and has been equally important in museum thinking, it has not made a major impact on museum display. Indeed, many displays may continue to reinforce the very ideas that postmodernism sought to challenge. Wood (1997, p. 62), for example, observes how, particularly in smaller museums, stereotypes of gender and gender roles persist in displays.

A few exhibitions using archaeological material have been explicitly postmodern in nature. In the United States, the work of Fred Wilson, a black New York-based artist, is most commonly referred to. His 1990 exhibition, *Mining the Museum* at the Museum of the Maryland Historical Society in Baltimore, included empty cases to represent "unknown" important African Americans. He also included labels describing "Plastic display mounts made c. 1960s, maker unknown." And perhaps most famously slave shackles positioned next to elegant silver ware captioned "Metalwork 1793–1800" (Wilson 1995). In a display of Iron Age finds at the Schloß Gottorp in Schleswig, Northern Germany, one case was left completely empty to demonstrate the missing evidence about the appearance of women (see Stig Sørensen 1999, p. 145, who also discusses displays in terms of gender). This ironic use of museum methods has seldom made it beyond the one-off exhibits.

The travelling *Stonehenge Exhibition* is another example of an attempt to challenge museum orthodoxy. This project was led by Barbara Bender (see Bender 1997 for a full description) with help from a journalist, some modern Druids, and some members of the Free Festival/Traveller community at the time when English Heritage were preventing pagans and travellers from using Stonehenge for solstice festivals.

In every sense, this was an attempt to deconstruct author-ative narratives and museum orthodoxy, and, although suc-cessful in many ways, Barbara Bender admits it required her own legitimisation and authority and as such simply cre-ated a new version of an authorative narrative. The exhibition involved nine large board trilothons each putting across a dif-ferent group's history of Stonehenge. Design quality was not considered paramount; it looked as if it had been put together by a group of school children with very limited resources.

A museum gallery that is often cited as an example of post-modern theory put into practice is the now replaced *People before London* gallery (1994–1999) at the Museum of London. The curators Jon Cotton and Barbara Wood were explicit in iden-tifying themselves as the creators of the history on show (see above); they intermixed modern items with the prehistoric, asked the visitors explicit questions, and interweaved inbe-ded gender and environmental narratives. Alan Saville (1999, pp. 106–107) provides a criticism of this approach where he states it is a mistake not to use curatorial confidence. The new prehistoric gallery at the Museum, *London before London*, has indeed stepped back from this approach. It may be that the failure of postmodernism to take a serious hold in museum displays either reflects the innate conservatism of museums or the weakness of postmodern ideas when they leave the rarefied confines of academia. Either way, it would be hoped that, at the very least, museum curators are engaging with theory of all types, and it is affecting design decisions.

The Elements of Display and Design

Too little is written on the design theory of museum galleries and exhibitions in general and archaeology displays in par-ticular. When debate does take place, it is normally between museum archaeologists rather than involving designers. The literature similarly is dominated by museum archaeologists rather than designers. Works, such as *Inside Out On Site In* (Staal and Martijn de Rijk 2003), which recounts the redesign of the Dutch National Museum of Ethnology and *Creating the British Galleries at the V&A* (Wilk and Humphrey 2005), neither of which deal with archaeology, recount the process of designing galleries that are valuable but rare.

The basic tools of communication are as they have ever been: objects, words, pictures, and assorted props that can be used to stimulate the different senses, sight, sound, touch, and (occasionally) smell. Added to this is something that is less easy to define. It is the way words, objects, and pictures are combined and grouped and added to by such elements as space, light, and colours – props, that help create a context, atmosphere, and ambience for displays. The rest of this chapter will look at some of these elements individually as they contribute to archaeological displays, while Chapter 13 looks in more detail at specific examples.

Objects

Objects will normally be the centrepieces of any archaeological display. Much has already been written about the particular strengths and weaknesses of archaeological objects. The way they may have physically changed in the ground will inevitably be a strong influence on their display. The nature of archaeological finds, recovered painstakingly from the ground often thousands of years after their original use and discard, makes them both a wonderful treasure but also often almost impossible to display without conservation and reconstruction. This robs them of their originality and confuses the museum visitor (this is similar to the great reconstructed dinosaurs of natural history museums that are often based on the cast of a few bones found thousands of miles away).

There is a danger that objects are given too much prominence, or too little, through the vagaries of preservation. It is almost impossible not to give the impression that early prehistoric people only used stone tools and that Neolithic farmers only used broken pots, and green knives, and that axes weighed down early metallurgists. Few museums have attempted major temporary exhibitions focussed entirely on early prehistoric archaeology, possibly because, although featuring complex ideas, it relies on unprepossessing collections.

Sometimes the sheer quantity of objects available to archaeologists means that not enough attention is given to individual finds. Stone (1994, pp. 197–199), in discussing the redisplay of the Alexander Keiller Museum in Avebury, Wiltshire, admits that a decision was made to reduce the number of objects on display because too many of those available were too similar. The implication is that only so many stories can be told from an object and only so many objects are needed to tell a particular story. Also, and perhaps more importantly, just because archaeological objects are in a collection they do not need to be displayed if they are not materially contributing to the story. Often, the very best displays are those centred around strong iconic objects such as that of the "Ice Man" and his possessions in the South Tyrol Museum of Archaeology in Bolzano, Italy, or the Bronze Age Boat in Dover. In each case, the displays concentrate on a single find or site and build a display around this, including the necessary background of chronological, cultural, and archaeological information.

Much classical archaeology has always been displayed, and continues to be displayed as art objects, decontextualised from its method of recovery and often from the social and cultural context of its creation, use, and loss. This is for historical reasons and the nature of the institutions in which it is displayed, and it is bound up with both of these, the value sets ascribed to the material. This process is perhaps seen in its most extreme with the antiquities that have been adopted by the modern art world such as Greek Cycladic figurines (Skeates 2005, pp. 313–314).

Words

Words remain the primary medium used by museums to explain their objects and stories and to give cohesion to a display. They normally come in the form of captions that describe groups or individual objects and text panels that tell the accompanying story. Again, much has been written about text in museums that is not specific to archaeology (again, see Hooper-Greenhill 1994). In the past, the temptation has been to write as much as possible, but there is now a move away from this "book on the wall" approach if only because evaluation has shown that most visitors were simply not reading it. Most museums now try to write less complex text and use more accessible and engaging writing in short blocks of words (see Grey et al. 2006 for a guide to approaches to museum text). The great challenge for curators is to condense their complex stories to fit this methodology. The museum must decide the tone of its voice as used in text and the type of writing that will work best with its visitors. Different writing can be used in different ways to communicate different messages (see Skeates 2002 for how text has changed in archaeology displays in recent years). In the Museum of London's *London before London* gallery, poetry is used as wall text alongside imaginary quotes from prehistoric people, whereas in the new *Medieval London* gallery, special captions have been written specifically for children (examples are given in Grey et al. 2006, p. 70).

The piece of museum interpretation perhaps most open to abuse is the humble label. This is the devise most close to the object, often the method by which the curator has the power to give the object meaning. Traditionally, labels have fulfilled a purely classificatory role and this lives on in many museums. Accession numbers, dimensions, and technical descriptions of the object are given that give no consideration to the needs of the visitor and use up valuable space.

New technology probably means labels are not this long for the world. At the National Museum of the American Indian in Washington, DC, several cases of objects exist without labels but rely on computer touch-screens placed outside and separate from the cases that show a photographic image of the case contents. The visitor touches the image of their object of choice for the traditional label information to appear. At NMAI, it is not obvious that the technology has been used to its full potential, the computer technology being used could give a more personalised interpretation of an object; and the case display freed of its words could be displayed more imaginatively. A similar approach has also been taken at the Inuit display in the National Museum of Denmark in Copenhagen, and will surely be the future for all galleries.

Probably the biggest challenge to archaeologists writing text is the vocabulary to use. As with all academic subjects, there is a vocabulary and nomenclature that is particular to the subject and is fully understood by practitioners even when its original meaning has disappeared. Should museums write about: "The Stone Age," "The Neolithic," "The Fifth Millennium B.C.," "The Agricultural Revolution," or "The time of the first farmers"? Different museums take different approaches, which of course has the potential to cause further confusion for the visitor. Museums are tending to move away from the more technical terms and towards descriptive ones.

Pictures and Other Visual Images

Painted and drawn reconstructions are a common way to illustrate archaeological interpretations of the past, making up for the shortcomings in the real material. Models, reconstructions, and mannequins are used to the same end. Examples of displays and galleries that have used reconstructions are discussed in Chapter 13. Such methods are used because they have an immediacy of communication that is attractive in its own right and also are an obvious short-hand way of communicating, which is particularly useful when it is known how few words museum visitors wish to read. For archaeology, galleries dealing in the ancient past, particularly prehistory, modern reconstructions are of course the only way of illustrating the past. Even for later periods, a decision has to be made as to whether contemporary images (medieval church paintings or Roman images on pottery) are a better way of illustrating the past than modern reconstructions. It is difficult to find an archaeology gallery that does not rely heavily on visual reconstructions of the past, and in some cases they dominate displays to the extent where the "authentic" objects become secondary. For example, in its prehistoric and Roman displays, the Dover Museum uses powerful mannequins, models, and reconstructions while objects are almost ignored. Similarly, in the Corinium Museum in Cirencester, large painted reconstructions and mannequins in sets dominate the design.

There are two main problems with most visual (and built) reconstructions of archaeological interpretations. First, they find it almost impossible not to give a level of certainty about what the past looked like that it is impossible to prove. Second, there is no passive or neutral artistic style in rendering images. All are particular to the artist who is creating them and also, in most cases, particular to a time and place. As such, when a visitor looks at a painting or drawing, of say a Roman town, or a Neanderthal camp, they see details that cannot be archaeologically substantiated and also will probably be thinking as much about the style of painting and the date and culture it derived from as the images it portrays. There is a detailed literature on how archaeological images have influenced views of the past as much as the archaeological discoveries they support (Moser 1998, 2003).

Some illustrative styles, perhaps, lend themselves more to breaking down these barriers. A more impressionistic sketchy approach like that of archaeological illustrator Victor Ambrose has both neutrality in terms of style and suggests the nebulous boundaries of archaeological evidence. Similarly, the use of "naïve" cartoons, such as those of Lucia Gaggiotti, in the new Museum of London *Medieval London* gallery (used with the children's captions, see above) and illustrated in Grey et al. (2006) may allow images to be used in a more neutral way, although of course they may introduce their own language to do with humour and triviality that may or may not always be wanted.

Sometimes pictures can be used to try and break from the interior space of the gallery. For the British Museum temporary exhibition *Sudan*, large images of the Sudanese landscape were a key design element to make a very explicit link between the artefacts and the monumental and beautiful desert landscapes where many had originated. In comparison, the *Gothic Art for England 1400–1547* exhibition at the Victoria & Albert Museum used poor-quality small images that failed to communicate the splendour of Gothic architecture to the extent where they detracted from the overall design. The

National Museum of Scotland's *Early Peoples* gallery uses hardly any photographs preferring to use modern art, an effect that can, at least initially, suggest it has decontextualised its objects from their original landscapes. The use of art as a way of supporting and interpreting archaeology overlaps with the use of images and is dealt with in more detail in Chapter 14. Perhaps the most powerful way images can be used to interpret archaeology displays is through an actual physical connection with the original landscape that will only come through the location of museum buildings and their design (see below).

The other type of image available to the archaeologist is the set of record drawings made onsite to interpret archaeological features. These drawings tend not to be a dominant feature of archaeological displays, even though they are so characteristic of archaeological evidence. This is probably because they are complex and difficult to understand. For *London before London*, the Museum of London created plans of sites using routed out timber to show major negative features. These were a development of models made by General Pitt Rivers of the sites he excavated and displayed in South Wiltshire Museum Salisbury. It is perhaps a shame that archaeological plans are not used more, even in a stylised and simplified way to make a direct connection, not only with the site itself but also the techniques of excavation and data recovery.

Chronology and the Presentation of Time

A problem of acute interest to archaeological displays is how to communicate chronology and the locating of particular, objects, interpretations, and displays in time. Along with geology and natural history, archaeology does not just need to deal with communicating chronologies it also needs to deal with concepts of "deep time." As noted elsewhere in Chapter 1, even if it only deals with the story of anatomically modern people the chronology is about 200,000 years. When dealing with human hominid ancestors the period is about 3,500,000 years. People cannot conceive of such huge time-scales and find it difficult to make sense of them in terms of understanding change through time. This is more acute with children who have to learn to understand the meanings and parameters of time. Even with adults, conceptualising deep time and changes within very long chronologies are very difficult, if not impossible. Human brains can compute ideas around personal time experience (tens of years) and possibly those that have affected direct ancestors and descendents (several tens of years) but not beyond. People are also used to major events occurring within the direct experience of an individual, and they construct narratives on this basis. Fictional narratives about the real past try and use personal experience. So, for example, the movie *The Day after Tomorrow* telescopes the effects of global warming into several weeks; the William Golding novel *The Inheritors* (1955) deals with the arrival of Homo sapiens and the end of Neanderthals in the personal experiences of a few protagonists. Although people know that many of the phenomena covered by archaeology happened over hundreds or thousands of years, they want to understand them in terms of their effects on individuals.

For children, the process of explaining how long ago something happened is made more complex by modern museological methods. Teachers have complained at how frustrating the actors used by the Museum of London are. These actors pretend to be Romano–British people for the children (see Chapter 14). This is a very powerful way of communicating ideas and the messages are retained in a way that glass case displays could not hope to. However, as a teacher has explained, "we spend ages in the classroom trying to explain how long ago the Roman period was, and then they come to the museum and meet one!"

A further problem is the ways historians, archaeologists, and museums compartmentalise up history into self-contained units (a failing shared with many other subjects). Thus, there is the Bronze Age and Iron Age as two distinct periods with a firm boundary between them. As a result, there are Bronze Age and Iron Age objects and monuments, and, of course, Bronze Age and Iron Age people. This methodology is so embedded in thinking that, even if one consciously knows it to be false, people do imagine that at the time people thought of themselves in these terms (as Bronze Age people in the ways we consider ourselves British or European people) and would have recognised the divide ("I went to bed last night and it was still the Bronze Age, I have woken up today and it has become the Iron Age").

So there is a past in which all events, objects, and people are divided up into clearly divided "blocks" and all events took place within time frames clearly understood and experienced by living individuals. And, yet, this was most clearly not the case. Almost all historic labels are applied after the event, and many major changes in human culture and experience (particularly at the macrolevel identified by archaeology) cannot be recognised as such at the time. How should the museum archaeologists deal with this challenge in terms of how ideas are communicated to audiences?

Some have gone to the extreme of almost giving up. David Clarke in the *Early Peoples* gallery at the National Museum of Scotland has moved away from chronology to a thematic approach for the very reason that in his opinion visitors do not think in terms of long time spans. He has also largely dispensed with the cultural labels that had been used to package up the past. Timelines identifying the age of objects are used, but these are very low down the hierarchy of interpretation and are mainly there for comparison between different objects rather than as major reference points.

Other attempts have been made to communicate past time in different more meaningful ways. The Museum of London's *London Bodies* exhibition (see also Chapters 8 and 13) produced a chronology based on generations, rather than years, and counted this backwards from the present. The exhibition design was also presented starting at the present and moving backwards. The general consensus from those involved was that the public did not really make sense of this methodology.

A backwards chronology is often used at the introduction of galleries and displays in order to "orientate" the visitor. The Jorvik Centre (see also Chapter 13) starts by taking visitors backwards in time cars through history until they arrive in the ninth century of Viking York when the time cars turn round and they then proceed to move forward in time, back towards the present. The *London before London* gallery at the Museum of London uses a similar approach. It moves forward in time for the main display, but starts with a short audio-visual presentation that goes back in time from the present to the beginning of the galleries chronology (c. 500,000 B.C.).

The modern history gallery at the National Museum of Denmark in Copenhagen (not an archaeology gallery) is laid out on a loop design that allows the visitor to either start at the beginning and move forwards in time, or start at the present and move backwards. The entrance and exit are at the same place.

Most museums use timelines of one sort or another. And they are generally accepted to be the most straightforward way of communicating easily a new and complex period or culture. For example, for its *Sudan* exhibition, the British Museum saw the timeline as the main way of introducing an unfamiliar period and subject. A timeline has also been used at the beginning of the new *Medieval London* gallery at the Museum of London. This is also used to reinforce the conceptual design of the gallery and make links to events elsewhere in the world. The timelines was approved by focus groups that said, if kept simple, it would help them use the gallery.

Another difficulty with time in museums is its uneven division. Every popular written "history of the world" or "history of humankind" on the TV gives the first chapter, or episode 1, to prehistory and the vast majority of time is given over to the short recent past for which there are written records. As a general rule in books, films, and, indeed, museums the nearer to the present you get, the more space is telescoped to give greater coverage to smaller amounts of time. At the Museum of London, roughly the same amount of gallery space is given to the 500,000 years of prehistory, 400 years of Roman rule, 1,000 years of Medieval London, 200 years of Stuart and Georgian London, and 100 years of Victorian London (why the Romans get more than they deserve relates to the relative importance of this period in British culture). This bias comes partly from a natural interest in the more recent and familiar past, but also from the nature of the evidence that increases exponentially as technology allowed for more and more words and events to be recorded. But, inevitably, it also means physical space is reinforcing the biases in dealing with the past already mentioned. See Davies (2005) for a detailed discussion of children's learning methods in relation to time and the example of a specific educational programme from the Crow Canyon Archaeological Centre in the United States.

Space

The way space is used in museum galleries and exhibitions is extremely important. It works in two quite separate, but obviously related ways. Space is used in a practical way in deciding how much room is available to display objects and in helping a visitor move through a gallery; the use of space influences which parts of the exhibition are used and viewed and in which ways. It can also be used to support the design ambience and, thus, how visitors perceive the subject being communicated. Pearce (1990, pp. 149–156) uses different archaeology gallery and exhibition plans to show how a linear and constrained space makes visitors confront the exhibitions story line in a different way than an open space that offers visitors a choice as to how they traverse it. Visitor tracking surveys have shown that visitors tend to move through a gallery using the quickest possible route. As such, the designer must choose whether they are going to use this by putting their interpretations along this route; or if they are going to try and thwart it by blocking easy through routes.

This idea works at both a practical level: not wanting to annoy visitors or lose them; but also at a philosophical one: wishing to give the visitor a prearranged single narrative; or to suggest a range of choices that are available with no single set narrative. Most archaeology galleries, for example, those at the Museum of London, and indeed the layout of the Museum as a whole, run chronologically and offer a single narrative. The *Early Peoples* gallery at the National Museum of Scotland, and the ethnography galleries at the Pitt Rivers Museum, Oxford offer a thematic approach that will make visitors think about the collections in quite different ways. Similarly, most of the galleries at the British Museum offer "snapshots" of different times and places rather than individual or collective narratives.

As noted, space can also be used to add to an overall design narrative. In the old layout at the Museum of London, the "Dark Age" displays were housed in a short, narrow, and low corridor between the much larger and more open Roman and Medieval galleries. As such, it suggested that the Dark Ages were a short, dark, and constricted period between better-understood and "larger" periods. Similarly, at the Corinium Museum in Cirencester, prehistory is squeezed into a narrow labyrinth like corridor that opens into wide, open, and double-storey galleries that deal with Roman Cirencestor, so a similar effect is created as at the Museum of London.

This use of space can be used with large objects to, in effect, create internal architecture. At the Museum in Arles, France, the interior space is divided into three open halls, in which objects are placed iconically and vistas are created by grouping objects in ways that echo characteristic spaces within the Roman city. So the rich sarcophagi, tombstones, and remains of mausolea are arranged on either side of an avenue that extends from the homes of the living residents of *Arelatum* (represented by a magnificent mosaic) to the world outside (symbolised more mundanely by the entrance foyer of the museum). Although the monuments could never have been seen in precisely this way in Roman times, the display nevertheless forces the visitor to contemplate their potential effect within the landscape (Francis Grew, personal communication).

A similar approach was taken by the British Museum for its *Sudan* and *Persia* exhibitions. As already noted for the *Sudan* exhibit, the grandeur of natural landscapes was seen as important and an open space was created with large photographic backdrops. Whereas for *Persia* it was the monumentality of the objects that was important, and the design filled the space with vertical masses. Similarly, at the Museum of London, the *London before London* gallery has low cases so the overall effect is of an open space – reflecting the open rural landscape – whereas in *Medieval London*, cases are massed vertically to mirror the closed-in urban space of the medieval city.

Light

Like space, light levels can be used both in a practical way (to safely navigate a visitor round a gallery and to protect objects) and to help create ambience. Some archaeological materials, particularly those with pigments, are sensitive to light levels that need to be controlled in display (see Chapter 10). Light can also generate heat, particularly within closed cases that can damage some objects, although modern technology means that this is now largely controllable. Correct lighting levels are also obviously important in ensuring that galleries are safe for visitors.

Lighting can also play an important role in creating the context and atmosphere in a gallery. Traditionally, archaeology, and, particularly, prehistory galleries are gloomy places lit as if the past was always in the "twilight zone." Therefore, the levels of light used have the ability to break down preconceptions, give different impressions of the past, and also add to a dynamic atmosphere. It is the case that in days before electricity, many interiors would have been dark and for building recreations this has the potential to create problems. For the Museum of London's *High Street Londinium* exhibition (see Chapter 13), the actual sources of light for the interior of Romano-British buildings, oil lamps, could not be used, and lighting was hidden in rafters where, hopefully visitors were not aware of it, but clearly the result was not authentic. Similarly, at Jorvik (also Chapter 13), it has been impossible to create anything resembling the daylight of Viking York in a basement space. At the Corinium museum in Cirencester, just as the way the space is used (see the section on Space above) creates a false distinction between prehistory and the Roman period, so does light. The Roman galleries are much *lighter*, which could, unintentionally suggest a more *enlightened* period. At the Museum of London's *London before London* exhibition, the gallery was purposefully made as light and airy as possible to spotlight the objects and their aesthetic and technological sophistication. In that gallery, coloured lighting was also used. Cases with objects from the River Thames have a blue-tinged light to signify water.

However, many visitors fail to make this link; many associated the blue with the sky.

At the planned displays at the Museum of High Altitude Archaeology in Argentina, it is proposed to have the lighting change throughout the day in the exhibition room, simulating sunrise through to sunset, to help create an atmosphere similar to that on the high mountain top at the time of the Inca pilgrimages the museum celebrates.

Models and Reconstructions

Models and reconstructions might be seen as a three-dimensional extension of images and pictures and share similar problems. Semantics seem to be important here. Museums use the terms *reconstructions*, *simulations*, and *evocations* all to mean slightly different things. The point is, as with painted reconstructions, museums rarely have the information for a perfect reconstruction, and even if they did, the materials and context would be wrong. Surveys show that models and reconstructions are extremely popular, and most museums use them in some form or another. Fullsize reconstructions using models and mannequins can be found at museums around the world. At Shenyang Museum in China, Neolithic buildings have been reconstructed and peopled with mannequins to reproduce life of the time. In delicious literal form, this includes (to use the translation from the guidebook) "scene of discussing among clannish members," "scene of cooking," and, best of all, in the corner of one timber and daub building "the scene of copulation." There are countless other examples used to show how buildings, settlements, and landscapes were once used and also how people looked and acted; and more and more these are being created virtually rather than as actual three-dimensional models.

However, for some, reconstructions are seen as detracting from the objects that should be at the centre of museum displays and contribute to "dumbing down" of museum interpretations, "the use of reconstructions in museums is a thorny issue with inherent ethical and conceptual problems" (Lucy and Herring 1999, p. 84). This statement reflects the museum archaeologist's lack of self-confidence when faced with using reconstructions to interpret their subject in an accessible and popular way. There are historic reasons for this. Reconstruction dioramas are sometimes associated with outdated "ethnographic" representations of "primitive" peoples akin to natural history displays and this may be one reason why some feel uncomfortable with them. Most natural history displays do feature stuffed animals in "lifelike settings." These seem to have become popular in early nineteenth century America (Moser 1999, pp. 96–97) but quickly spread and have become the norm. Although some museums, such as the London Natural History Museum, have moved away from using stuffed animals to a greater use of other interpretation methods, their use remains ubiquitous and has seen a resurgence in some recent redisplays such as at the Muséum National d'Historie Naturelle, Paris, and the Mammal gallery at the Smithsonian Museum of Natural History, Washington, DC. From the early natural history dioramas, ethnographic examples developed, often initially at the great world fares of the late nineteenth century (Moser 1999) and then onto dioramas of early people in the early twentieth century. For example, see Momin and Pratrap (1994, p. 293), for India.

More generally, reconstructions are associated with theme parks and attractions such as Madame Tussauds and the London (and other) Dungeon that are primarily entertainment rather than educational venues. This uncomfortable distinction has already been discussed in terms of the history and development of museums (see Chapter 2). The academic argument against reconstructions is that they imply "we know exactly how it was" (James 1999, p. 119). As James (1999, p. 118) has pointed out, museum and archaeological reconstructions are not really reconstructions at all, because the term implies a certainty that is never there (see also Moser 1999 for a discussion of this for reconstruction dioramas for early peoples).

Different ways might be used to try and make clear that reconstructions are only one possible version of events, either by offering alternatives as was done with drawn reconstructions of excavated remains at Durrington Walls (e.g., as shown in Parker Pearson 1993, p. 72, figure 58) and Cowdery's Down (Millet with James 1983, figures 70–71), detailed explanatory text (but would it be read?), or as suggested by James and yet to be realised, through computer technology (James 1999, p. 131). Visitors like reconstructions and models. They have the ability to provide a different and accessible way of communicating information. However, they should support not overpower objects, and it is the designers role to ensure that they stimulate thought about the nature of evidence rather than offer up history on a plate.

Aids and Interactives

It is now almost essential to accompany a new exhibition with an audio–visual (AV) show of some kind. These AVs normally act as an introduction to the displays, explaining how finds were uncovered, conserved, and displayed (e.g., the *Bronze Age Boat* gallery at Dover Museum and the *Mary Rose* Museum). They can also be used to present part of the story that cannot be easily explained through the objects (for example, at Sutton Hoo where the AV tries to communicate the nature, texture, and complexity of Saxon life at the time). Sometimes AVs have been used as the central part of an exhibition, such as The British Museum's *Mummy, the Inside Story* (see Pes 2004 for a review). At the Museum of London, the AV at the beginning of the *London before London* gallery is used to introduce visitors to the deep time that the gallery deals with and the very unfamiliar landscapes, and to emphasise that the place being dealt with is the same space now occupied by Greater London. These AVs have the same strengths and weaknesses as reconstructions. They are popular and have the ability to communicate ideas that would be difficult to communicate with objects. On the other hand, they run the danger of overpowering the real evidence and projecting images that by their nature will have to rely on conjecture and will not be in any sense real, while appearing very real.

Interactivity is defined as "acting on each other" (Owen 1999, p. 174) and as such at one level or another could be used to describe any type of museum interpretation in that it is hoped that the visitor does not receive information in a purely passive way. In the definition of the word that museums normally use, *interactivity* involves some form of physical interaction. Interactives offer an opportunity to bring visitors into physical, tactile, contact with real objects and to support interpretation through a two-way rather than one-way communication. For archaeology, this often means replicas, sometimes clothes that visitors can handle and try on, and occasionally real objects can be touched. Stone tools are perhaps most suitable for this, and much has been done to find ways of securing flint tools in such a way that they can be handled but not removed. In addition, computer and electronic technology is being used more and more to provide games and activities that are often aimed directly at children or families. At the Bronze Age Boat gallery at Dover Museum, visitors can do a giant jigsaw of the pieces of the boat as excavated and study environmental evidence under microscopes. At the Canterbury Roman Museum, there are handling collections of real artefacts and magnetic mosaics to make. At the *Stonehenge* gallery at South Wiltshire Museum in Salisbury you can demonstrate how a sarcen stone was lifted. At the new *Medieval London* gallery at the Museum of London, there are clothes to try on, a touch screen "game of life," and push-button electronic quizzes to explore the origin of words and medieval eating habits.

The perennial criticism of these devices is that they are always breaking-down or wearing-out and are not used in the way they are designed. Conversely, they are seen as a way of capturing and holding the attention of children who would otherwise learn nothing from static displays.

Another area where technology has the potential to improve and widen visitor experience is with audio guides and more-sophisticated digital AV technology. Audio guides have been in existence for some time and offer the ability of a more varied visitor experience. At Battle Abbey in Sussex, the site of the Battle of Hastings, visitors can take an audio tour where they can choose to hear the account of a Saxon warrior, a Norman warrior, or a Saxon woman. This offer of choice is undoubtedly the future. The technology for personalised tours of a museum delivered through a mobile phone or palm held computer already exists. It is only a mater of time before it becomes the norm.

Locations and Buildings

Sometimes the strongest interpretative tool in an archaeology museum can be the location of the museum and how this location is used. Many archaeology museums are based on the site of the original excavation or monument, and the remains or backdrop are built into the museum design for dramatic and contextual effect. In fact, so important is context for archaeology that such museums have a natural advantage and often provide the most memorable visits. Examples of this kind of use abound. The Roskilde Viking Ship Museum in Denmark has one entire wall of the museum as a window that looks out onto the estuary where the ships displayed were excavated and once sailed. Similarly, at the Jewry Wall Museum in Leicester, the archaeology museum looks out onto the ruins of a Roman bathhouse including the eponymous wall. The Le Musée de la Civilisation Gallo-Romaine in Lyon is landscaped into the steep Fourvière hill and has been enormously influential in terms of museum architecture and design. Visitors enter on a level with the top of the adjacent theatre seating-bank, and slowly make their way down through four gently sloping gallery floors and two mezzanines to the final rooms, which, fittingly, contain the funerary displays. The intention is to create a sense of exploration, of digging down to the very heart of Lugdunum (Francis Grew, personal communication).

Key Text

Grey, A., Gardom, T., and Booth, C. (2006). *Saying it differently, a handbook for museums refreshing their displays*. London: London Museums Hub.

CHAPTER 13
DISPLAYING ARCHAEOLOGY: EXAMPLES

Examples of the galleries, exhibitions, displays, and sites that interpret archaeological information.

Introduction

This chapter discusses the range of exhibitions and how they go about interpreting archaeology to the public. It complements Chapter 12 which looks at the methods and elements of exhibition design and Chapter 14 which looks at public programmes and education in their wider sense, and indeed other examples can be found throughout the book particularly in Chapters 2 and 5. Chapter 16 lists all of the museums and exhibitions mentioned in the book alphabetically for ease of reference.

The majority of a museum's collection is not on display and never will be. In a survey of British museums in 1991, the SMA found that 64 percent of museums had less than 10 percent of their collections on display (Merriman 1993b, p. 13). For archaeology, very reasonably, the percentage will be smaller than some other types of museum as the vast majority of archaeological material is collected as contextualised evidence rather than as display, or even research, items in their own right. But, nevertheless, it is to museum galleries that most go to see collections and objects. A survey of museum displays illustrates just how different archaeology museums are, but how, as already discussed, they use very similar methods for communication.

The *Uber*-Museums

A few museums stand out as exceptional in terms of their size, the range and excellence of their collections, their buildings, and their reputation as world tourist attractions. For archaeology, the most obvious members of this list are the British Museum in London, the Louvre in Paris, the Hermitage in St Petersburg, the Museum of the Ancient Near East (Pergamon Museum) in Berlin, the Metropolitan Museum of Art in New York, the Smithsonian Institution in Washington, DC, and the Egyptian Museum in Cairo. These museums (Cairo aside) are the national museums of the world powers in the eighteenth and nineteenth century when the concepts of displaying power through great museums were born. These nations also possessed the Imperial power and economic wealth to obtain collections from wherever they wanted. As such they now stand either as treasure houses of world history, civilization, and art or post-Imperial anachronisms to past discredited values. The visiting public, on the whole, takes the former line. These museums float above all others and live by different rules. They are visited by millions wishing to see their famous treasures but seldom seeking to understand the world from which they came, let-alone the circumstances by which they found their way into these city-centre, classic-style buildings.

These museums do not tend to be the place to find innovative displays and interpretation. Although building developments, such as the Grand Pyramid at the Louvre and the Great Court at the British Museum are innovative, they tend to be about visitor circulation and grand gestures rather than about interpretation. In most of these museums, great works are displayed as decorative or fine art with very little information about the cultures from which they have come. They also through the nature of their collections promote old models of civilization and value. So, even though the British Museum has recently moved its ethnography displays into its main building, it is still dominated by Greek, Roman, Egyptian, Near Eastern, and Middle Eastern collections. Its galleries rely on the power of objects, and interpretation tends to be scholarly and didactic. It, therefore, remains the case that the world's most famous archaeological objects are primarily understood as works of iconic art, as museum pieces rather than pieces in museums.

Temporary exhibitions allow a more innovative approach and the *uber*-museums have the pulling power and political weight to put on "blockbuster" shows. The British Museum has recently held a series of major archaeological exhibitions. *Mummy, the Inside Story* (2005) attempted to use new technology in dealing with a popular and well-rehearsed subject: unwrapping Egyptian mummies. The exhibition was built around a three-dimensional film describing how modern medical techniques, including body scans, had been used to investigate the contents of a mummy without unwrapping it. The actual mummy and associated artefacts were displayed in a room next to the cinema (see Pes 2004 for a review). Although extremely popular, and offering an example of how museums can break from static object and written word based exhibitions, the content offered little more than can be found on a National Geographic or Discovery Channel TV programme.

Other recent major blockbuster exhibitions at the British Museum have perhaps shown what the British Museum can do best, and what they should be doing: bringing the archaeology of major world cultures to new audiences. Recent exhibitions have included *Sudan* (2004) and *Persia* (2005). Both brought major collections to London for the first time and shed light on otherwise little-known (in the case of Sudan) or misunderstood (in the case of Persian) cultures. However, both were also unimaginatively displayed in crowded and uninspiring surroundings, and shown primarily as fine art rather than within any display context. This has been a continual failing of the British Museum that is partly hindered by poor temporary exhibition space. Another example was *Gladiators and Caesars: The Power of Spectacle in Ancient Rome* (2000) that, despite its popular subject matter bolstered by the recently released movie *Gladiator* and an incredibly rich object list, was again let down by conservative design and interpretation.

Sudan was staged with support from the Sudanese National Museum, while that Museum was being renovated with aid from UNESCO. Similarly, *Persia* brought objects from the Iranian National Museum to London. In both cases, there were political sensitivities to deal with to bring the material to the United Kingdom. With *Sudan*, there was the political and humanitarian tragedy of Dafour happening at the same time as the exhibition. This led to the British Museum not charging for entry to the exhibition, having charity collecting boxes in the space and working particularly hard with modern Sudanese communities. Similarly, the Persian artefacts almost did not travel to London due to political tensions (see Lotz 2005 for a discussion of this process). For both exhibitions, cultures were being introduced to UK audiences that were largely unknown or were only known from a traditional Western perspective. With *Persia*, there was a particular will to present the civilization on its own terms not from the familiar Western or, more particularly, Ancient Greek perspective. For both exhibitions, British Museum teams travelled to the countries in question to gain a feel for the subject and this permeated the final design. With *Sudan*, in particular, the scale and nature of the landscape were made a key feature of the exhibition design.

Perhaps a less successful exhibition for the British Museum was *Buried Treasure*, although it proved more popular on its UK tour. The exhibition showcased archaeological finds found by the public, often with metal detectors to support the Portable Antiquities Scheme and Treasure Act (see Chapter 6).

Smaller National and Large Regional Museums

The large regional museums and smaller national museums are a step down from the *uber*-museums. These are often miniversions of the former. The large regional museums are also in nineteenth-century classical buildings and hold collections of world archaeology dominated by the Classical world and Near and Middle East that are displayed as decorative and fine art. Examples can be found across North America and Europe. The prime difference is that these museums tend also to collect and display regional and, in some cases, national collections of archaeology.

PLATE 4. Displays in the *Early Peoples* gallery at the National Museum of Scotland. (Copyright, NMS.)

Of recent galleries, perhaps the most interesting is the *Early Peoples* gallery at the National Museum of Scotland (opened in 1999; see Spalding 1999 and Ascherson 2000 for reviews; Plates 4 and 5). Superficially conservative in its lack of modern technology (the gallery has one monochrome silent AV presentation), the lack of interactives, and the high design values of its cases and mounts, it nevertheless attempts several new ways of communicating to its audience. The gallery breaks with most archaeology galleries desire to put objects into a strong typological, chronological, and environmental context. Covering a period of about 10,000 years from the end of the Mesolithic to 1100 A.D., the gallery displays its exceptionally rich collections thematically and by technology, not chronologically. These displays are also largely devoid of any supporting contextual information; there are hardly any photographs of sites or landscapes. What the curator David Clarke has included in the gallery is modern art.

Plate 5. Sculptures by Eduardo Paolozzi containing arte-facts in the entrance area of the *Early Peoples* gallery at the National Museum of Scotland. (Copyright, NMS.)

Modern art has often been used in relation to archaeological displays. This may have its origins in the modern art movements adoption of archaeological and anthropological motifs in the early twentieth century, and may also be related to the abstract but physical nature of many archaeological objects whose aesthetics can be appreciated even though their original meaning is now lost. More recently, artists have also taken an interest in archaeological methods, and archaeologists have turned to art to help empathise with ancient people (see Chapter 14). At the NMS, specially commissioned art by major Scottish artists, such as Andy Goldsworthy and Eduardo Paolozzi, feature in the gallery and contribute to a complex shift in how the artefacts might be viewed by moving away from objects that reflect technology, and instead telling stories about objects that somehow hold secrets about those who once used them. The NMS does though have clear references with the past. Its display of items by types of object rather than cultures has resonance with early displays such as that at the Pitt Rivers Museum in Oxford. The gallery has received mixed reviews and is undoubtedly complex: "... not a hands-on but a brains-on museum" (inexact quote from Ascherson 2000, p. 83). Linked to the NMS is the Royal Museum. This is still a place for grand blockbusters that bring beautiful, new, and exotic objects to a new audience, which when combined with high design and interpretation values, communicate effectively a summary of knowledge about parts of human past. *Treasures from Tuscany* at the Royal Museum in Edinburgh in 2004 was an excellent example of this.

The Museum of London is comparable to the National Museum of Scotland in size. It was founded in 1976 out of two previous institutions: the London Museum and the Guildhall Museum. It is also unusual for Britain in that it has a relatively modern, purpose-built building. Its permanent galleries have always attempted to cover chronologically London's prehistory and history and merge from archaeology into social history somewhere in the sixteenth century with exceptions before and after.

It is currently on its third prehistory gallery. The second, called *People before London*, in place between 1994 and 2000, and was highly thought of, being one of the first large museum galleries to embrace some elements of post modernism (see Cotton 1997 and Chapter 3). The current gallery *London before London* was opened in 2002 and, although arguably more conservative than its predecessor in interpretation, it has tried to take a more radical approach to design that echoes the *Early Peoples* gallery at NMS (see Schadla-Hall 2002 for a review; see also Plate 6).

Like the National Museum of Scotland and the Museum of London, the large regional museums tend to be a mix of the traditional and innovative. This, perhaps, reflects the need to work harder at attracting audiences, particularly families and children. In some museums, archaeology has suffered, because it has had to compete for space with fine art and social history that often appear more appealing. Currently, both the National Museums and Galleries of Wales in Cardiff and the

Plate 6. The River Wall, part of the *London before London* gallery at the Museum of London (2002). (Photo: Museum of London.)

Ulster Museum in Belfast are seeing archaeology take a reduced role in their main buildings to allow for other displays.

Attempting to make archaeology of direct relevance by melding it with social history is still rare. The most notable example is probably the *Peopling of London* exhibition developed by Nick Merriman (1993a) at the Museum of London in 1993 (see Merriman 1990 for a discussion of the thinking behind the exhibition). The exhibition used archaeology and social history to chart immigration into London through history. At the time considered a groundbreaking project (it is still much referred to), its greatest success was to bring members of immigrant communities into the Museum. A different take on this approach was made in 1998 with the Museum's *London Bodies* exhibition (Werner 1998; Swain and Werner 1998; Swain 1998b; Chapter 8).

Museums in Australia and North America have a greater imperative to make their archaeology of direct social value as so much of it has derived from Indigenous communities or the contact between European immigrants and Indigenous communities. The National Museum of Australia uses its *Horizons* exhibition to deal with the European settlement of Australia to remind visitors that the land was already settled when they arrived. In the *Gallery of First Australians*, the Museum's Indigenous curators used archaeology to make a strong statement about early cultural achievements (the oldest rock art, the first boomerangs, etc.). In *Tangled Destinies*, a gallery that gave a history of ideas about the Australian environment, the Museum used the story of archaeologists' discovery of deep time and its impact on the national imagination (Mike Smith, personal communication). The Museum has also put on archaeological exhibitions of a more traditional type. These have included displays on Tutankhamen, Treasures from Southeast Asian shipwrecks, and Pompeii, developed overseas and brought into the museum. In 2005, the museum staged *Extremes* that looked at the archaeology and environmental history of major world deserts along the Tropic of Capricorn: the African Namib and Kalahari, Australian deserts' and South America's Atacama. The exhibition was very strong in its use of objects and sumptuous visuals, and it received very good reviews. Unfortunately, visitor numbers were only 20 percent of what the museum was used to for big temporary exhibitions, perhaps suggesting that this was an exhibition for a specialist audience (Mike Smith, personal communication).

The National Museum of the American Indian, part of the Smithsonian Institution in Washington, DC, opened in 2004 (as discussed in Chapter 16). It combines innovative architecture and interpretation with more traditional galleries that mix social and contemporary history with archaeological material to discuss the place of native Americans in the modern world.

Smaller Regional Museums

One level down, again, are smaller regional museums, often in larger towns or smaller cities and collecting and displaying archaeology from a local region. In some cases, these museums are purely archaeological in nature. Perhaps the "benchmark" example in the United Kingdom is the Corinium Museum in Cirencester (Plate 7). Cirencestor is on the site of what was one of the major towns of Roman Britain and finds and objects have been accumulated for several centuries including several large mosaic pavements. The Corinium Museum was created in the mid-nineteenth century from private collections and private bequests and became publicly owned in the early twentieth century again with aid from rich benefactors and collectors. It has benefited from ongoing archaeological excavations in and around the town.

The displays trace the story of Cirencester and its region from prehistory to the eighteenth century but are completely dominated by the Roman displays that take up approximately 80 percent of the display area. The exhibits are displayed chronologically with a closed passage-type display for prehistory and the Saxon and later periods but a more open thematic approach to the Roman displays. Human remains feature throughout the displays and include reconstructions of graves and the now obligatory "fleshed out" heads of clay showing visitors what certain ancient individuals would have looked like.

The museum in its current manifestation (a major redisplay took place in 2004) has all the ingredients discussed elsewhere of a model modern museum. The rich collections are well-displayed in good-quality, secure, and well-lit cases with ample captions and accompanied by colour-coded attractive graphic panels that use a hierarchy of text aimed at a general reading and ability level. The objects are supplemented, possibly slightly overpowered, by sets and reconstructions that use life-size realistic mannequins. In addition, there are computer terminals offering more detailed information about the collections and, in some cases, touch-screen supplementing displays; children's activities and interactives including specialist activity sheets and trails. There is a widespread use of painted reconstructions in a modern style that provide the dominant visual message for the gallery. Consideration has been given to disabled visitors, including some text in braille and tactile exhibits. As a museum dominated by archaeology, there is also some information on archaeological techniques, most notably a reconstruction of an archaeological section showing stratigraphy and finds back through the town's history.

Corinium is an example of all current established museological approaches for archaeology taken to their natural conclusion. The only thing it lacks is an introductory film, present at places like the Museum of London *London before London* gallery, Sutton Hoo, and Dover (see below and Chapter 12). It explicitly accepts the premise that visitors should be given as much help as possible in "realising the past" and that the actual objects need to be very heavily supplemented by realistic sets of one kind or another. It also presents an unquestioned and established past.

Similar museums to Cirencester can be found around Britain (such as Dorchester, Colchester, and Norwich). Some present a slightly more didactic "adult" approach such as Devizes, while others present galleries more geared for children, such as the *Stonehenge* gallery at South Wiltshire Museum Salisbury. A similar pattern can be found across Europe.

University Museums

University museums are those that have developed from teaching and research collections. By this very nature they will be for "an academic audience, and its core audience is an internal one" (MacDonald 2000, p. 75 referring to the Petrie

PLATE 7. The new *Roman* galleries at the Corinium Museum, Cirencester. (Copyright, Cotswold District Council.)

Museum). However, most university museums now also see themselves as having an important public role to play. They often hold very important and eclectic collections reflecting the role of university academics in much early archaeology.

There remains a tension within university museums over their role. At one extreme, they should be free to be experimental and radical in their approach, and to use the academic skills of staff to try new approaches to museology. However, in reality, university museums tend to be conservative and there remains a concern that pandering to children or public might lead to "dumming down" (MacDonald 2000, p. 79). There have been honourable exceptions to this rule such as the *Digging for Dreams* (2000), exhibition created in partnership among the Petrie Museum, the Croydon Museum and Heritage Centre, and Glasgow Cultural and Leisure Services which explored the modern fascination with ancient Egypt. It included the juxtaposition of modern objects with ancient artefacts from the collections. The Petrie Museum of Egyptian Archaeology is part of University College London. Its collections of Egyptian antiquities came from the fieldwork and collecting of Flinders Petrie and his patron Amelia Edwards (MacDonald 2000 gives an introduction to the museum its origins and aims; MacDonald and Shaw 2004 looks at its audience).

Many university museums, developed in the nineteenth century, have primarily classical archaeology collections for which innovative display, even if affordable and desirable is problematic. A recent exception has been *Colour among Greeks and Etruscans* (2005–2006) at the Allard Pierson Museum, Amsterdam. This used modern replicas alongside original pieces to illustrate how gaudily coloured ancient sculptures would have been.

Site Museums

The very best archaeology museums are often those that are based around a single site or find. They have the advantage of being focused on a single subject and often innovative or exciting architecture to make a direct link to the site. They will also highlight context, that key ingredient of archaeological meaning. It is also, by nature, only exceptional archaeological sites and finds that will warrant their own museum. So, key discoveries such as the *Mary Rose* and *Dover Bronze Age Boat* in England, the Roskilde Viking Ships in Denmark (Plate 8), the Ice Man Museum in Italy, the site of Neanderthal in Germany, La Tene in Switzerland and the Hubei Museum, and Museum

PLATE 8. The boat yard at the Roskilde Viking Ship Museum, Denmark, where the public can see traditional shipbuilding. (Photo: Nikola Burdon.)

of Qin Terracota Warriors and Horses in China, to name but a few, all have exceptional finds in exceptional settings.

The very particular conservation needs of key finds can often add to the drama of their locations and displays, and add to the interpretation. The *Mary Rose* in its great hanger-like space being constantly sprayed with water and PEG is an example (see also Chapter 10). Similarly, the massive glass and steel case that holds the conserved Dover Bronze Age Boat is almost like a modern art installation.

Site museums have also often brought out the best in museum architects. The great glass wall of the Roskilde Viking Ship museum acts as a wonderful backdrop to the ships and makes a direct link to their find spot and original context: the open water. The Laténium Museum in Switzerland (Plate 9) and Neanderthal Museum in Germany also offer exceptional architecture that makes a direct link to the landscape. This is, of course, not always the case. The architecture of older site museums can be a detraction. The Roman Palace of Fishbourne in Sussex looks like a 1960s bus garage. The site is due for refurbishment. It provides an interesting contrast to the nearby Bignor villa that is surrounded by thatch and timber and provides a completely different atmosphere.

At Bibracte, meanwhile, Au Musée de la Civilisation Celtique, the curators have gone a stage further by recreating a small funerary enclosure of the Gallo-Roman transitional period, exactly as it was when under excavation in 1992. This exhibit forms part of a remarkable museum on the slopes of Mont Beuvray, near Autun in Burgundy. The building is spacious and entirely glass-sided, with extensive use of wood and black marble, forcing the visitor to conceptualise it as part of the landscape – to look outwards rather than inwards. The original funerary enclosure lay directly under the museum and was excavated in advance of its construction.

Perhaps partly because the museum is twinned with a research centre that coordinates the international programme of fieldwork on Mont Beuvray, there is one of the most comprehensive presentations of archaeological practice and of current academic concerns. Maps and aerial photographs illustrate points of topographical interest; the facsimile of the site is complete down to details of burning in a ditch terminal and spoil from the excavated pit; and the pots themselves are available for study in an adjoining case – although, surprisingly, they seem not to match precisely the replicas in the model (Francis Grew, personal communication).

Reconstructions

As already discussed in Chapter 12, reconstructions are a key part of archaeological interpretation in museums. Although they are rare in the larger museums, they are very common in almost all other museums. Some museums and displays have been completely based around reconstructions of one type or another.

The best known example in the United Kingdom is probably the Jorvik Viking Centre. First opened in the early 1980s, it has been a well-publicised model of a particular model for

PLATE 9. Latènium, Switzerland. The architecture of the museum in sympathy with the landscape. (Photo: Jack Lohman.)

interpretation whose success led to a number of imitators but also some criticism from within the profession (see, e.g., Schadla-Hall 1984; Gathercole and Lowenthal 1990, p. 245; and Plates 10 and 11).

Jorvik was the brainchild of the then Director of the York Archaeological Trust Peter Addyman following the excavation of part of Anglo-Scandinavian York at Coppergate between 1976 and 1981. Excellent organic conditions led to exceptional preservation and a wealth of structural, artefactual, and environmental finds. During the excavation, more than 500,000 members of the public visited the site (Addyman 1990, pp. 76–81). It was this public interest that prompted the Trust to develop Jorvik that was opened to the public in 1984. Jorvik is not a traditional museum, and there is no collection directly associated with it (although The York Archaeological Trust is a Registered Museum under the British Government MLA-run scheme). It was the first so-called dark ride that took visitors on small moving cars through a reconstruction of Viking York

PLATE 10. The Jorvik Viking Centre York. (Photos courtesy of the York Archaeological Trust.)

as revealed by the Coppergate excavations. At the beginning the visitors are taken back through history (literally in that the time cars go backwards) in order to orientate them, and at the end of the Viking reconstruction is a reconstruction of the excavation and then finally a more traditional museum-style display of the actual finds from the dig.

The reconstructed section includes complete houses, streets, and even ships. These are not built using authentic materials but every attempt is made to create an "authentic" look and feel. Mannequins, in some cases, using actual Viking skulls to build up facial likenesses populate the site. The whole thing, which is enclosed in a huge dark basement space, is further supplemented by a soundtrack and smells to conjure a real-time experience of the Viking town.

Jorvik was heavily influenced by visitor surveys that were undertaken during the dig that identified "public misconceptions about the past and archaeology" (Addyman 1990,

PLATE 11. The Jorvik Viking Centre, York. (Photos courtesy of the York Archaeological Trust.)

pp. 258–259). This led to a very literal approach to interpretation that have left some pure museologists uncomfortable, believing Jorvik goes too far, both in terms of the archaeological interpretation and museum interpretation methods. But this museum has been hugely popular with the public, almost 900,000 people visiting in each of its first two years of opening (Addyman 1990, p. 262). Pearce (1997, p. 54) has suggested that the combination of Jorvik and the Archaeological Resource Centre (ARC) in York (see Chapter 14) would provide a near-full archaeological experience.

Jorvik offers an extreme example of one type of archaeological interpretation. The Museum of London used a similar approach in its 2000 temporary exhibition *High Street Londinium* (Hall and Swain 2000a; Swain 2004a; Plates 12 and 13). For this 6-month exhibition, the museum reconstructed three houses from the first century A.D. based on the results of archaeological excavations at 1 Poultry between 1994 and 1996 in the City of London (Rowsome 2000). Like at Coppergate, the level of survival on the site allowed the archaeologists to be able to make

PLATE 12. *High Street Londinium*: Reconstructing Roman London at the Museum of London (2000). (Photo: Museum of London.)

a detailed plan of the site, and artefacts allowed a detailed reconstruction of how the buildings were made and used.

The aim was to show the public how archaeology could be used to reconstruct the past and also to try and give an indication as to what it would really have been like to live in first-century Roman London. Here the Museum was also conscious (as with Jorvik and the Vikings) that it would be trying to correct a popular conception of the Roman world.

PLATE 13. Roman actor and school children in the *High Street Londinium* exhibition. (Photo: Museum of London.)

As designed, the exhibition was divided into three distinct spaces: an introductory area, the reconstructed buildings, and finally a display of the finds from the excavation. The main part of the exhibition was the area of reconstructed buildings. The idea here was to take the ground plan of part of Roman London, as revealed at 1 Poultry, lay it out to exact scale in the exhibition space and then, using the archaeological evidence, reconstruct this part of the first-century town. The aim was to give visitors an "experience" of Roman London so the reconstruction not only had to look real but also feel and smell real. There would be no real objects in this space, and there would be no captions or explanatory text. Instead, visitors were handed a large leaflet, which acted as a guided map to the space and provided explanations of areas through which they were walking. Unlike other exhibitions, such as Jorvik, visitors were allowed to walk through the reconstructed spaces at their leisure, touching everything. This obviously called for a reconstruction that would "feel real" at a very detailed level, and would also be extremely hardy.

Although no attempt was made at total authenticity in the reconstruction, it was policy to use original materials and techniques wherever possible in order to create the most realistic experience. So, newly felled oak prepared with adzes was used for the roofs, windows, and doors. Forged iron was used for the door hinges. But mud brick and daub were not used for the walls and most nails were modern with resin copies of Roman nail heads hiding them.

It was realised that it was easier to create a sense of reality by producing internal spaces with light shining in, than external spaces, so the Roman building plans were used to fill as much of the exhibition space as possible with building interiors. In fact, however, so strong were the recreations, and so used are the public to dealing with "un-real realities" that none of them seemed put off by the small areas of the exhibition which revealed the walls and ceiling of the gallery.

The entrance area of the exhibition included a 5-minute video that explained the nature of the Poultry development and excavation, and how the reconstruction was realised. The purpose of this was to put what visitors would see in the reconstruction into the context of the archaeological process, to explain to them that the reconstruction was based on actual archaeological evidence from an actual site within the City. To emphasise this sense of place and context, large graphics showed the location of the site in relation to both Roman and modern London.

The final area of the exhibition was a display of the actual finds from the 1 Poultry site, including many items that the visitors would have seen as replicas in the reconstructed area. It was incredibly gratifying how much time visitors spent poring over these objects after having had them put into context within the reconstruction.

It was felt strongly that mannequins would intrude into the sense of reality. It was also impossible to people the space with real people full-time, even if this were desirable. Three partial solutions were found. Trained actors dressed as Roman-Britons inhabited certain rooms on certain days – aimed primarily at school groups. This simply expanded on the arrangements the Museum of London already had in place for the permanent Roman gallery and its room settings. Craft demonstrators (pottery, wood, bone, and, leather workers) were also used on certain days in one of the rooms. A sound-track was also used to give background atmosphere. However, the most ambitious attempt at introducing life into the exhibition involved a film. One of the three buildings, a pottery shop, included the shop-front facing onto the *via Decumana* – the high street of the exhibition's name. Onto the view out of this front was projected a continuously running 10-minute loop of film. This was of about seventy individuals from Roman reconstruction groups walking past a Roman street set. Despite the obvious artifice of this process, it proved hugely popular with visitors and helped make the link between the interiors, the people of Roman London, and the town in which the buildings were set.

High Street Londinium was a great success by many criteria. It received very favourable media coverage, excellent visitor figures, and supported very good commercial sales. Visitor comments were also extremely favourable. The one continuing complaint from visitors was that it was only a temporary exhibition and should have been made permanent! Is this, however, the wrong way to be explaining archaeological evidence? In an article in *The Independent*, Mark Ryan described it as "tacky literalism at its worst." His complaint was that this was a museum giving the visitor too much, taking away their need to imagine the Roman world for themselves. Was *High Street Londinium* leaning too far towards being a theme park? Were there too few real objects? Was it a museum exhibition at all in the true sense? All archaeological interpretations are just that, interpretations. There was much in the exhibition that could not be guaranteed as accurate.

The museum was aware of these possible accusations but would argue that they come from the wrong perspective. The prime aims were: (1) to give visitors a new, different, and enjoyable experience that they would remember; (2) to convey to them the nature of the archaeological process and how a modern office development can lead eventually to a revised understanding of the past; and (3) to convey what it would have been like to live in first-century Roman London, and how different this would have been to most people's impression of the Roman world. It was argued that the methods used achieved these aims more successfully than a more traditional exhibition type. Visitors clearly did enjoy the exhibition and did not think they were being patronised, deprived of using their imagination. Archaeologists often underestimate how intelligent and discerning the public can be but also how much help is needed in understanding the deep past.

Living Museums

It is in the United States where reconstructions have been taken to their most extreme form. Here, several major sites are based entirely around full-scale reconstructions that "recreate the past" and people it with professional living historians. There are many examples of this kind of museum, at different scales, for example, the Old Sturbridge Village, Massachusetts (Simmons, 2000), that creates a vision of early nineteenth-century U.S. rural life and advertises "re-created original homes," "authentically costumed villagers," and "celebrations of nineteenth-century Americans." Here historical archaeologists have been part of the project for more than 20 years. A full-size reconstruction has also been made of the first pilgrim settlement at Plymouth, Massachusetts, where actors or living historians dressed in part take on the complete personas of the documented settlers, including their original accents and refuse to come out of part when talking to visitors.

Perhaps the most extreme examples of U.S. living-history sites can be found in the so-called historic triangle in Virginia. Here, within a 20-mile radius can be found Colonial Williamsburg, Historic Yorktown, and the Jamestown Settlement. James Fort, and Jamestown that developed from it, is where the first English settlement in North America and was founded in 1607 by an expedition of 105 men in three ships that arrived from London. The story of Jamestown is now firmly embedded in the American national myth through the story of Pocahontas and John Smith. Since 1996, the Association for the Preservation of Virginia Antiquity (APVA) has been excavating the actual 1607 James Fort, and a museum and visitor centre have been built for the 2007 anniversary. The site is located within a U.S. National Park and is close to the APVA site the U.S. National Park Service has also built a new visitor centre for 2007. A few hundred yards away, and off of the island, is Jamestown Settlement. This is a state-funded facility that has also been largely rebuilt for 2007, including a huge museum and education complex. However, the most evocative part of Jamestown Settlement is a 1:1 reconstruction of the James Fort featuring living history actors in seventeenth-century costume. Close by and moored on the James River are full-scale reconstructions of the three original ships, the *Susan Constant*, the *Godspeed*, and the *Discovery*. In the woods beside the centre is a reconstructed Indian village. The ships and Indian village also feature living history actors (Plates 14 and 15).

About 5 miles from Jamestown is Colonial Williamsburg. Williamsburg takes a bit of time to work out. Is it a theme park, a living museum, or just a historic town? And how did it get to be like this? Could an eighteenth-century town (and particularly such an important one, Williamsburg was the capital of Virginia at the time of the War of Independence) really survive the ravages of time and remain perfectly preserved in the early twenty-first century?

Colonial Williamsburg is the creation of two men: Revd. Dr W. A. R. Goodwin who brought the original vision, and John D. Rockefeller, Jr., who brought the money.

Later nineteenth- and twentieth-century houses were demolished and most of the surviving eighteenth-century houses were completely refurbished. Several key buildings, including the Governor's House, were built from scratch using eighteenth-century plans and drawings. The result was a version of the eighteenth-century state capital in twentieth-century America, surrounded by hotels, modern roads, and shopping centres and featuring a large visitor centre, two major museums, and a conservation centre. The Colonial

PLATE 14. Jamestown Settlement, Virginia, USA. The Living History reconstruction of James Fort. (Photo courtesy of the Jamestown Settlement, Williamsburg, Virginia.)

Williamsburg Foundation that is in turn owned by the Rockefeller family manages it. Eighteenth-century living history actors who take on the characters of its original inhabitants and who live out daily life as well as major events in the town's history populate it.

It is almost impossible not to like Williamsburg (at least initially). It not only represents a very attractive ideal of history, it also represents a very attractive and comfortable present. Around the anglophone world, developers and individuals are trying to create living surroundings similar to Williamsburg: traffic free; tree-lined; redbrick Queen Anne architecture with early colonial clapboard vernacular. But it is also false, and, to a degree, sinister. It creates and perpetuates a very particular version of American history. See Handler and Gable (1997) for a strong critique of the methods and motives of Williamsburg's owners. For the museum archaeologist, it is equally disconcerting. Nothing tries harder to create a true picture of the past

PLATE 15. Jamestown Settlement, Virginia, USA. The Living History reconstruction of The Indian Village. (Photo courtesy of the Jamestown Settlement, Williamsburg, Virginia.)

through physical material culture, architecture, and landscape but still ends up so far from it.

Beyond the Museum: Museum Archaeology in the Landscape

The point has already been made that archaeology is inextricably linked to sites, landscape, and context. And it is one of the criticisms of museums in general that they are boxed off from the outside world and fail to make proper connections with it. It, therefore, seems logical that wherever possible archaeological museums, and the delivery of museum archaeology, should be linked to actual sites, monuments, and landscapes. "By definition, sites are in situ: their context does not need to be re-created ab initio as in the case of museum exhibits. Since context is a valuable asset, not to be squandered by transfer of the remains to another setting" (Stanley Price 1990, p. 287). The ability to do this will of course be dependent on whether sites survive and are accessible. In the last few decades, there has also been a shift in philosophy away from individual sites and objects to emphasis the importance of landscapes. However, obviously the ability to interpret archaeology in landscapes will be effected by how much the ancient landscapes and sites have survived, and the modern access that can be given to them.

The subject of archaeological site and landscape management, preservation, and interpretation is a discipline in its own right, but, needless to say, questions of archaeological authenticity are equally as relevant at any scale, whether considering single objects, displays, sites, or landscapes. As Pearce (1990, p. 174) has noted, "archaeologists may have to accept that the public wish to experience the cultural heritage is not really about understanding the past at all, but rather about feeling better about the present."

This states what should be the obvious. When visiting a castle, or hill fort or monastery, beautiful lawns for children to play on, a good gift shop, a good restaurant, convenient parking, and an aesthetic view all contribute to a "good day out" or worthwhile visit. These may all distract from a "true" understanding of the past, but a thoughtful and sympathetic interpretation to the site will contribute to the good day out *and* give visitors an insight into the past and how it has been created, *and* probably contributes to the long-term sympathetic management of the site. This echoes similar debates about museums.

Many sites fit into a Western concept of the picturesque, the idea of romantic ruins, that have been preserved in the eighteenth and nineteenth century for this reason and then been overlaid later with a didactic interpretation in the twentieth century. The tradition of the romantic ruin is very much an English one and was countered in the late nineteenth and early twentieth centuries by French ideas that favoured restoration. The debate was partly fought out over the "restoration" of Knossos by the Britain Arthur Evans. His use of reinforced concrete to allow "essential" restoration, or "reconstitution" as Evans termed it so that the original state of the palace could be understood by visitors was initially welcomed by almost all. Only with time did the dangers of making a conceptual leap from archaeological interpretation to reconstruction lead to doubts (see Lapourtas 1997 for a full discussion). Evans and others felt they needed to compensate for the shortcomings of visitor imagination (Lapourtas 1997, pp. 76–77). It is currently fashionable not to underestimate the imagination of visitors, and this has led to a certain level of snobbery about reconstruction discussed elsewhere.

Whatever the reasons, any claim that managed historic landscapes and sites offer a more authentic picture of the past than a museum is relative: "As it now stands, the site exemplifies two very different approaches to a medieval ruin. From the eighteenth century comes the overall woodedness and greenness with terraces, cascades, and asymmetrical plantings; from the twentieth century come the severe exposure of walls and the stripped lineaments of plan, set off by shaved lawns and framed by earthen verges. One is evocative, the other didactic – neither is medieval" (Peter Fergusson, 1990, p. 31, in his guide to Roche Abbey, Yorkshire).

There are many types of historic landscapes and many ways that monuments can be preserved, interpreted, and experienced, and museums fitted into them. They range from the traditional "heritage venues" in Western countries like England's monasteries and castles that are often "overmanaged" and interpreted but do offer the full family experience, to the famous archaeological sites in the Mediterranean and Middle East often excavated and interpreted in the nineteenth century. These often contain a confusing mix of original ruin, original reconstruction, more recent dilapidation, and recent attempts at reconstruction. Examples include world famous sites such as Knossos, Pompeii, and Babylon and thousands of lesser-known sites. Most of these sites are associated with traditional museums that are beside or within the monuments and display objects and sometimes offer interpretation.

In other, often urban, examples, the sites and their remains need to live beside the modern world and modern functions. A common sight in and around new developments in cities, are the attempts to preserve, display, and interpret ancient ruins that have been disturbed or discovered. Here, there is a need to balance modern use and the desire to preserve.

Caroline Sandes (personal communication), looking at such sites in the City of London, has shown convincingly that it is not enough to preserve a piece of a historic structure simply because it has an academic value. It must take on an aesthetic value within its new setting in order to be valued by its new users.

The construction of the Athens Metro, completed in 2000, allowed for the creation of five archaeological displays in train stations. These take the form of relatively conventional showcase-based displays. They include both real objects excavated from the area of the station and replicas. They stand out through their number, size, and ambition. Surveys (Penny Kalligerou, personal communication; Hamilakis 2001) have suggested that they are popular with Athenians, being visited and appreciated by a cross section of the local population including many who do not regularly visit museums. They also include recreated sections of stratigraphy with objects, and skeletons from burials built in.

Ideally, museums will supplement a range of methods that will encourage the understanding of historic landscapes. The Carnac region of Brittany in Northwest France is a rich landscape of Neolithic and early Bronze Age sites. Impressive chambered tombs, often including stone carvings, litter the countryside. However, the area is most famous for a series of megalithic avenues and arrangements that dissect the countryside, the exact meaning of which remains (and will remain) a mystery. The area is also a tourist destination for its coastline and peaceful countryside and historic towns and villages. Therefore, many of those who visit the area will be doing so in a relatively "passive" manner. One would hope that any interpretation of the sites would try to communicate how the different sites work within the wider landscape and relate to each other both spatially and chronologically. A greater challenge is to communicate the possible significances of the sites to those who constructed them and used them.

A visitor looking to understand the archaeology of the region and its interpretation is greeted by a variety of options that highlight the ways archaeology can be interpreted. The stone avenues have spent much of the last few decades fenced-off to avoid erosion. Visitors can view them from a distance, read graphic panels, and occasionally climb onto wooden platforms for a better view. As the stones are spread over many miles, maps are needed both to find them all and get a feel for their scale and significance; however, they are well advertised and through their size are easy to find. The chambered tombs are on the whole quite different. Most are not advertised or signposted and maps and guides are needed to find most. The search initially seems very worthwhile as in most cases the chambers, built in the forth millennium B.C., are largely intact and can be entered. It is only after visiting several that it is realised that most were "reconstructed" by antiquarians at the time when they were excavated.

In the town of Carnac is the small Musée de la Pré-histoire, an archaeological museum that seeks to interpret the region in the Neolithic and Bronze Age. It is painfully tradi-tional relying on the largely antiquarian investigation of the areas sites. It is dominated by objects, many of them very fine but there is hardly anything to link them directly to the sites or the landscape, and absolutely nothing to help visitors understand the meaning of the sites.

An alternative to the museum is Archeoscope. This is not a museum and has no original artefacts. Instead, it is an enclosed, narrated, sound and light show, not entirely unrem-inisant of a 1970s heavy rock concert set involving dry ice and megaliths rising through a stage. What Archeoscape does try to do is communicate the wonder of the stones and what their spiritual meaning might have been to those who built them.

Another site that seeks to interpret a megalithic landscape is Archaeolink in Grampian, Scotland. This is a controversial site that is a private enterprise, using much public money to try and encourage investment to the area through increased tourism. Archaeolink involves a new purpose-built site within a themed park and with a series of exhibits largely lacking real archaeological objects. Again, its problem is making the link between a particular site and a much wider and complex land-scape. Computers within the centre provide an innovative and imaginary solution. When leaving the site a visitor can enter their destination, a type of monument that interest them (for example, stone circles or castles), and the time they have available, into a computer. They will then be given an itinerary of sites they can visit, with directions for their journey home. Thus, relatively basic geographically based computer technology makes a link between landscape museum and information. In time, PDAs and mobile phones (see Chapter 14) will vastly increase these kinds of options.

Key Texts

Addyman, P. (1990). Reconstruction as interpretation: The example of the Jorvik Viking Centre, York. In P. Gathercole and D. Lowenthal (Eds.). *The politics of the past*. London: Unwin.

Ascherson, N. (2000). Notes and reviews, The National Museum of Scotland. *Public Archaeology, 19*(1), 82–84.

Clarke, D. (2000). Creating the Museum of Scotland: a response to Neal Ascherson. *Public Archaeology, 1*(3), 220–221.

Denford, G. T. (1997). *Representing Archaeology in Museums, The Museum Archaeologist, 22.* Society of Museum Archaeologists.

Swain, H. (2004a). High Street Londinium: Reconstructing Roman London. In Paul Frodsham (Ed.), *Interpreting the ambiguous: Archaeology and Interpretation in early 21st-century Britain.* British Archaeological Reports 362, 89–93.

CHAPTER 14
SCHOOL, PUBLIC, AND COMMUNITY PROGRAMMES

This chapter discusses the place of archaeology in formal and informal educational programmes: how museums deliver educational programmes to support the teaching of archaeology in schools and for life long learning and public programmes support galleries and exhibitions. Types of public programmes include traditional approaches and more innovative ideas, such as community excavations and the use of actors – ways of reaching new and less traditional audiences.

Introduction

As already discussed in Chapter 2, there remains an unfortunate, and self-imposed, divide in museum concepts between formal education and entertainment. Such a divide also exists between education aimed specifically for schools and education for other audiences, although the philosophy of life-long learning is at least eroding this. Most museums provide programmes of events for school children, adult learners, families, and other groups of visitors. A further false divide is the current concern with "communities" and the need to address problems of "social exclusion." All of these subjects, formal education, public programmes, and community initiatives overlap and are often not addressed directly through museum galleries and exhibitions (although these play an important part and are dealt with in Chapters 12 and 13) but through associated initiatives. These are the subject of this chapter.

265

Formal Education For Children

Most museums have an explicitly educational role, employ specialist educational staff, and rely heavily on educational visits to justify their existence. During school-term times, for example, about half the visitors to, for example, the Museum of London are school groups. Formal education at school is also where the vast majority of people are given the framework of understanding in archaeology and history that they will rely on in adult life. In a depressingly self-fulfilling cycle, the only "archaeology" most English school children study are the Roman and Egyptians. These then become the archaeological subjects of most interest to English adults so these feature prominently in popular culture, books, and museums. And this high profile and interest feeds back into their place in the school curriculum. Surveys have often shown (e.g., Wood and Cotton 1999) how tenuous most adults understanding of early history and prehistory is, and, in most cases, this goes back to what they were taught (or not taught) at school. Although, as Susan Pearce has observed (1990, p. 15), there has never been a formal link in Britain between state education and public museums, and this has left the museums to develop programmes to attract schools almost on a market basis rather than through a formal relationship.

The English example is repeated with variations in different countries. National myths are created and promulgated through the history taught in schools, and consciously or inadvertently the way a nation thinks about its past will be shaped by how and what it teaches of history and prehistory in schools. In France, for example, prehistory is given more prominence, and the Romans downplayed. Sometimes this trend has caused much harm; sometimes it has the ability to do much good. For example, the National Standards for History in the United States have done much to improve the understanding of Native Americans and the role of African Americans. The current controversy in America, about the teaching of "intelligent design" for the origins of life, adds a new facet to this debate.

School programmes are very important for those who promote the importance of history because formal education is the only time when, on the whole, a captive and formative, if challenging, audience is available. Archaeology as a subject would appear to be perfect for teaching. It is multidisciplinary and questioning and goes to the heart of what it is to be human. However, in the United Kingdom, archaeology as a subject is hardly taught in schools, and where it is used, it tends to be used as a source of evidence in the teaching of traditional history subjects that reinforce the "classic" model of Western development.

Observing a hoard of noisy 8 year olds invading a museum gallery can be an exhilarating or a depressing experience. A teacher has been observed at the Museum of London telling a class: "learn as much as you can and be back here for lunch in one hour." None of the children would have learned anything by the end of the hour other than how to lose a pencil behind a showcase. Alternatively, a noisy class of children has often been completely silenced by the performance of an actor in a Roman room setting. The ability of children to enter another world and ignore their superficial modern surroundings when engaged properly is astonishing.

As part of a survey for the redisplay of the Alexander Keiller Museum in Avebury, Wiltshire (Stone 1994; see also Chapters 11 and 12), English Heritage asked school children what they wanted to know about prehistory. Stone's rather pessimistic take on the responses is perhaps misfounded. Answers that included "where did they go to the toilet?", "how did they get rid of it?", "did children go to school?", and "what toys did they have?" help to identify ways of engaging children, and these are all questions that archaeologists could be asked to answer, or at least speculate on. However, it is interesting to note that despite undertaking this survey, the "key concepts" developed for the redisplay (Stone 1994, p. 196) pretty much ignore its findings and descends into archaeobabble, talking of "prehistoric cosmologies" as the central concept for the displays. It is true, as discussed elsewhere in Chapter 11, that most museum galleries need to appeal to a wide range of audiences and, thus, cannot be too heavily aimed at children. The solution for most museums is to provide a school service that supplements the gallery displays.

Current education provision in England was developed from the 1988 Education Reform Act (ERA). This made a provision for the development of a national Curriculum that is compulsory for almost all children of school age in England and Wales. It has three core subjects (English, mathematics, and science) and seven foundation subjects that include history (see Stone 1990 for a discussion). A working group developed each subject curriculum. Although archaeologists argued hard for the relevance of their discipline to most subjects, it was obviously to history that they looked to for most involvement. In this event, archaeology does not appear as a discreet subject in the history curriculum but is included in a number of its topics. Most children end up studying the Romans in Britain, Ancient Egypt, the Middle Ages, and sometimes the Vikings and the Saxons. Children also get to go on school trips, and here museums can play an important role. "Field trips, and museum and site visits, form an integral part of the school curriculum for history [and] have enormous potential for bringing history to life and creating a lasting impression" (Stone 1990, p. 55 quoting from DES 1990, sections 10.2, and 10.16).

Where a gallery or subject does not feature directly in the curriculum, museums can try and find other ways of making it relevant. In developing the *People before London* gallery at the Museum of London, even though very little prehistory has found its way into the National Curriculum, a specially designed technology section was introduced to try to woo school groups (Cotton 1997). In the most recent *London before London* gallery, geography modules are taught through the gallery.

In Britain, it is often left to the imagination and enthusiasm of individual teachers as to how much archaeology is used in the classroom. Bonham (1997) provides one example of how archaeology can be built into the secondary school history curriculum including pretend excavations using carpet tiles. She also makes the point that there are a wide range of educational resources now available from organizations, such as English Heritage, should teachers wish to make use of them.

In the developing world, education is still seen very much in vocational terms for most, and the study of archaeology seen as a luxury. Stone and Molyneaux (1994) give a wide and eclectic range of attempts from around the world to use archaeology and specifically museum archaeology to deliver educational programmes.

As in the United Kingdom, in the United States, archaeology has struggled to make an impact on formal preuniversity education or to be taken seriously as a profession by the general public. This is despite its strength as a cross curriculum, or in U.S. parlance "cocurriculum," subject that mixes science and arts in a unique way. This has also meant that attempts to involve school children in archaeology projects are often done in the isolation of an overarching learning framework (see Zimmerman et al. 1994 and Smardz Frost 2004 for examples in the United States.) In the United Kingdom, projects, such as the Shoreditch park community project (see below) similarly sit outside a wider archaeological educational framework. What these examples also illustrate is the great benefit of involving children, or for that matter anyone, in actual digging as part of archaeological education.

Corbishley and Stone (1994) present an excellent, if somewhat depressing, review of how archaeology has continually failed over time to make an impact on formal education in the United Kingdom. But they are considering this from an archaeologist's perspective. One reason why archaeology has failed to have the influence it should on formal education is that archaeologists seem primarily interested in promoting their own concerns: agendas concerned with preserving and managing sites, rather than in helping teachers deliver their programmes and agendas (Zimmerman et al. 1994). However, despite their frustrations, many museums do offer formal educational programmes directly aimed at school children that do draw on archaeological evidence and materials. These projects tend to be very "task orientated" and dominated by questions about how people did things rather than about how they felt. This becomes even more the case when practical exercises are attempted. Object handling and craft exercises, making Roman lamps and mosaics, and so forth, dominate these programmes. Projects that do involve people's thoughts often involve actors and storytellers that are very popular with children. In the United Kingdom, the Group of Educators in Museums (GEM) acts as a specialist network for the promotion of museum education.

Public Programmes

Public programmes can take many forms and often overlap or are identical to services being offered by schools. Here are the different types of activities that museum archaeology can provide to supplement and expand on gallery displays is discussed.

Displaying New Discoveries

One way to make archaeology of more immediate interest to the public is through new discoveries. Archaeology's "unique selling point" is the discovery of past treasures from the ground. It is, therefore, a tragedy if archaeologists fail to involve members of the public in these discoveries. Modern developer-funded, professionalised archaeology has conspired to make archaeological excavations inaccessible to most. It, therefore, comes as a surprise to many just how excited and engaged the public can become over a new find. It is also the case that if the members of the public feel more excited about a find, the more attached they are to it. And this attachment comes from their nearness in space and time. Being shown a relatively unimportant find that was found on their street yesterday becomes as important as a famous ancient treasure found hundreds of years ago in another country. Archaeologists need to use this. The closer they can get the public to the point of discovery, the more they will engage the public with the past and what it can tell them.

The Museum of London has, for some time, had an explicit policy of trying to attract new visitors, and raise its profile,

PLATE 16. *The Spitalfields Roman.* Ten thousand members of the public queued to see this new discovery at the Museum of London in 1999. (Photo: Museum of London.)

by trying to advertise and display new archaeological discoveries as quickly as possible after discovery. Its most successful example of this approach was the so-called Spitalfields Roman (Roberts and Swain 2001; Swain 2000; Thomas 2004, pp. 18–26; Plate 16; Chapter 7). A rare Roman stone sarcophagus was discovered on 12 March 1999 at excavations in Spitalfields close to the city. The removal of the lid revealed a decorated and well-preserved lead coffin contained within. This was only the third find of this type ever made in London and the first since the nineteenth century. Recognising the importance of the discovery, its potential to reveal new evidence about the Roman period, and the interest it was likely to generate amongst the general public, the decision was taken to bring the sarcophagus, still containing the unopened coffin into the Museum. This was done on 19 March. The coffin was installed in one of the galleries, interpretation boards were hastily prepared, and the public were allowed to see the coffin. Curators gave regular short talks about the finds and were always present to explain their significance to visitors. Indeed, this was the principal method by which the finds were interpreted.

Arrangements were made to open the coffin on the evening of 14 April in the presence of a small audience and two TV camera teams. Very complex preparations had to be made to ensure the well-being of the coffin, its contents, and of those involved in its opening. National and local press and radio also covered the whole process.

The coffin was found to contain the well-preserved skeleton of a young woman lying in a layer of silt that contained rich organic remains. New interpretation panels were prepared and, in effect, *the Late Stuart* gallery of the Museum was turned into a temporary exhibition space for the coffin, skeleton, and associated finds. Work continued on the coffin while the public were allowed to view the finds. At one point, a curator was able to announce to the public the discovery of a glass phial in the silts – between the sarcophagus and coffin – literally minutes after conservators had first found it. As analysis work continued, the organic silts in the coffin revealed evidence for leaves and textiles, including gold thread.

It is estimated that an extra 10,000 people visited the Museum specifically to see the finds, some of them queuing for one and a half hours to file past the coffin. After 2 weeks, all was removed for further conservation and analysis. Some material was temporarily redisplayed to coincide with a special local TV programme. All was put back on show for the first showing of a national TV programme in January 2000. This had 4.3 million viewers. The whole exercise proved beyond doubt the huge interest there is in archaeology, especially if finds can be brought to public attention rapidly after discovery and can be interpreted in an imaginative way.

Since *The Spitalfields Roman*, the museum has regularly displayed new finds, normally combining them with press releases, public events, and lectures. Finds put on display include waterlogged medieval ship timbers, a hoard of Roman gold coins, and parts of a Roman water-lifting mechanism.

However, the policy of displaying the finds straight after discovery and luring visitors through media coverage is not without risks. Conservation needs can be problematic, although these can also add to the attraction. In the past, the museum has created a special water tank in its medieval gallery to hold waterlogged timbers and, on several occasions, has included ongoing conservation as part of displays of new finds (see also Chapter 10). More worrying is the need to display and interpret objects before they are fully researched and to find associated stories that will woo the media. In 2000, the museum displayed Roman artefacts and human cremated remains that despite attempts at careful press management were described in the media as evidence for a female gladiator, something they were probably not. Similarly, in 1999, the museum displayed a preserved banana skin that stratigraphy had shown to be Tudor (sixteenth century) in date. Subsequent scientific dating suggested it was much later. In both cases, it was realised that a tension existed between wishing to share discoveries with the public as soon as possible and the recognition that only stories of a particular kind would attract the media attention needed to give displays the publicity they needed, and sometimes risks would be taken with scholarship.

Handling

The figures quoted are never quite the same, but, as a general rule, it is observed that something like only 20 percent of what is read is remembered; 30 percent of what is heard; 40 percent of what is seen; 50 percent of what is said; 60 percent of what is done; but a full 90 percent of what is seen, heard, said, and done. The obvious conclusion from this is that most museum displays are not the best way of communicating and the more a museum can do to involve their visitors more actively the better. The great strength of museums, in general, and archaeology, in particular, is that they have real things for visitors to interact with. With all the obvious caveats about the protection of collections accepted, allowing visitors to handle and come into direct contact with objects is a powerful medium for communication, and most archaeology museums have some form of object handling in their programmes. The ability to handle objects is also accepted as being a powerful method of education for school children (e.g., Durbin et al. 1990). Several institutions have taken this to its logical conclusion and made interaction with objects the main focus of a visit including the Archaeological Resource Centre (ARC), York (now transformed as *The Dig*).

The Archaeological Resource Centre (ARC) in York was a further brainchild of the York Archaeological Trust (YAT) (see Chapter 13) and was developed, in particular, by Andrew Jones and Dominic Tweddle. Opened in the late 1980s, the ARC was housed in the restored medieval St Saviours church near the centre of the city (see Kadrow 1990 for an introduction to the ARC). When first opened, the building doubled as a store for the YAT and included glass walled offices for specialist staff so their work could be viewed as part of the visitor attraction. The purpose of the ARC was to introduce the general public, and school groups to archaeological methods through a series of interactives and activities. It was based on the premise that the public is interested in how archaeologists do things, not just what they find, and the public will engage with this often complex subject best through hands-on activities.

The ARC visit began with an audio–visual presentation titled "What is "archaeology?" It then had three further "zones." The first zone dealt with finds research and gave visitors the opportunity to handle and sort actual finds from York excavations. The next section dealt with experimental archaeology and included replicas of such things as Viking shoes. The final section contained computers.

The ARC was primarily staffed by trained volunteers. This gave an opportunity for a further group of highly motivated people to become involved but also greatly reduced the costs of running the centre. The volunteers took a very hands-on role in mediating the centre. There were no traditional graphic panels or glass case displays. In 2005, a major redevelopment of the ARC begun to create *The Dig*. This develops the concepts of the ARC to create an educational interactive reconstruction of an excavation. Similar facilities to the ARC exist in different places and at different scales. For example, *New York Unearthed*, is part of the South Street Seaport Museum, New York.

The nature of many archaeological finds also makes them suitable for being taken out of the museum and for the creation of handling collections that can be moved around as needed. Such schemes have been running in some museum services for many years, normally linked to formal educational programmes. Most services involve the creation of some form of object container that can be loaned to schools with accompanying learning aids and returned when finished. However, the sheer quantity of bulk mundane archaeological material offers the opportunity for permanent loans or gifts of such material. In 1999, the Museum of London developed a Roman School Box scheme that allowed finds to be donated to local schools.

Using the vast amount of unstratified and residual material in its archaeological archive (see Chapter 7) and in response to a survey that showed a real demand from schools, the Museum developed a scheme to deliver boxes of Roman finds to state schools in Greater London. The initial project was for 200 boxes (in total there are 1,800 state primary schools for 5–11 year olds in London). Each box was made of metal and had a hinged top and several draws. The boxes were purposely designed to look good and be durable so they would not be forgotten or undervalued by the schools. These contained a selection of real artefacts including pottery sherds, oyster shells, and building materials, including tessera and tiles. The box also contained a teaching pack to explain how to use the box including a videotape and a series of replica items, in some cases relating directly to the actual artefacts (so a large sherd of mortaria would be accompanied by a complete replica). The boxes were donated to the schools on the condition that they would return them if they were ever not wanted (Plate 17).

The evaluation of the scheme 1 year after starting showed that the boxes were really valued by the schools and were being used for a range of teaching including art and science, not just Roman history. However, the scheme was very

PLATE 17. A Roman school box designed to be given to junior schools in London and including real Roman artefacts. (Photo: Museum of London.)

expensive and external sponsorship and funding was needed even for the trial. So far, no funding has been found for the whole scheme. It is also recognised that even with their use for other subjects most boxes will spend most of the year not being actively used. For a full review of the scheme, see Hall and Swain (2000b).

PLATE 18. *The Dig*, at the Museum of London in 2001. An event designed to help children understand how archaeology works. (Photo: Museum of London.)

Doing

As noted above, archaeology lends itself to "doing" activities, and these are a popular way of engaging, in particular, children. This type of activity can take a myriad of forms and, in many cases, can be developed to be taken off-site and be done without supervision. Smith (2002) offers a very traditional list of "cheap and cheerful" and safe and predictable events and methodologies to get members of the public involved in archaeology. They can be used to teach about ancient technology, such as pottery making and leatherworking, more generally about aspects of life in the past, or about archaeological techniques. Many of these methods are well-tried and tested and remain popular, for example, dressing up in costumes. It is sometimes unclear exactly what the learning outcomes are for such activities, but, if nothing else, they encourage museum visits and an interest in archaeology and can be a focus for museum publicity. Smith (2002) summarises National Archaeology Days (NADs) in the United Kingdom, organised annually by the CBA, previously weekends in July and now whole weeks, they provide a focus around hands-on events for museums and other archaeological bodies.

Many different museums around the world have developed their own examples of learning aids based around the idea of handling material. The Museum of Prehistory, Zug, Switzerland (Museum Für Urgeschichten), has a wonderful selection of child friendly booklets and playing card-sized painted reconstructions that make up into sets of images. The Neanderthal Museum in Germany has a series of preplanned activity sessions each aimed at a different learning outcome.

In 2001, The Museum of London developed *The Dig*, in effect a fake archaeological excavation for children to teach them about archaeological methods (Martin 2002; Plate 18). Built as a series of small units within the Museum, it allowed children, supervised by real archaeologists, to excavate a section of a site, uncover and identify real finds, and interpret simple stratigraphy. At a debrief, the different parts of *The Dig* were put together to reveal the complete plan of the site. Because it is dismountable, *The Dig* is still used and the idea has been widely copied.

Living History

Another popular form of archaeology programme involves actors and "living historians." These fall into several related but distinct groups. Throughout much of the Western world, there are a growing number of hobbyists who spend time dressing up in period costume and "reenacting" past events. These are often associated with men and warfare, so, in the United Kingdom, the most popular groups are based on the Romans, Vikings, English Civil War, Napoleonic Wars, and World War II. In the United States, the American Civil War is very popular. However, so popular has this become that groups exist that are based on almost all periods of history. The exact motivations for this activity are complex, and it is not the place of this book to explore. Needless to say, it is a subject that has provided rich-pickings for postmodern analysis (see, e.g., Appleby 2005). However, those who get involved often take their subject extremely seriously, often going to great lengths to create authentic looking costumes and accessories. These reenactment groups are much used by museums either to put on one-off grand events (the Museum of London, for example, has held a "medieval muster" and gladiatorial combats) and also to provide small-scale events that allow children to try on armour and talk to experts. As inferred, the role of reenactors forms a subset of the wider debate about authenticity, realism, and how museums should communicate (see Chapters 12 and 13). They present a very particular picture of the past that is comfortable and unchallenging. The subjects covered reflect popular subjects dominated by aggressive men and fighting, but they all talk English and are visitor-friendly. The gladiators may get the clothes and weapons perfectly correct, but none of them get to die. However, reenactors are very popular with the public and do give displays and sites a sense of life, movement, and colour that will never come from static displays.

In the United Kingdom, reenactment tends to be an amateur or partly professional activity. In the United States, it has been taken to a new level of realism through professionalisation. At sites, such as the Jamestown Settlement and Williamsburg (see Chapter 13), the detailed historical evidence available, supplemented by the archaeology is used to make living history one of the prime methods of interpretation, and those involved spend years training and perfecting accents, crafts and behaviour. The effect is very powerful, but the same criticisms persist. At Colonial Williamsburg, for example, there is a decided shortage of black slaves present (although they are not completely absent).

Another aspect of living history is the employment of actors to perform specific programmes for public audiences and school parties. Similar to the U.S. examples, such actors can take on the role of actual or imagined characters from the past and tell their own stories to audiences. As noted above, although adults often feel uncomfortable with such performances, children often adore them, and they are a powerful way of holding children's attention and leaving them with a lasting impression.

Art and Archaeology

This chapter has so far dealt with the traditional ways that museums enhance their static displays and exhibitions with educational and entertainment programmes. This section gives two examples of more imaginative public programme that show just how clever museum education can be if it seeks to think differently.

One area where museum archaeologists are looking to use their subject in a more imaginative way as part of public learning programmes is through art. Archaeology and art work together at several different levels. First, there is the example of artists using archaeology for inspiration. See Pearce (1997, pp. 52–53) for examples of artists who have drawn on archaeology and ethnography, mainly as a way of questioning the established practice of museums and the authentication of objects, including the work of Fred Wilson in the United States (see Chapter 12). See Pearce (1999, pp. 21–24) for a discussion of artists using archaeology as their own creative muse. However, perhaps more interesting is the use of art and artistic activity to try and understand and maybe even empathise with people in the past, particularly those who have left no written records. Some artists have found inspiration in archaeological methods and practices and in the nature of archaeological material. The more recent use of art in museum exhibitions and programmes may be a reflection of the move away from scientific empirical study and towards a more intuitive approach.

As already discussed in Chapter 13, museums have used art in different ways in their displays. These include the Roskilde Museum in Denmark and the *Early Peoples* gallery at the National Museum of Scotland. In 2000, the Museum of London hosted a poet-in-residence, Bernadine Evaristo, who was funded by the Poetry Society. She produced a verse novel, *The Emperor's Babe* (2001) that dealt, amongst other issues, with the identity of black people within the Roman Empire. Some of Bernadine's poetry was also used in the Museum's 2002 *London before London* gallery as part of a range of writing to communicate the ideas of prehistory to different audiences in different ways.

The American artist Mark Dion has carried out a number of projects that create installations based around the ideas of archaeological collecting. His most ambitious project, *Tate Thames Dig*, involved a fieldwork project on the Thames foreshore culminating in the creation of a "cabinet" displaying his finds in a way that developed ideas about collecting, typology, and antiquarianism to a primarily aesthetic end (Dion 1999). Here, his main concern was not what archaeologists found but what they do with their finds. British artist Neil Brownsword in his 2005 *Collaging History* exhibition at the Potteries Museum, Stoke-on-Trent also took his inspiration from what archaeologists found rather than the past itself, although he concentrated on the nature of the objects found in Stoke and how these related to the rapidly disappearing ceramics industry that for more than 200 years had made the city world-famous.

Art has also been used to help visitors engage with archaeological subjects. From 2000 to 2001, the British Society of Museum Archaeologists, under the guidance of Janet Owen, undertook a major *Art of Archaeology* project funded by the Heritage Lottery fund. This included a range of projects of different types undertaken in nine different UK venues. The project is described in detail in Wise 2003.

As a final twist to art and archaeology, in 2005 the antiestablishment graffiti artist "Banksy," unbeknown to staff, hung one of his works on the walls of the British Museum where it remained unnoticed for 3 days. The work included a fake caption: "early man venturing towards the out-of-town hunting ground." The work was an imitation of a cave painting showing a man pushing a shopping trolley. The caption further noted the date of the work as "from the post-catotonic era." In a postmodern twist, the artist later displayed the work in his own exhibition as "on loan from the British Museum," and the British Museum was hoping to acquire the piece once this exhibition ended (*Current World Archaeology* 2005, p. 10).

Raising the Dead

Despite the current ethical debates about the place of human remains in museums (see Chapter 8), it is a fact that most children adore skeletons and the ancient dead, and ancient burials are a powerful way of making a direct contact with ancient peoples and their beliefs in a very intimate way. Two imaginative projects illustrate how this can be used.

In France, a school project was developed to study Bronze Age society and beliefs, and the nature of archaeological evidence (described in Masson and Guillot 1994). A class of children was divided into two. In isolation, one group considered the nature of a burial based on known and conjectured evidence and then constructed the burial using an actual skeleton from a teaching collection and associated artefacts. The burial was then covered in earth. The second group then undertook an archaeological excavation of the grave, initially being led to believe that it was a real grave. Once the skeleton was found (including its identifying museum catalogue number), the children were told the nature of the conceit, but rather than being disappointed they redoubled their efforts wishing to solve the puzzle of what the burial and its artefacts were trying to tell them about the past.

This imaginative exercise allowed the children to think about how people might furnish a grave to reflect their beliefs and circumstances, how such objects might be uncovered and understood, and the divergence between the two obviously allowed the children to question archaeological methods and shortcomings.

PLATE 19. The "Celtic" warrior presentation developed by the National Museums and galleries of Wales and designed to teach children about how objects survive (or don't survive in the ground). (Photo: Museum of London.)

The National Museums and Galleries of Wales Conservation Department developed a similar project in 1998 (Plate 19). This *Celtic Warrior* exercise involved a live actor dressed as a late Iron Age warrior who talks to and interacts with a school party before he "dies." Using a false back to a constructed burial cyst of the type used by magicians, the real actor, once "buried" disappears and is replaced by a model skeleton and a series of replica artefacts resembling those the warrior had but now as they would be after 2,000 years under the ground. Once the initial shock of the children is overcome (and although most are thrilled, there is always one who is deeply distressed by the process!), they have to analyse what has happened by the process of long burial: organics disappearing, metals corroding. Again, this is an imaginative way of helping children in a very immediate and exciting way to think about the nature of archaeological evidence and why we know what we do about prehistory.

Community Archaeology

Community archaeology as a definable concept is relatively new but, as a practice, is as old as archaeology itself (see Holgate 1993 for a discussion of its history). Its recent popularity is based on the recognition that much current archaeology is undertaken by a small closed profession, by itself for itself, even though most within the profession would profess that archaeology is all about a public service. The concept of community archaeology has taken on an even more urgent vogue very recently within the wider call for social inclusion, the measuring of the cultural value of heritage, and the championing of the value of places to local communities. The theory goes that archaeology is only undertaken for the greater good of a public community and involving that community in archaeology will give them an improved quality of life and most specifically will increase the value they put into the places where they live, thus increasing the overall well-being of society.

Communities can of course be difficult to define. Pearce (1990, p. 181) suggests they are "those people who are neither professional curators nor professional archaeologists." This of course oversimplifies and avoids the most complex issue about communities: their ability to self-define, overlap, and take on a political dimension. Ideas also work at different levels and in different ways in different parts of the world. Some indigenous communities are very clearly defined from within and play a fundamental role in the archaeology of their past (see Chapter 8 in relation to human remains). In other places, communities are defined from without and have no direct relationship with archaeology. It is the case that archaeologists ignore communities at their peril, and they have a duty to consider their views in relation to what they plan to do.

Museums do not need to play a part in community archaeology, and some work carries on without their input, either run by communities themselves or other archaeological organisations. However, museums are perfectly placed to perform a role. They often represent a visible and tangible focus for archaeology in an area and have a public service remit that allows them to put resources into such projects. Indeed, any public museum with local archaeology collections not performing some community role is surely not fulfilling its duties? Community work also tends to take place *in* the community thus giving museums an opportunity to break away from their buildings and reach people who might not, for a number of reasons, feel comfortable or able to come to the museum itself.

The most obvious manifestation of the archaeological community is the local archaeological society, and these continue to exist and prosper throughout Britain and elsewhere. However, the aging white, middle classes mainly populate many local societies to their own admission, and political dogma, as well as basic democracy, would hope for involvement from a much wider segment of the population and many other communities (see also Chapter 11 for a discussion of museum publics).

Many small-scale community projects carry on based around the enthusiasm of individual archaeologists, often without resources and relying on discretionary effort, and working with small, motivated groups of the public, sometimes members of local societies, or people gathered together around specific projects. For example, see Waller (2000) for work by the borough archaeologist in an urban and largely poor area of the West Midlands; and Russell (2000) for work in Southampton that includes community digs, pot washing groups, Young Archaeologist clubs (YACs), and fieldwork; and Faulkner (2000) for a discussion of the community excavation at Sedgeford.

The community archaeology project that is most often cited in Britain is the one developed in Leicestershire at the beginning of the 1980s by Peter Liddle of Leicestershire Museum Service (see Liddle 2002). This scheme (which is still going strong) recruited members of the public into parish groups to undertake fieldwalking and associated activities. It saw local people actually taking ownership of the research into, and management of, their areas' past.

In London, the Museum of London has attempted a number of initiatives to engage with nontraditional audiences using local archaeology. *Outsites* are an attempt to display some of London's archaeology back where it was excavated. It relies on the good will and often the finances of property developers or other organisations. In effect, small museum displays are installed in public areas where they can be maintained and are deemed secure. Some are permanent, some temporary. A number are already in place, including one at a railway station. It is hoped that they will both help to communicate archaeology to those who don't visit museums, enhance the sense of community in the places they are located, and act as useful adverts for the museum. Another project was known as *Look ahead with Archaeology*. This was undertaken with a group of homeless men with special care needs. The museum worked with them at the hostel in which they lived to develop an exhibition on the archaeology from the surrounding area. The men were totally involved in the process, thereby gaining a whole series of skills and hopefully increased self-confidence as well as finding out about the past. Only a few people were involved in the project; although many more saw the exhibition once it was installed in the hostel and then moved to a local community centre.

The museum has also supported and undertaken community excavations. Most notably, in the summer of 2005, it undertook the excavation of part of Shoreditch Park opposite its Mortimer Wheeler Resource centre and LAARC (see Chapter 7). The site had previously held nineteenth-century housing that had been largely destroyed during bombing in World War II. The project was a huge success and showed how viable research could be combined with educational and community projects (*Current Archaeology* 2006).

New Technology

A final, obvious way to undertake museum programmes that will reach new audiences outside the museum building is through the internet. Most museums, and indeed most museum projects, already take an associated website to be an essential prerequisite. These sites take many forms and are aimed at many types of audiences. Perhaps most powerfully for museums, it gives a way of making large collections that cannot be displayed in a traditional way accessible (see also Chapter 9). Several museums, in the late 1990s, created VCTs (virtual teaching collections) based on a new software package *Cabinet* (Boast 1997). This was based on images of objects but more importantly the ability to add any kind of associated data in any form of relationships. The Petrie Museum has put all of its 80,000 objects online and has created *Digital Egypt for Universities* to "encourage multi-disciplinary collections based teaching and learning" (MacDonald 2002, pp. 13–14). A trawl through some of the museum websites offered in Chapter 16 shows just how varied this type of interpretation is and how exciting the prospects are for the future.

Key Texts

Stone, P. G., and Molynaeux, B. L. (1994). *The presented past*. London: Routledge.

Wise, P. J. (Ed.). (2000). *Significant Others, The Museum Archaeologist*, 25, Society of Museum Archaeologists.

Wise, P. J. (Ed.). (2002). *Public Archaeology: Remains to be Seen, The Museum Archaeologist*, 27, Society of Museum Archaeologists.

Wise, P. J. (Ed.). (2003). *The Art of Archaeology, The Museum Archaeologist*, 28, Society of Museum Archaeologists.

PART 4

CONCLUSIONS

*Indeed an interest in the past seems to be
a universal human characteristic.*
J. D. Evans (1981, p. 13)

CHAPTER 15
CONCLUSIONS

Museum archaeology at the start of the twenty-first century and a discussion of likely future trends.

The National Museum of the American Indian (NMAI), part of the Smithsonian Institution in Washington, DC, might be considered the nearest thing to the future for one type of archaeology museum. It attempts to meld the Western model of museums with the voice of the Indigenous peoples from whom its collections originate. On entering, it has everything that would be expected of an early twenty-first-century museum: two shops (one with quality souvenirs, the other with original Indian art); two restaurants (again, one selling Indian recipes); a cavernous and architecturally stunning lobby (with no ancient objects in site); cutting-edge technology in its displays (touch screens mean there is no need for numbers or words to interfere with the aesthetics of display); a cinema; a study room; and very nice toilets.

The building itself, designed by Douglas Cardinal, is glorious. It is built in sympathy with Indian culture and, externally, it makes a firm and complete break with the classic temple model of museum design. The whole building and its surroundings, including materials and orientations, are designed with Indian beliefs in mind. However, it also adheres to the quasisacred rules of the Smithsonian that demands that each museum has windows that look out at their neighbours on the Mall (in this case the eastern wing of the National Gallery).

So far so good. . . . But what about its displays? After some very beautiful, but rather superficial wall-case displays showing a thematic range of objects, the main galleries are found, almost apologetically, hidden at the back of the building. They contain no clear didactic or typological, or geographic, or historical account of the Indian nations that can be navigated in order to understand or explain American Indians in a way Western museum audiences would expect. Instead, there are a series of modular displays that try primarily to put across Indian views of their current place in the world. Objects are hard to find, and a mix of graphic styles and poor orientation makes navigation difficult and tiring.

Some displays do manage to work at two levels, or in two symbolic languages: a long case of guns through time (from flint-locks to Kalashnikovs) works as a classic typology (a similar typology of firearms exists in the Pitt Rivers Museum, Oxford) and an aesthetic musing on the way Indians have suffered from Western aggressive technology. But such clarity is rare.

Perhaps the fault here is not with the museum but with the Western museumgoer. Perhaps in time we will learn to understand and sympathise with a new type of museum. In fact, is this the museum acting as an "engine of social change" that we had all promised, but, perhaps, the majority of us had not taken too seriously? But for now, the NMAI suggests that museums really are a product of the Western enlightenment world and only makes sense within this context. This would certainly explain the geographical and historical distribution of museums and how the non-Western world has failed to embrace them except when aspiring to Western values or by reinventing them as is perhaps happening in Africa.

Interestingly, the NMAI repository at Suitland, MD, in the Washington suburbs works perfectly. It too is a combination of Indian-sympathetic design with state-of-the-art storage and conservation for the collections. But here, there is no clash of cultures – only sympathetic design. Perhaps because no messages, explicit or implicit are being attempted, the building is simply designed to work for both communities (Indians and museologists), uninterrupted by the troublesome public.

The NMAI tells the story of a living Indigenous people who, up until recently, have been primarily studied through archaeology. The exact links between the "archaeological Indians" and their living communities might be up for discussion, but importantly the archaeological people have living, modern, empowered representatives in the here and now. One role of archaeology in the twenty-first century is to find an accommodation between traditional Western museums and archaeology and such people. Te Papa in New Zealand, the National Museum of Australia, and the Australian Museum are the other obvious places where this negotiation is being worked out. However, many other museums still have to come to terms with this need.

Then there are the archaeologies of orphaned cultures: the museums of Egyptian, Greek, Roman, Viking, and other ancient peoples. Despite our loud, vehement, and prolonged assertions to the contrary, it is tempting to conclude that most living people do not consider what happened in the distant past to be, in any way, relevant to the present and future. Studying prehistory will not provide a cure for cancer. Knowing that there has been dramatic climate change in the past will not help solve global warming. But this is not to say that archaeology is without value. When they have the luxury to allow it, people who are interested in the past do choose to spend leisure time pursuing and pondering it. Museums are one of the arenas in which a society and the individuals within that society can negotiate with the past in order to decide what relevance it will have to the present and future.

The past can and does tell fascinating stories that make us ponder the world around us, and real objects have the ability to compliment, and even tell, these stories in different ways. The most imaginative public programmes and community projects have also shown that museum archaeology really can be classless and can "make a difference" to normal people. There is simply a need for museum archaeologists to fully embrace their potential. At the macroscale, museums do thrive, and millions of people do choose to visit them and to value archaeological evidence.

Susan Pearce, one of the great minds of late-twentieth-century museum studies, was unfortunate enough to write her book *Archaeological Curatorship* (1990) just as the world was changing. Although it hints at the effects of postproces-sualism, developer funding and market forces, the birth of contract archaeology, and the globalisation of archaeological and museum politics; the book was written just before these influences had been felt. One can only hope that this book does not suffer the same fate. Scanning the horizon for the type of cataclysmic change that these phenomena have brought to museum archaeology, it is difficult to spot anything as extreme. But I do not, as yet, have hindsight to reassure me.

In trying to identify what will effect future changes, three interlinked but distinct debates emerge:

1. How to best collect and curate archaeological material? (see Chapters 7, 9, and 10);
2. How to negotiate the value to be put on archaeological material? (see Chapters 6 and 8); and
3. How to interpret and communicate archaeology to the public (Chapters 11–14).

These questions will inevitably be addressed within the wider context of archaeology and museologies past and present (see Chapters 1–5).

It would seem clear that in the West we are now collecting too much and not putting to full use that which we already have. Museum archaeology is not sustainable. We must some-how find a way to stop archaeology from being a linear pro-duction line and have it become a holistic system. Only then will what we are doing with past excavated material affect how we generate new material. A solution to this has not yet been found. This is primarily because market forces now drive the majority of archaeology, but the products of excavations (the archives and collections) have no market value. However, this challenge is now recognised and being written about and debated. Progress is being made.

This is a key time in the development of archaeological thought and practise in relation to excavation archives. It has long been accepted and unchallenged that an attempt should be made to fully record and fully recover the results of excavation and that this material should be stored forever as a testament to the initial work and as a research resource for future generations. Three things undermine this model. Post-modernism has questioned the nature of the record in the first place. Developer-funded, developer-planned, and developer-led archaeology has generated more material than was ever thought possible, this has led to a huge burden of expense and effort being put on those expected to keep the artefacts – who are very seldom the organisations digging them up. Finally, it has been shown that, in many cases, archives have not been used as the incredible research resource they are thought to be.

For museums, with the many competing demands on their resources, the problem is acute. How do museums justify ever more stores and ever more curators and conservators when the direct benefit to public programmes is often difficult to see? The model of the LAARC in London points to one solu-tion. The economies of scale and critical mass are used to ensure that archaeological material is cared for at the appro-priate regional level by staff that can maximise its benefit. But, clearly, more is needed; it is not enough simply to care for material well. A time has come when it may be reason-able to be more critical in terms of what is kept. Also, even more imagination is needed in using new technology to make records more accessible and more economical to curate.

Archives will continue to be core to museum archaeolog-ical activity because archaeological excavation, with its won-derful combination of real material culture put into context through association to identify past human activity, is what archaeology and archaeological interpretation is all about. But new methodologies are needed to take it viably into the twenty-first century.

The great civilizations of the past most coveted by the mod-ern West are located in the poorer developing nations. Iron-ically, outside the West archaeological material often does have a market value because it is rare, not adequately pro-tected, and in demand by collectors. One would hope that, in time, individuals, communities, and nations will come to value and protect their archaeology because of its cultural value to communities rather than its market value to individuals. It may be a long wait, and we can only hope that destruction has not gone too far. The West has a responsibility to help protect threatened non-Western archaeologies.

The West also has a responsibility of a different kind over human remains. Human remains are, for the present, the most contentious issue in museum archaeology. However, the debate divides into two main areas that are arguably self-contained. In the Western, Christian, and humanist traditions, human remains are not inherently sacred, they only acquire this status through association: by belonging to a close relative, a war victim, a great leader, and so forth. Without this association, human remains are seen as valuable scientific evidence and as a potentially powerful method of interpretation in museums. For other peoples and cultures, human remains are inherently sacred or are imbued with powerful cultural associations that make their use by museums unacceptable. The test for museums is recognising which group any particular human remains falls into, and ensuring that the barriers between the groups are not unnecessarily blurred.

It is ironic that it is in the interface with the public that change and evolution seem most orderly. Museum displays are only subtly different now from a hundred years ago, but they are cumulatively better, and I am sure that displays will continue to improve. The greatest fear is that homogeneity will take hold and a point will come where all displays and public programmes look the same wherever you go. The greatest joy of museum archaeology is its variety and range. By striving for excellence and quality, I hope that this would increase, not narrow, over time. Exhibitions, galleries, and programmes also tend to be inherently conservative and tend to legitimise familiar uncontroversial views of the past. But they do evolve, and they do respond to developing audiences and theory. A review of the newer museum archaeology galleries (e.g., *Early Peoples* at NMS, *London before London* at MoL, Corinium, and NMAI) shows a refreshing and exciting mix of different takes on what an exhibit should be and how we can respond to different audiences.

In Chapter 6, I referred to the concept of the "Total Collection" (Thomas 1991, p. 3) where conceptually every item in a collection is given equal value whatever its material, origin, or use. Thomas used the term to raise the humble potsherd to the heights of the complete pot. I would suggest it should be used to mean that any object has the potential to be given any meaning. For the future, a new degree of fluidity of thinking and a new confidence is needed from the archaeological curator: a fluidity of thinking about the meanings and values that are attached to objects and a fluidity and confidence in dealings with audiences. Instead of using relativism as an excuse for giving up authority, curators need to use it to allow themselves to develop new and imaginative ways to deal with their collections and their audiences. Different objects will be given different meanings at different times and by different groups. This runs counter to the traditional model of tying objects down ever more tightly to created meanings. However, it has the potential to allow the museum archaeologist to fully embrace the challenges they face and to reinvent the relevance of their collections and role. New technology, if used imaginatively, will contribute to this freedom.

Archaeology is important, and museums are of value. Museum archaeologists have a role to play in society. They have a responsibility to be outward looking, imaginative, and relevant. They are the guardians of collective lost memory as it is revealed through the objects that have survived from the past. It is their responsibility to help rediscover the lost memory in a way that contributes to society and is not a burden on it.

CHAPTER 16
MUSEUMS AND EXHIBITIONS

All Museums and Galleries Mentioned in This Book

Above all, museums are places to visit. No description, photograph, or webpage ever equals the experience of actually travelling to, arriving at, and walking round a display. This chapter provides a list of all the museums, sites, and exhibitions mentioned in the text. For temporary exhibitions that no longer exist, an opening date is given. Museums are in the United Kingdom unless stated otherwise. Where one exists, a link has been given to the museum webpage; where these do not exist, and where appropriate, I have included a link to the best possible webpage for factual information on the museum.

THE ABBEY MUSEUM OF ART AND ARCHAEOLOGY. Brisbane, Australia. Independent museum with collections from European archaeology.
www.abbeymuseum.asn.au.

THE ALEXANDER KEILLER MUSEUM. Avebury, Wiltshire. Small site-based archaeology museum on a prehistoric World Heritage Site. Collections are from local sites.
www.english-heritage.org.uk.

THE ALICANTE ARCHAEOLOGICAL MUSEUM. Alicante, Spain. A new museum showing regional and maritime archaeology. It was named *European Museum of the Year* in 2004.
www.marqalicante.com.

ALLARD PIERSON MUSEUM. Amsterdam, Netherlands. Archaeology museum of Amsterdam University, collection of classical antiquities.
http://cf.uba.uva.nl/ap.

Colour among Greeks and Etruscans (2005–2006). Temporary exhibition on how ancient statues would have been painted.

ARCHAEOLOGICAL MUSEUM OF IOANNINA. Epiras, Greece. Regional state museum, built in the 1960s and currently being renovated. Prehistoric and classical period collections.
www.culture.gr.

THE ARCHAEOLOGICAL MUSEUM OF PALERMO. Sicily, Italy. Museum of classical antiquities. Located in previous convent buildings.
www.comune.palermo.it/siti_esteri/english/museum.htm.

THE ARCHAEOLOGICAL MUSEUM OF SAN PEDRO DE ATACAMA. Chile. University museum with displays of local archaeology, including Andean mummies of Atacama peoples.
www.sanpedroatacama.com/ingles/museo.htm.

THE ARCHAEOLOGICAL RESOURCE CENTRE (ARC). York. Activity centre based on excavations in York. Now closed and redesigned as The Dig, an excavation based activity centre.
www.digyork.co.uk/.

ARCHEOSCOPE DE CARNAC. Carnac, France. Light, sound, and object presentation on the Carnac megalithic alignments.
http://www2.ac-rennes.fr/cst/doc/dossiers/archeo/enbret/musees_sites.htm.

THE MUSÉE D'ARLES ET DE LA PROVENCE ANTIQUE. Arles, France. Regional archaeology museum with antiquities from a Roman town.
http://www.tourisme.ville-arles.fr/a2/a2f.htm.

ASHMOLEAN MUSEUM. Oxford. University museum and Britain's oldest public museum. Collections of European and Western Mediterranean antiquities.
www.ashmol.ox.ac.uk.

AUCKLAND MUSEUM (Auckland War Memorial Museum). Auckland, Australia. Regional museum including Maori collections.
www.aucklandmuseum.com.

AU MUSÉE DE LA CIVILISATION CELTIQUE. Bibracte, Mont Beuvray, near Autun, France. Late Iron Age and Roman site. Includes

research centre, ongoing excavations, and museum with education programmes.
www.bibracte.fr.

THE AUSTRALIAN MUSEUM. Sydney, Australia. Major Aboriginal collections. Undertakes partnership programmes with Indigenous communities.
www.austmus.gov.au.

BATTLE ABBEY, SUSSEX. Site of Battle of Hastings. Includes museum and audio guide to site.
http://www.english-heritage.org.uk/battleabbey/.

Bodies, the Exhibition. Touring exhibition. Similar to Body Worlds (below), it uses "plastinated" and dissected human remains to explain anatomy.
http://www.bodiestheexhibition.com/.

Body Worlds . Touring exhibition. Gunther von Hagens' much publicised and much written about travelling exhibition of "plastinated" human remains.
www.bodyworlds.com.

BOTSWANA NATIONAL MUSEUM. Gaborone, Botswana. National museum includes archaeology collections.
www.botswana-museum.gov.bw.

BRISTOL CITY MUSEUM AND ART GALLERY. Bristol. Local authority museum with permanent displays on local archaeology and Egyptology. Currently undergoing refurbishment.
www.bristol-city.gov.uk.

THE BRITISH MUSEUM. London. National museum. World collections of archaeology including European prehistory, Roman Britain, Central America, Africa, Far East, medieval and renaissance Europe, Roman Empire, classical Greece, Mesopotamia, and Egypt.
www.thebritishmuseum.ac.uk.

Archaeology in Britain since 1945: New Views of the Past (1986). Temporary exhibition highlighting postwar archaeological discoveries in Britain including Lindow Man.

Enlightenment: Discovering The World in the 18th Century. Permanent gallery which, opened in 2003, that explores development of archaeology, science, and collecting.
www.thebritishmuseum.ac.uk/enlightenment,

African Galleries. Permanent gallery opened in 2001 displaying the Museum's African collections for the first time within the main Museum building.
www.thebritishmuseum.ac.uk/africangalleries,

Living and Dying. Gallery funded by the Wellcome Trust using ethnographic, archaeological, and modern art installations.
www.thebritishmuseum.ac.uk/livinganddying.

Gladiators and Caesars: The Power of Spectacle in Ancient Rome (2000). Temporary touring exhibition.

Mummy, the Inside Story (2005). Temporary exhibition that used a 3-D film to illustrate the nonintrusive study of a British Museum Egyptian mummy.

Buried Treasure (2004). Temporary exhibition linked to Portable Antiquities Scheme and Treasure Act that then travelled in a different form to other UK locations.
www.thebritishmuseum.ac.uk/buriedtreasure.

Sudan (2004). Major temporary exhibition with loaned material from Sudan.
www.thebritishmuseum.ac.uk/sudan.

Persia (2005). Major temporary exhibition with loaned material from Tehran.
www.thebritishmuseum.ac.uk/persia.

BIGNOR ROMAN VILLA. Bignor, Sussex. Remains of Roman villa including accompanying museum.
www.romansinsussex.co.uk/sussex/bignor.

THE BURKE MUSEUM OF NATURAL HISTORY AND CULTURE. University of Washington, Seattle, USA. Holds collections of north western

U.S. archaeology including the remains of "Kennewick Man."
www.washington.edu/burkemuseum.

THE BURRELL COLLECTION. Glasgow. Previous private collection of art
and archaeology, now part of Glasgow Museums.
www.glasgowmuseums.com.

THE BUTRINT MUSEUM. Butrint, Albania. Regional museum recently
redisplayed after a history of suffering under different political
regimes. Includes displays of Greek, Roman and medieval finds.
www.butrintfound.dial.pipex.com.

CANADIAN MUSEUM OF CIVILIZATION. Quebec, Canada. Major new
museum with displays on First Nation peoples.
www.civilization.ca/visit/cmcvisite.aspx.

CANTERBURY ROMAN MUSEUM. Canterbury, Kent. Tells the story of
Roman Canterbury on the site of actual excavations in town a
centre basement. Includes in situ Roman floors.
www.canterbury.gov.uk.

CAPITAL MUSEUM. Beijing, China. Grand new museum, opened in
2005, telling the story of the city's history.
www.capitalmuseum.org.cn/en.

CEREN SITE AND MUSEUM. El Salvador. Open air museum showing
aspects of every day life in the Maya world prior to the Spanish
arrival.
www.meierweb.us/ceren.

CHATHAM ISLANDS MUSEUM. Waitangi, New Zealand. Small museum
featuring the Morirori, Maori, and European history of the Chatham
Islands.
www.nzmuseums.co.nz.

CHECHEN ITZA. MEXICO. Mayan temple ruins.

THE CLEVELAND MUSEUM OF ART. Cleveland, USA. Fine-art museum
includes large classical and other archaeological collections. Currently being renovated with completion planned for 2010.
www.clemusart.com.

COLCHESTER MUSEUM. Colchester. Regional museum with archaeology displays from prehistory to the seventeenth century but
concentrating on Roman. Built within a medieval castle.
www.colchestermuseums.org.uk.

COLONIAL WILLIAMSBURG. Williamsburg, Virginia, USA. "Living history" reconstructed eighteenth-century capital of Virginia.
www.history.org.

THE COLLECTION. Lincoln. New museum with archaeology galleries
on Lincolnshire's prehistory and history.
www.lincolnshire.gov.uk/ccm/.

CONSERVATION CENTRE. National Museums Liverpool, Liverpool.
Museum service conservation facility that includes exhibition,
study, and learning centre.
www.liverpoolmuseums.org.uk/conservation.

COPAN SITE AND MUSEUM. Honduras. Major Maya complex. On-site
and open-air museum.
http://www.copanhonduras.org/ruins.htm.

CORINIUM MUSEUM. Cirencester, Gloucestershire. Regional museum
with archaeology collections from prehistory to the seventeenth
century but concentrating on Roman.
www.cotswold.gov.uk.

CROCODILE MUSEUM. Kom Ombo, Egypt. One of a series of planned
new museums.

CROW CANYON ARCHAEOLOGICAL CENTER. Cortez, Colorado, USA.
Archaeology centre for study of Pueblo Indians.
www.crowcanyon.org/.

DENNIS SEVERS HOUSE. Spitalfields, London. "Reconstruction" of a
period house interior by the late artist Dennis Severs.
Dennissevershouse.co.uk.

THE DIG. York. See The Archaeological Resource Centre entry.

DORSET COUNTY MUSEUM. Dorchester, Dorset. Regional museum
with archaeology collections from prehistory to the Middle Ages;

includes material from Maiden Castle hill fort.
www.dorsetcountymuseum.org

THE DOVER MUSEUM, Dover, Kent. Regional museum with archaeology displays from prehistory to Middle Ages. Includes Dover
Bronze Age Boat gallery.
www.dovermuseum.co.uk.

DROTTEN ARCHAEOLOGICAL MUSEUM. Lund, Sweden. City-centre
museum built around (and displaying) medieval excavations
including the foundations of a church.
www.kulturen.com/eng.

EGYPTIAN MUSEUM. Cairo, Egypt. Established by the Egyptian Government in 1835, this is the major world holder of Ancient Egyptian
artifacts, including the objects from the tomb of Tutankhamen.
The museum is due to be renovated during the building of the
new Grand Museum of Egypt.
www.egyptianmuseum.gov.eg.

THE EGYPTIAN MUSEUM. Turin. Important collection of Egyptian antiquities includes innovative new design and display techniques.
http://www.museoegizio.it.

ETRUSCAN GUARNACCI MUSEUM. Volterra, Italy. Traditional museum
of local Etruscan antiquities. One of the earliest public museums
in Europe (1761).
www.comune.volterra.pi.it/english/museiit/metru.html.

THE FIELD MUSEUM. Chicago, USA. Major museum of natural history,
archaeology, anthropology, and world cultures.
www.fieldmuseum.org.

FISHBOURNE ROMAN PALACE. Chichester, Sussex. Roman palace includes accompanying museum.
www.sussexpast.co.uk.

FITZWILLIAM MUSEUM. Cambridge. Part of Cambridge University, it is
one of the world's oldest public museums. Includes collections of
classic archaeology and ceramics.
www.fitzmuseum.cam.ac.uk.

Flag Fen Bronze Age Centre. Peterborough. Site of excavation that continues during summer months. Also includes a conservation facility for wet wood, a museum of finds, and reconstructions of round house in park setting.
www.flagfen.com.

Fornsal Museum. Gotland, Sweden. Regional museum including Viking and medieval collections. Display of osteoarchaeology.
www.lansmuseetgotland.se.

Geneva Cathedral. Switzerland. Archaeological site preserved, with interpretation, located below a medieval cathedral floor.

Genocide Memorial Centre. Kigali, Rwanda. The centre is built on a site where 250,000 people are buried. The site acts as a memorial to the Rwandan genocide and other genocides.
www.kigalimemorialcentre.org.

The Getty Center and Getty Villa. California, USA. Education and research centre as well as museums of classic antiquities based on the personal collections and wealth of the late John Paul Getty.
www.getty.edu.

Glenbow Museum. Calgary, Canada. Major collection of Western Canadian artefacts, and of world cultures.
www.glenbow.org/.

The Great Barn Exhibition. Avebury, Wiltshire. Interactive exhibition about history of Avebury site within a historic timber barn. The site is within Avebury village and close to the Alexander Keiller Museum.
www.nationaltrust.org.uk.

The Grand Museum of Egypt. Cairo, Egypt. Currently under construction. It will hold national collections of Pharonic antiquities, including the finds from the tomb of Tutankhamen.

Guidford Museum. Guildford, Surrey. District museum with archaeology galleries and collections.
www.guildford.gov.uk/GuildfordWeb/Leisure/Guildford+Museum/.

HASLEMERE EDUCATIONAL MUSEUM. Haslemere, Surrey. Includes collections and displays of world archaeology.
www.haslemeremuseum.co.uk.

THE STATE HERMITAGE MUSEUM. St Petersburg, Russia. One of the great world museums, includes major classical and Russian archaeological collections.
www.hermitagemuseum.org.

HISTORISKA MUSEET. The Museum of National Antiquities, Stockholm, Sweden. Part of museum complex, it includes Viking displays and treasury of antiquities.
www.historiska.se.

> *The Maya Game (2006–2008).* Temporary exhibition using Mayan antiquities to explore the nature of history and historical evidence.
> *www.historiska.se/exhibitions/2006/maya/.*

HUBEI PROVINCE MUSEUM. Wuhan, China. The Chime-Bells museum holding objects excavated from nearby tombs including 2,400 bells. Museum includes daily demonstrations of ancient music.
http://grid.hust.edu.cn/npc04/about_wuhan/museum.htm.

THE HUHAGAM HERITAGE CENTRE. Chandler, Arizona, USA. Archaeological and community centre for the Gila River Indian Community. It opened in 2004 in a specially designed building.
www.griccrmp.com/Huhugam.htm.

IMHOTEP MUSEUM. Saqqara, Egypt. New museum opened in 2006.

INDIAN MUSEUM. Calcutta, India. Ex-Colonial museum holding Indian antiquities.
http://userpages.umbc.edu/~achatt1/Calcutta/indmus.html.

JAMESTOWN SETTLEMENT. Williamsburg, Virginia, USA. Museum, visitor centre, and "living history" reconstructions centred around the 1607 founding of Jamestown as the first English settlement in America.
www.historyisfun.org.

JEWRY WALL MUSEUM. Leicester. Museum purposely built on the site of Roman remains. Covers the archaeology of Leicester from

prehistory through the Middle Ages.
www.leicestermuseums.ac.uk.

JOHN SOANE MUSEUM. London. Collection of antiquities displayed in their original eighteenth-century setting and format.
www.soane.org.

JORVIK VIKING CENTRE. York. "Dark ride" experience and museum display of Viking York based on Coppergate archaeological excavations.
www.vikingjorvik.com.

KILMARTIN HOUSE. Argyll, Scotland. Small independent museum set in a prehistoric landscape.
www.kilmartin.org.

KULTUREN I LUND. Lund, Sweden. Regional museum with archaeological displays of medieval remains is part of larger partly open-air complex.
www.kulturen.com/eng/.

LATÉNIUM ARCHAEOLOGY PARK AND MUSEUM. Neuchâtel, Switzerland. New, purposely built museum celebrating the La Tene archaeological site, and its cultural significance.
www.latenium.ch.

LE MUSÉE DE LA CIVILISATION GALLO-ROMAINE. Lyon, France. Museum of Roman antiquities.
www.lyon.fr/vdl/sections/fr/culture/musee_civilisation_gallo_romaine_1.

THE LONDON DUNGEON. London. Horror-based visitor experience on London history.
www.Thedungeons.com.

LOUVRE. Paris, France. World-famous collection of classical and Egyptian antiquities. Also includes preserved remains of a medieval castle.
www.louvre.fr.

MADAME TUSSAUDS. London. Visitor experience featuring wax-work figures.
www.madame-tussauds.co.uk.

MARY ROSE Museum. Portsmouth, Hampshire. The remains of the Tudor warship and museum of objects.
www.maryrose.org.

Metropolitan Museum of Art. New York. USA. Internationally important collections of classical antiquities.
www.metmuseum.org.

Musée des Antiquités Nationales de Saint Germain en Laye. Paris, France. National museum of French antiquities covering Palaeolithic through to the Middle Ages.
www.musee-antiquitesnationales.fr.

Musée du quai Branley. Paris, France. New national museum of "tribal art."
www.quaibranly.fr/.

Musée de la Préhistoire. Carnac, France. Small regional museum with important Neolithic and early Bronze Age collections from Carnac area.
www.museedecarnac.com.

Musée de Tautavel, European Center of Prehistory. Tautavel, France. Museum developed on site of palaeolithic cave excavations. Includes finds, dioramas, and reconstructions.
www.tautavel.com/tau-5100.php.

Musée National de Préshistoire. Les Eyzies De Tayac, France. National museum of prehistory, concentrating on upper palaeolithic.
http://www.musee-prehistoire-eyzies.fr/.

Museum of Anthropology at the University of British Columbia. Vancouver, Canada. Major university museum housing collections of First Nations material.
www.moa.ubc.ca/.

Museum of Archaeology and Anthropology. Cambridge, UK. University museum contains collections of British and foreign archaeology.
Museum-server.archanth.cam.ac.uk.

MUSEUM OF FINE ARTS. BOSTON, USA. Major fine- and decorative-arts museum including large collections of classical antiquities.
www.mfa.org

MUSEUM OF HIGH ALTITUDE ARCHAEOLOGY. Salta Province, Argentina. Museum created to house and display three Inca child mummies and their associated artefacts.
www.maam.org.ar.

MUSEUM OF THE IRON AGE. Andover, Hampshire. Local authority museum displaying finds from the nearby Iron Age Hillfort of Danebury.
www.hants.gov.uk/museum/ironagem.

MUSEUM OF ISLAMIC ART. Doha, Qatar. New museum on a huge scale holding art and archaeology from across the Islamic world from all periods. To be completed in 2007.

MUSEUM OF LONDON. London. National and regional museum. Archaeology collections from prehistory to the Middle Ages. Also includes the London Archaeological Archive and Research Centre (LAARC).
www.museumoflondon.org.uk.

London Bodies (1998). Temporary exhibition that used excavated skeletons to illustrate how Londoners have changed physically through time.

High Street Londinium (2000). Temporary exhibition that reconstructed part of first-century Roman London as excavated at 1 Poultry.

The Dig (2000). Temporary exhibition and activity for families. Included a reconstruction of an excavation for children to undertake and learn about archaeological techniques.

Capital Gains! Archaeology in London 1970–86 (1986). Exhibition that summarised archaeological discoveries in Greater London.

London before London (2002–). Permanent gallery of the Greater London area in prehistory.

Medieval London gallery (2005–). Permanent gallery tracing London history from 410 to 1558.

People before London (1994–2000). Previous prehistoric gallery. This exhibit used several innovative interpretation techniques.

The Museum of the Ancient Near East (Pergamon Museum). Berlin. Museum of classical antiquities as part of Berlin museum complex on Museum Island. Includes internationally important collection of Middle Eastern antiquities.
www.smb.spk-berlin.de.

Museum of the Maryland Historical Society. Baltimore, Maryland, USA. Hosted the influential temporary exhibition *Mining the Museum*.
www.mdhs.org.

Museum of Prehistory. Zug, Switzerland. Regional museum. Features life-size dioramas and a strong educational programme.
http://www.museenzug.ch.

The Museum of World Culture. Gothenburg, Sweden. New museum that attempts to use ethnographic and archaeological collections from around the world, in a series of changing temporary exhibitions, to address current debates.
www.varldskulturmuseet.se.

National Army Museum. London, England. National museum tells the story of the British army.
www.national-army-museum.ac.uk.

Finding the Fallen (2005–2006). Exhibition about archaeological excavations to identify missing World War I soldiers in France and Belgium.

National Museum of Afghanistan. Kabul. Museum seriously damaged during recent wars.
www.afghan-web.com/kabul-museum.

National Museum of the American Indian. Washington, DC, USA. New (2004). Smithsonian Institution museum dedicated to American Indian culture.
www.nmai.si.edu.

National Museum of Australia. Canberra, Australia. Archaeology is included as part of thematic displays. A holding place for

Aboriginal sacred objects and human remains.
www.nma.gov.au.

THE NATIONAL MUSEUM OF DENMARK. Copenhagen, Denmark. Important displays of prehistoric and medieval objects including well preserved Bronze Age burials. Where the Three Age System was developed and first used in the nineteenth century.
www.natmus.dk.

THE NATIONAL MUSEUM OF GREENLAND. Nuuk, Greenland. Museum includes archaeological displays and collections. These include a fifteenth-century group of human remains preserved by freezing conditions.
www.natmus.gl.

NATIONAL MUSEUM OF IRAQ. Baghdad. Holder of important ancient Mesopotamian antiquities. Looted during 2003 U.S. invasion.
www.baghdadmuseum.org/wmcd_index.htm.

NATIONAL MUSEUMS OF KENYA. Nairobi. Several museums include prehistory galleries in Nairobi.
www.museums.or.ke.

NATIONAL MUSEUM OF LEBANON. Beirut. Contains important regional collections. Seriously damaged during the Civil War and now largely restored.
www.lebanon.com/where/lebanonguide/nationalmuseum.htm.

NATIONAL MUSEUM OF NATURAL HISTORY. Washington, DC, USA. Smithsonian Institution museum dedicated to natural history including human evolution and ethnographic collections.
www.mnh.si.edu.

NATIONAL MUSEUM OF RWANDA. Butare, Rwanda. Historic, ethnographic, and archaeological collections.
www.museum.gov.rw.

THE NATIONAL MUSEUM OF SCOTLAND AND THE ROYAL MUSEUM. Edinburgh. National museum with archaeology collections from prehistory to the Middle Ages. Includes the *Early Peoples* gallery. The Royal Museum includes Egyptian and ethnography collections.
www.nms.ac.uk.

Symbols of Power at the Time of Stonehenge (1985). At the National Museum of Antiquities, Edinburgh (previous incarnation of the NMS). Highly influential temporary exhibition that brought together prehistoric objects and argued their symbolic importance in expressing power.

Etruscans *(2004)*. Major loan exhibition from Italy.

National Museum of Tanzania. Dar-es-Salaam, Tanzania. Includes several different sites. The Museum and House of Culture includes displays on human evolution.
www.museum.or.tz

The Natural History Museum. London. National museum includes displays on human evolution.
www.nhm.ac.uk.

Muséum National d'Historie Naturelle. Paris, France. Recently refurbished with beautifully designed galleries.
www.mnhm.fr/.

Neanderthal Museum. Germany. Site museum on location of a hominid find.
www.neanderthal.de.

New Walk Museum. Leicester. City museum includes innovative display of ancient Egyptian material.
www.leicestermuseums.ac.uk/museums/newwalk.

New York Unearthed. South Street Seaport Museum, New York, USA. Archaeological material from the City used for educational purposes. Limited opening and access.
www.southstseaport.org/places/nyunearthed.

Nicholas P. Goulandris Foundation Museum of Cycladic [and Ancient Greek] Art. Greece. Private collection of Greek antiquities.

Norwich Castle Museum. Norwich, Norfolk. Local authority museum in medieval castle keep. Regional archaeology displays.
www.museums.norfolk.gov.uk.

OLD STURBRIDGE VILLAGE. Massachusetts, USA. Living museum depicting early nineteenth-century rural life.
www.osv.org.

OSAKE HISTORY MUSEUM. Osaka, Japan. New museum in tower block with archaeological remains preserved in basement, and excavation replica activity centre.
http://www.mus-his.city.osaka.jp/english_iso-8859-1/index.html.

PALAZZO GRASSI. Venice. Held the influential exhibition *Celts, the Origins of Europe* in 1991.
www.palazzograssi.it.

PALENQUE MUSEUM. Mexico. Innovative regional state museum.
www.bluffton.edu/~sullivanm/mexico/palenquemuseo/museo.html.

PARC ASTERIX. Paris, France. Children's theme park based around the cartoon character.
www.parcasterix.com.

PARC DE PRÉHISTOIRE DE BRETAGNE. Vannes, France. Open-air park containing life-size dioramas of prehistoric life, as well as dinosaurs.
www.prehistoire.com.

PAULOS AND ALEXANDRA CANELLOPOLOS MUSEUM. Greece. Privately owned collection of Greek antiquities.

PEABODY MUSEUM OF ARCHAEOLOGY AND ETHNOLOGY. Harvard University, Cambridge, Massachusetts, USA. University museum with major collections from North America, Meso-America, Europe and Eurasia.
www.peabody.harvard.edu.

PERTH MUSEUM AND ART GALLERY. Perth, Scotland. Local authority museum with wide-ranging collections, which include local archaeology, ethnography, and Egyptology.
www.perthshire.com/residents/Arts+and+Culture/Museums/Museums.htm.

PETRIE MUSEUM OF EGYPTIAN ARCHAEOLOGY. London. Part of University College London, this museum houses Egyptian collections gathered by Flinders Petrie and his patron Amelia Edwards.

Currently awaiting redisplay, the Museum is noted for its innovative outreach and collaborative work.
www.petrie.ucl.ac.uk.

Ancient Egypt: Digging For Dreams (2000). Temporary exhibition created in partnership between The Petrie Museum, Croydon Museum and Heritage Centre, and Glasgow Cultural and Leisure Services. Explores modern fascination with ancient Egypt.

PITT RIVERS MUSEUM, Oxford. Ethnographic collection of the nineteenth-century archaeologist and collector still displayed to his original thematic groupings.
www.prm.ox.ac.uk.

PLYMOUTH PLANTATION. Massachusetts, USA. Living history reconstruction of a seventeenth-century settlement that has an associated museum.
www.plimoth.org.

POMPEII, Italy. Roman town preserved by eruption of volcano in the first century A.D. Includes on-site museum.

POMPEJANUM. Bavaria, Germany. Museum building is a nineteenth-century copy of the so-called Castor and Pollux house in Pompeii. Houses some of the state collections of Roman antiquities. Fully restored and reopened as a museum in 1994.
http://www.schloesser.bayern.de/deutsch/schloss/objekte/as_pom.htm.

POTTERIES MUSEUM. Stoke-on-Trent. Local authority museum with important collections and galleries recording the history of the town's internationally important ceramics industry, as well as its earlier history.
www.stoke.gov.uk/museums.

Collaging History (2005). Temporary exhibition by modern artist Neil Brownsword based on the archaeology of Stoke's ceramics industry.

PREHISTO PARC. Tursac, France. Open-air park containing life-size dioramas of prehistoric life.
www.prehistoparc.fr/.

QIANLING MUSEUM AND SITE. Qianxian County, China. Museum on site of Royal mausoloea excavations.
www.chinamuseums.com/qianlingm.htm.

MUSEUM OF QIN TERRA-COTTA WARRIORS AND HORSES. Lintong County, Shaanxi Province, China. Excavation site of tomb of Emperor Qin Shi Huang and the (so far) 7,000 terracotta life-size figures buried with him.
www.bmy.com.cn.

ROSKILDE VIKING SHIP MUSEUM. Roskilde, Denmark. Museum purpose built to take a group of excavated tenth-century Viking ships. Includes shipyard that makes modern replicas and conserves new finds.
www.vikingeskibsmuseet.dk.

ROSKILDE MUSEUM. Roskilde, Denmark. A small, regional museum that worked with modern artists for the redisplay of its collections.
www.roskildemuseum.dk.

SAALBURG. Taunus Mountains. Germany. Reconstructed gate to Roman frontier built in 1890.
www.saalburgmuseum.de.

SAINSBURY CENTRE FOR VISUAL ARTS. Norwich. Gallery holding a private collection including many ethnographic pieces displayed as fine art.
www.scva.org.uk/.

SCHLOß GOTTORP. Schleswig, Northern Germany. Regional museum with archaeology collections.
www.schloss-gottorf.de.

SEGEDUNUM. Tyneside, England. Site of Roman fort, reconstructed bath house, and museum.
www.twmuseums.org.uk/segedunum.

SEOUL MUSEUM OF HISTORY. Seoul, South Korea. National museum with archaeology displays.
www.museum.seoul.kr.

SHENYANG MUSEUM. Shenyang City, China. Museum including open-air full-size reconstructions of buildings on site of Neolithic excavations.
www.chinamuseums.com/shenyang.htm.

SUTTON HOO. Woodbridge, Suffolk. Site of Saxon royal burial ground and associated visitor centre includes display and some artefacts.
www.nationaltrust.org.uk and *www.suttonhoo.org.*

SOUTH TYROL MUSEUM OF ARCHAEOLOGY. Balzano, Italy. Houses the body and the equipment of the "Ice Man."
www.archaeologiemuseum.it/fo1_ice_uk.html.

STADSMUSEUM. Gothenburg, Sweden. Includes displays of archaeological finds from the city and a beautifully designed Viking gallery.
www.stadsmuseum.goteborg.se.

SOUTH WILTSHIRE MUSEUM. Salisbury. Local authority museum with displays on Stonehenge and local archaeology. Also includes original models and archives from Pitt Rivers' excavations.
www.salisburymuseum.org.uk.

STREHLOW RESEARCH CENTRE. Alice Springs, Australia. Community and research centre of Aboriginal material in central Australia.
www.nt.gov.au/nreta/museums/strehlow/index.html.

EL TAJIN MUSEUM. Mexico. State museum with innovative new displays.

TEOTUHACAN. Mexico. Site of Aztec ruins with on-site museum.

TE PAPA TONGAREWA MUSEUM OF NEW ZEALAND. Wellington, New Zealand. National museum with important Maori collections and well-regarded approach to ethnic and cultural integration.
www.tepapa.govt.nz/TePapa/.

TIKAL MUSEUM. Guatemala. Site museum.
www.tikalpark.com.

TURPAN MUSEUM. China. Regional archaeology museum.

UNIVERSITY OF PENNSYLVANIA MUSEUM OF ARCHAEOLOGY AND AN-
THROPOLOGY. Philadelphia, USA. Leading U.S. university-based
museum. Collections of Classical and Native American archaeology.
www.museum.upenn.edu.

USAK MUSEUM. Northern Turkey. Home of the "Lydian Hoard" of
sixth-century B.C. antiquities.

VARUSSCHLACHT MUSEUM AND PARK KALKRIESE. Osnabrücker, Germany. Museum and park marking the site of German victory over
Roman legions.
www.kalkriese-varusschlacht.de.

VASAMUSEET. Stockholm, Sweden. Built to hold the early seventeenth-century warship Vasa that was lifted in 1961.
www.vasamuseet.se.

LA VENTA. Mexico. Site of ruins with on-site museum.

VICTORIA & ALBERT MUSEUM. London. National museum of decorative arts.
www.vam.ac.uk.

Gothic, Art for England 1400–1547 (2003). Major temporary exhibition.

VILLAHERMOSA. Mexico. Olmec site moved to allow for the continued
exploitation of the original site for oil.

WILTSHIRE HERITAGE MUSEUM. Devizes, Wiltshire. Small regional
museum with archaeology collections from prehistory to the Medieval period.
www.wiltshireheritage.org.uk.

Appendix
Working in Museum Archaeology

When I grow up, I don't think I would like to be an archaeologist at all.
Harbans Manku, school child quoted by Bonham (1997, p. 86)

Museum Archaeology as a Profession

In Britain, there is no museum archaeological profession. Numbers are too small and are jobs too diverse. The UK Society of Museum Archaeologists has about 250 members, some of these members are not working as museum archaeologists, and some museum archaeologists will not become members. It is probably unlikely that there are more than 300 people in the United Kingdom who could call themselves by this title. The jobs museum archaeologists are likely to hold range from curator of archaeology in a medium-sized museum service, curators of specific period areas in larger museums (such as curator of Roman collections), as more generic curators of human culture, or as curators of collections in smaller museums. Many of the museum staff with archaeological degrees find themselves working in other areas of museum work such as education, marketing, and collections care. In England, the recent Portable Antiquities Scheme has created forty-seven Finds Liaison Officers, most, but not all of which, are based in a museum.

Those who seek to be recognised professionally tend to end up as members of both the Institute of Field Archaeologists (IFA) and the Museums Association (MA). Both have formal membership grades and accreditation of different kinds, and membership in either or both is often referred to in job descriptions. Both of these professional organizations bring different advantages, and, between them, they do offer the professional support that a museum archaeologist needs. It is just unfortunate that two subscription fees are needed. Within the IFA, the Finds Group most closely aligns to the interests of museum staff, and many museum staff are members.

The group that supports museum archaeology most closely is the Society of Museum Archaeologists (SMA). This organisation was founded in 1984, and its relatively modest size and close-knit and active nature reflects the museum archaeological community in the United Kingdom. (A far smaller Society of Scottish Museum Archaeologists is currently in the process of remerging with the UK body.)

A Career Path?

Because it spans two disciplines, museum archaeology normally requires its protagonists to seek expertise from two sources. In Britain, most of those who end up as museum archaeologists have obtained a first degree in archaeology and then further qualifications in specific museum studies. The number of British universities that offer a first degree in archaeology increases all the time. There are a relatively large number of well-established archaeology departments with overlapping courses. Joint degrees are often possible with, in particular, classical history but also with other arts and science-based subjects. In North America, almost all archaeology is taught within anthropology departments (Calgary and Boston are unusual in having archaeology departments not linked to anthropology). As in the UK universities, some North American universities also offer archaeology linked to classical history departments.

As the number of universities that offer archaeology has increased so too have the number offering courses in museum studies. These courses have also expanded to include heritage and cultural studies and public archaeology. Further professional development is offered through National

Vocational Qualifications (NVQs) and by becoming an Associate or fellow of the Museum Associations (AMA and FMA).

In some other countries, such as France, career progression is more formalised and organised as part of the statesystem.

Curators

Nick Merriman (1990, p. 38) notes how some museums have moved away from old-fashioned discipline-based departments and divisions to create human history subject areas. Although this might be seen as a negative development in diminishing archaeological specialism, and indeed it is difficult not to see it primarily in terms of museum cut backs, Merriman notes that it does bring archaeology into a more relevant mainstream concern with people now. He suggests that museums could go even further and combine archaeology with biological sciences for landscape and environmental projects. In larger museums, traditional curator posts continue, and in the largest museums, particularly the nationals, the "curator scholar" still exists. However, these are often not directly linked to a museum career progression as they rely on academic expertise that will, at least partially, come from a university background.

In small museums, curators tend to do everything from caring for their collections to organising exhibitions and educational programmes. See Wood (1997) for a summary of the perepetetic tasks required of curators of small museums.

Archaeological Conservation

Archaeological conservators represent a subprofession in their own right with specific degree courses and professional membership organisations. In the United Kingdom, they are overseen by the United Kingdom Institute of Conservation (UKIC) that publishes guidance on practise and on issues such as ethics.

The discipline requires "a high degree of manual dexterity . . . an understanding of the processes and preoccupations of modern archaeology, a knowledge of material science and early technology, combined with an aesthetic sense" (Kronyn, 1990, p. 8).

Most conservators would expect to have a first degree in archaeology or a related subject and a second degree specifically in conservation or archaeological conservation. The number of universities that offer degrees in conservation remains small and these degree programmes are threatened because such degrees are expensive to teach and attract relatively few students. Most archaeology conservation courses tend to be in the United Kingdom, with University College in London and in Cardiff being the best known. There is only a short tradition of archaeological conservation training in the United States. This may well change with the new emphasis in the United States on historical, and particularly, maritime, archaeology.

Most museums of a medium size or above employ a team of conservators and archaeologists who find themselves working alongside painting conservators, furniture conservators, or others depending on the range of the museums collections. Large institutions, such as the British Museum, employ very large teams.

REFERENCES

The Abbey Museum of Art and Archaeology. (1989). *A pageant of the centuries.* Brisbane: The Abbey Museum of Art and Archaeology.

Addyman, P. (1990). Reconstruction as interpretation: The example of the Jorvik Viking Centre, York. In P. Gathercole and D. Lowenthal (Eds.), *The Politics of The Past.* London: Unwin, pp. 257–264.

Addyman, P. V., and Brodie, N. (2002). Metal detecting in Britain: Catastrophe or compromise. In N. Brodie and K. Walker Tubb (Eds.), *Illicit Antiquities.* London: Routledge, pp. 179–184.

Agnew, N., and Bridgland, J. (Eds.). (2006). *Of the Past, for the Future: Integrating Archaeology and Conservation.* Los Angeles: Getty Conservation Institute.

Aitchison, K. (2004). *Disaster Management Planning for Archaeological Archives,* IFA Paper No. 8. Reading: Institute of Field Archaeologists.

All-Party Parliamentary Archaeology Group. (APPAG). (2003). *The Current State of Archaeology in the United Kingdom, First Report of the All Party Parliamentary Archaeology Group.* London: APPAG.

Anderson, G. (Ed.). (2004). *Reinventing the Museum.* Walnut Creek: Alta-Mira Press.

Anderton, M., and Schofield, J. (2000). The queer archaeology of Green Gate: interpreting contested space at Greenham Common Airbase. *World Archaeology, 32*(2), 236–251.

Andrews, G., Barrett, J., and Lewis, J. S. C. (2000). Interpretation not record: The practice of archaeology, *Antiquity, 74,* 525–530.

Anglia Publishing. (1993). *London Museum Medieval Catalogue 1940.* Ipswich: Anglia Publishing.

Annable, F. K., and Simpson, D. D. A. (1964). *Guide Catalogue of the Neolithic and Bronze Age Collections in Devizes Museum*. Devizes: Wiltshire Archaeological and Natural History Society.

Appleby, G. A. (2005). Crossing the rubicon: Fact or fiction in Roman reenactment, *Public Archaeology*, 4, 257–265.

Arnold, K. (2006). *Cabinets for the Curious, Looking Back at Early English Museums*. Aldershot: Ashgate.

Ascherson, N. (2000). Notes and reviews, the National Museum of Scotland, *Public Archaeology*, 1(1), 82–84.

Ascherson, N. (2002). Archaeology and the British media. In P. J. Wise (Ed.), *Public Archaeology: Remains to be Seen, The Museum Archaeologist*, 27, 35–45.

Acherson, N. (2004). Archaeology in the British media. In N. Merriman (Ed.), *Public Archaeology*. London and New York: Routledge, pp. 145–158.

Ashton, N. M., Cook, J., and Lewis, S. G. (1992). *High Lodge Excavations by G. de G. Sieveking 1962–1968 and J. Cook 1988*. London: British Museum.

Barrett, D.(2001). Sites and monuments records — an underused archaeological resource? In P. J. Wise (Ed.) *Indulgence or Necessity? Research in Museum Archaeology, The Museum Archaeologist* 26, 44–47.

Barrett, J. C. (1994). *Fragments from antiquity*. Oxford: Blackwell.

BCRPM (2005). *Marbles reunited news*, No. 1, December 2005, British Committee for the Reunification of the Parthenon Marbles.

Beagrie, N. (1998). The Arts and Humanities Data Service: A multi-disciplinary resource for archaeologists. In G. Denford (Ed.), *Museums for the 21st Century, The Museum Archaeologist*, 24, 3–6.

Beard, M., and Henderson, J. (1999). Rule(d) Britannia: Displaying Roman Britain in the museum. In N. Merriman (Ed.), *Making early histories in museums*. Leicester: Leicester University Press, pp. 44–73.

Bender, B. (1997). Multivocalism in practise: Alternative views of Stonehenge. In G. T. Genford (Ed.) *Representing Archaeology in Museums, the Museum Archaeologist 22*, 55–58.

Bernick, L. (1998). Art and antiquities theft. *Transnational Organized Crime*, 4(2): 91–116.

Bevan, R. (2005). *The Destruction of memory*. London: Reaktion.

Black, G. (2006). *The engaging museum, developing museums for visitor involvement*. London and New York: Routledge.

Blakey, M. L. (1990). American nationality and ethnicity in the deepest past. In P. Gathercole and D. Lowenthal (Eds.), *The politics of the past*. London: Unwin, pp. 38–48.

Blancke, S., and Cjigkitoonuppa, J. P. Slow Turtle. (1994). Traditional American Indian education as a palliative to western education. In P. G. Stone, and B. L. Molynaeux (Eds.), *The presented past*. London: Routledge, pp. 438–452.

Boast, R. (1997). Virtual collections, in G. T. Genford ed. Representing archaeology in museums, the Museum Archaeologist volume 22, 94–100.

Bogdanos, M. (with Patrick, W.) (2005). *Thieves of Baghdad*. New York and London: Bloomsbury.

Bonham, M. (1997). Artefacts in school history. In G. T. Denford (Ed.), *Representing Archaeology in Museums, The Museum Archaeologist*, 22, 86–93.

Boylan, P. (2002). The concept of cultural protection in times of armed conflict: From the crusades to the new millennium. In N. Brodie and K. Walker Tubb (Eds.), *Illicit antiquities*. London: Routledge.

Brading, R. (2000). The final frontier. In P. J. Wise (Ed.), *Significant Others, The Museum Archaeologist*, 25, 11–12.

Breeze, D. (1993). Ancient monuments legislation. In J. Hunter and I. Ralston (Eds.), *Archaeological resource management in the UK*. Stroud: Alan Sutton, pp. 44–55.

References

British Archaeology. (2006). No synthesis of British prehistory is right. *British Archaeology*, (March–April), 7.

British Museum. (1982). *Selection and retention of environmental and artefactual material from excavations*. London: British Museum. (The Longworth report.)

Brodie, N., and Walker Tubb, K. (Eds.). (2002). *Illicit antiquities*. London: Routledge.

Brodie, N. J., Doole, J., and Watson, P. (2000). *Stealing history: The illicit trade in cultural property*. Cambridge, UK: McDonald Institute.

Bromwich, J. (1997). Displaying archaeology in Britain and France. In G. T. Denford, (Ed.), *Representing Archaeology in Museums, The Museum Archaeologist*, 22, 29–38.

Brown, D. (2000). Putting it away properly. In P. J. Wise (Ed.), *Significant Others, The Museum Archaeologist*, 25, 13–19.

Brown, D. (2005). Everybody's got to have standards – haven't they? *The Archaeologist*, 58(Autumn), 11.

Burden, L. (2006). Pot report *British Archaeology*, (May–June), 44–47.

Burdon, N. (2004). Hindu finds from the Thames. *London Archaeology*, 10(10), 276–280.

Burdon, N., Green, A., and Smith, C. (2000). Portable antiquities from the Thames foreshore. *London Archaeology*, 9(5), 123–127.

Capon, J. (2002). *Guide to museums in China*. Hong Kong: Orientations. Magazine Ltd.

Carroll, Q. (2005). Who wants to rebury old skeletons? *British Archaeology*, (May–June), 10–12.

Cartledge, P. (2005). Book review: *The Elgin Marbles* by Dorothy King. *The Independent, Arts and Books Review*, Friday, 13 January 2005, 22.

Cassman, V., and Odegaard, N. (2004). Human remains and the conservator's role. *Studies in Conservation*, 49(4), 2004, 271–282.

Cassman, V., Odegaard, N., and Powell, J. (2007) *Human Remains, Guide for Museums and Academic Institutions*. Lanham MD: Altimira.

Caygill, M. (1996). *The story of the British Museum*. London: British Museum Press.

Chambers (1999). *21st Century dictionary*. Edinburgh: Chambers.

Charles-Picard, G. (Ed.). (1972). *Larousse encyclopedia of archaeology*. London: Hamlyn.

Cherry, J., and Longworth, I. (1986). *Archaeology in Britain since 1945: New directions*. London: British Museum.

Childs, T. (1995). The crisis. *Federal Archaeology, Special Training Issue: The Curation Crisis*, 7(4), 11–15.

Church of England and English Heritage. (2005). *Guidance for best practice for treatment of human remains excavated from Christian burial grounds in England*, CofE/EH.

Clark, J. G. D. (1954). *Excavations at Star Carr*. Cambridge, UK: Cambridge University Press.

Clarke, D. (2000). Creating the museum of Scotland: A response to Neal Ascherson. *Public Archaeology*, 1(3), 220–221.

Clarke, D. V., Cowie, T. G., and Foxon, A. (1985). *Symbols of power at the time of Stonehenge*. Edinburgh: HMSO.

Clarke, D. L. (1971). *Analytical archaeology*. London: Methuen & Co. Ltd.

Clarke, D. L. (1970). *Beaker pottery of Great Britain and Ireland*. Cambridge, UK: Cambridge University Press.

Clark, K. (Ed.). (2006). *Capturing the public value of heritage, the proceedings of the London conference 25–26 January 2006*. Swindon: English Heritage.

Cleere, H. (1991). The law relating to ownership and archaeological collecting in England and Wales. In E. Southworth (Ed.), *What's Mine is Yours! – Museum Collecting Policies, The Museum Archaeologist*, 16, 30–34.

Cocroft, W., and Thomas, R. (2003). *The Cold War: Building for nuclear confrontation 1946–1989*. London: English Heritage.

Cookson, N. (2000). *Archaeological heritage law*. Chichester: Barry Rose Law Publishing Ltd.

Condron, F., Richards, J., Robinson, D., and Wise, A. (1999). *Strategies for digital data, findings and recommendations from digital data in archaeology: A survey of user needs*. York UK: Archaeological Data Service.

Corbishley, M., and Stone, P. G. (1994). The teaching of the past in formal school curricula in England. In P. G. Stone, and B. L. Molynaeux (Eds.), *The presented past*, London: Routledge, pp. 383–397.

Corfield, M. (1988). The reshaping of archaeological objects: Some ethical considerations. *Antiquity, 62*, 261–265.

Cotton, J. F. (1997). Illuminating the twilight zone? The new prehistory gallery at the Museum of London. In G. T. Denford, (Ed.), *Representing Archaeology in Museums, The Museum Archaeologist, 22*, 6–12.

Council of Europe. (1969/2001). *The European convention on the protection of the archaeological heritage*. Strasbourg: Council of Europe (Valetta Convention). Revision of the 1969 edition.

Council of Europe. (2005). *The draft framework convention of the council of Europe on the value of cultural heritage for society*. Strasbourg: Council of Europe.

Cox, M. (Ed.). (1998). *Grave concerns*. York UK: Council for British Archaeology.

Cronyn, J. M. (1990). *The elements of archaeological conservation*. London: Routledge.

Cunliffe, B. (1981). Introduction: the public face of archaeology. In J. D. Evans, B. Cunliffe, and C. Renfrew (Eds.), *Antiquity and man, essays in honour of Glyn Daniel*. London: Thames and Hudson.

Cunliffe, B. W. (1984). *Danebury: An Iron Age Hillfort in Hampshire, Volume 1, The excavation 1969–1978: The Site*, CBA Research Report 52a.

Current Archaeology. (2006). The archaeology of the Blitz. *Current Archaeology, 206*, 487–492.

Current World Archaeology. (2005). Crock art. *Current World Archaeology, 12*, 10.

Daniel, G. (1978). *150 Years of archaeology*. London: Duckworth.

Darvill, T., Saunders, A., and Startin, B. (1987). A question of national importance: Approaches to the evaluation of ancient monuments for the monuments protection programme in England. *Antiquity, 61*, 393–408.

Davies, H. (2002). Looting graves/buying and selling artefacts: Facing reality in the US. In N. Brodie and K. Walker Tubb (Eds.), *Illicit Antiquities*. London: Routledge, pp. 235–240.

Davies, M. (1986). Setting the scene. In A. J. White (Ed.), *Dust to Dust, Field Archaeology and Museums Conference Proceedings Vol. 2*, pp. 1–8.

Davies, M. E. (2005). *How students understand the past*. Walnut Creek: Altimira.

DEMOS HLF. (2004). *Challenge and change: HLF and Cultural Value, a Report to the Heritage lottery fund*. London: HLF.

Denford, G. T. (Ed.). (1997). *Representing Archaeology in Museums, The Museum Archaeologist, 22*.

Denford, G. T. (Ed.). (1998). *Museums for the 21st Century, The Museum Archaeologist, 24*.

Department for Culture, Media, and Sport. (DCMS). (2000). *Centres for social change: Museums, galleries and archives for all*. London: DCMS.

Department for Culture, Media, and Sport. (DCMS). (2002). *The Treasure Act 1996, Code of practice (revised)*. London: DCMS.

Department for Culture, Media, and Sport. (DCMS). (2003). *The report of the working group on human remains*. London: DCMS. (The Palmer report.)

Department for Culture, Media, and Sport. (DCMS). (2004). *The care of historic human remains, a consultation on the report of the Working Group on Human Remains*. London: DCMS.

Department for Culture, Media, and Sport. (DCMS). (2005a). *Understanding the future: Museums and 21st century life*. London: DCMS.

REFERENCES

Department for Culture, Media, and Sport. (DCMS). (2005b). *Guidance for the care of human remains in museums.* London: DCMS.

Department for Culture, Media, and Sport. (DCMS). (2005c) *Combating illegal trade: Due diligence guidelines for museums, libraries and archives on collecting and borrowing cultural material.* London: DCMS.

Department of Education and Skills (1990). *Final report of the history working group.* London: HMSO.

Department of the Environment. (DoE). (1975). *Principles of publication in field archaeology.* London: DoE. (The Frere report.)

Department of the Environment. (DoE). (1978). *The scientific treatment of material from rescue excavations.* London: DoE. (The Dimbleby report.)

Department of the Environment. (DoE). (1983). *Publication of archaeological excavations.* London: DoE. (The Cunliffe report.)

Department of the Environment. (DoE). (1990). *Planning and policy guidance note 16, archaeology and planning.* London: DoE (PPG16).

Department of Health (2005). *The Human Tissue Act 2004, New legislation on human organs and tissue.* London: Department of Health

Devine, H. (1994). Archaeology, prehistory, and the Native Learning Resources Project: Alberta, Canada. In P. G. Stone and B. L. Molynaeux (Eds.), *The presented past.* London: Routledge, pp. 478–494.

Devonshire, A., and Wood, B. (Eds.). (1996). *Woman in industry and technology: Current research and the museum experience.* London: Museum of London/WHAM.

Dion, M. (1999). *Archaeology.* London: Black Dog.

Dobinson, C., and Denison, S. (1995). *Metal detecting and archaeology in England.* London: CBA and EH.

Dome, S. (1997). Our greatest national treasure, for our homeland's sake you must live forever" — the destruction of Românîa. In G. T. Genford (Ed.) *Representing Archaeology in Museums, the Museum Archaeologist 22,* 39–46.

Durbin, G., Morris, S., and Wilkinson, S. (1990). *A teachers guide to learning from objects*. London: English Heritage.

English Heritage. (1991a). *Management of archaeological projects*. London: English Heritage (MAP2).

English Heritage. (1991b). *Exploring our past, strategies for the archaeology of England*. London: English Heritage.

English Heritage. (1997). *English Heritage archaeology division research agenda*. London: English Heritage (external draft consultation document).

English Heritage. (2000). *Power of place, the future of the historic environment*. London: English Heritage.

English Heritage. (2005). *Discovering the past, shaping the future: Research strategy 2005–2010*. London: English Heritage.

English Heritage. (2006a). *Management of Research Projects in the Historic Environment*. Swindon: English Heritage (MoRPHE).

English Heritage. (2006b). Heritage protection review. *Conservation Bulletin*, 52, (Summer).

Evans, J. D. (1981). Introduction: On the prehistory of archaeology. In J. D. Evans, B. Cunliffe, and C. Renfrew (Eds.), *Antiquity and man, essays in honour of Glyn Daniel*. London: Thames and Hudson, pp. 12–18.

Evans, J. D., Cunliffe, B. and Renfrew, C. (Eds.). (1981). *Antiquity and man, essays in honour of Glyn Daniel*. London: Thames and Hudson.

Evaristo, B. (2001). *The Emperor's babe*. New York: Viking.

Fagan, G. G. (2006). *Archaeological fantasies*. London and New York: Routledge.

Fahy, A. (Ed.). (1995). *Collections management*. London and New York: Routledge.

Faulkner, N. (2000). Sedgeford, exploring an early English village. *Current Archaeology*, 171, 122–129.

REFERENCES

Ferguson, L., and Murray, D. (1997). *Archaeological documentary archives, IFA Paper No. 1.* Edinburgh: RCAHMS.

Fergusson, P. (1990). *Roche Abbey.* London: English Heritage.

Fforde, C. (2004). *Collecting the dead, archaeology and the reburial issue.* London: Duckworth.

Fforde, C., Hubert, J., and Turnbull, P. (Eds.). (2002). *The dead and their possessions, repatriation in principle, policy, and practice,* London: Routledge.

Fine-Dare, K. I. (2002). *Grave injustice, the American Indian Repatriation movement and NAGPRA.* Lincoln: University of Nebraska Press.

Fisher, M. (2004). *Britain's best museums and galleries.* London: Penguin.

Flynn, T. (2006a). Possession order. *Museums Journal,* (April), 22–25.

Flynn, T. (2006b). Book review: *The Elgin Marbles* by Dorothy King, *Museums Journal.* (May), 52–53.

Foanaota, L. (1990). Archaeology and museums work in the Solomon Islands. In P. Gathercole and D. Lowenthal (Eds.), *The politics of the past,* London: Unwin, pp. 224–232.

Folsom, F., and Folsom, M. (1983). *American ancient treasures.* Albuquerque: University of New Mexico.

Fyfe, G., and Ross, M. (1996). Decoding the visitors gaze: rethinking museum visiting. In S. MacDonald and G. Fyfe (Eds.), *Theorizing museums: Representing identity and diversity in a changing world.* Oxford: Blackwell, pp. 130–154.

Galt-Smith, B. (unpublished). *Access and its dilemmas at the Strehlow Research Centre in Alice Springs* (unpublished conference paper).

Ganiaris, H. (2001). *London bodies*: An exhibition at the Museum of London. In E. Williams, (Ed.), *Human Remains, Conservation, Retrieval, and Analysis,* BAR International Series 934, pp. 267–274.

Gathercole, P. (1990). Introduction. In P. Gathercole and D. Lowenthal (Eds.), *The politics of The Past.* London: Unwin, PP. 257–264.

Gathercole, P., and Lowenthal, D. (Eds.). (1990). *The politics of the past.* London: Unwin.

Gerrard, C. (2003). *Medieval archaeology, understanding traditions and contemporary approaches.* London: Routledge.

Gilchrist, R. (1999). *Gender and material culture: The archaeology of religious women.* London and New York: Routledge.

Golding, W. (1955). *The inheritors.* London: Faber and Faber.

Goni, U. (2005). Frozen in time, protest over child mummies. *The Guardian,* Wednesday, 21 September 2005.

Goodnow, K. (2006). *Challenge and transformation: Museums in Cape Town and Sydney,* Paris: UNESCO.

Government Accounting Office. (1987). *Cultural resources – Problems protecting and preserving federal archaeological resources.* Washington, DC: United States Government Accounting Office.

Green, B. (1991). East Anglia, the treasure scramble. In E. Southworth (Ed.), *What's mine is yours! – Museum collecting policies. The Museum Archaeologist, 16,* 20–22.

Greenhalgh, P. (1989). Education, entertainment, and politics: Lessons from the great international exhibitions. In P. Vergo (Ed.), *The New Museology.* London: Reaktion.

Grey, A., Gardom, T., and Booth, C. (2006). *Saying it differently, a handbook for museums refreshing their displays.* London: London Museums Hub.

Gumbel, A. (2006). The glory of Getty (and the smell of scandal). *The Independent,* Friday, 27 January 2006, 28–29.

Hall, J., and Swain, H. (2000a). *High Street Londinium, reconstructing Roman London.* London: Museum of London.

Hall, J., and Swain, H. (2000b). Roman boxes for London's schools: An outreach service by the Museum of London. In P. M. McManus (Ed.), *Archaeological displays and the public.* London: Architype Publications Ltd., pp. 87–96.

REFERENCES

Hall, M. (2002). Archaeology in fiction: The past as popcorn?. In P. J. Wise (Ed.), *Public Archaeology: Remains to be Seen, The Museum Archaeologist*, 27, 29–34.

Hamilakis, Y. (2001). Antiquities underground. *Antiquity*, 75(287), 35–36.

Hamlin, A. (1997). Presenting historic monuments in a divided society: Northern Ireland. In G. T. Denford, (Ed.), *Representing archaeology in Museums, The Museum Archaeologist*, 22, 3–5.

Hancock, G. (1995). *Fingerprints of the Gods*. London: Heinemann.

Handler, R., and Gable, E. (1997). *The new history in an old museum: Creating the past at Colonial Williamsburg*. Durham, NC and London: Duke University Press.

Heywood, F. (2006). Crossing continents. *Museums Journal*, (June), 35–37.

Hinchcliffe, J., and Schadla-Hall, T. (1986). Excavation archives: The relationship of field archaeologists and museums. In A. J. White (Ed.), *Dust to Dust, Field Archaeology and Museums Conference Proceedings*, 2, 42–51.

Hinton, P. (1993). Archives and publication in the real world. In E. Southworth, (Ed.), *Picking up the Pieces–Adapting to Change in Museums and Archaeology, The Museum Archaeologist*, 18, 6–9.

Hinton, P., and Swain, H. (1999). Registered archaeological organisations 1999/2000. *Archaeologist*, 35, 13.

Historic Scotland (1997). *The treatment of human remains in archaeology, Historic Scotland Occasional Papers 5*. Edinburgh: Historic Scotland.

Hodder, I. (2001). *Towards reflexive archaeology: The example of Çatalhöyük*, McDonald institute for Archaeological Research/British Institute of Archaeology at Ankara, Monograph no. 28.

Hodder, I. (Ed.). (2002a). *Archaeological theory today*. Cambridge UK: Polity Press.

Hodder, I. (2002b). Introduction: A review of contemporary theoretical debates in archaeology. In I. Hodder (Ed.), *Archaeological theory Today*. Cambridge UK: Polity Press, pp. 1–13.

Holgate, R. (1993). Community archaeology and museums. In E. Southworth (Ed.) *Picking up the Pieces — Adapting to Change in Museum and Archaeology, The Museum Archaeologist 18*, 36–41.

Holtorf, C. (2000). Sculptures in captivity and monkeys on megaliths, observations in zoo archaeology. *Public Archaeology, 1*, 195–210.

Holtorf, C. (2005). *From Stonehenge to Las Vegas: Archaeology as popular culture*. Walnut Creek: AltaMira Press.

Hooper-Greenhill, E. (1994). *Museums and their visitors*. London: Routledge.

Hopkins, D. (2000). The role of the county archaeologist. In P. J. Wise (Ed.), *Significant Others, The Museum Archaeologist, 25*, 3–6.

Hunter, J., and Ralston, I. (Eds.). (1993). *Archaeological resource management in the UK*. Stroud: Alan Sutton.

Hurst Thomas, D. (2002). Roadside ruins, does America still need archaeology museums?. In B. J. Little (Ed.), *Public benefits of archaeology*. Gainesville: University Press of Florida, pp. 130–145.

Impey, O., and MacGregor, A. (Eds.). (1985). *The origins of museums*. Oxford: Clarendon Press.

Institute of Field Archaeologists. (IFA). (1999). *By-laws, standards and policy statements of the Institute of Field Archaeologists*, Reading: IFA.

International Council of Museums. (ICOM). (1986). *Code of Ethics for Museums*, Paris: International Council Of Museums. Revised several times.

ICOMOS. (1931). *The Athens Charter for the Restoration of Historic Monuments*. Paris: ICOMOS.

ICOMOS. (1964). *International Charter for the Conservation and Restoration of Monuments and Sites*. Paris: ICOMOS. (The Venice charter.)

ICOMOS. (1990). *Charter for the Protection and Management of the Archaeological Heritage*. Paris: ICOMOS.

ICOMOS. (1996). *Principles for the recording of monuments, groups of buildings and sites*. Paris: ICOMOS.

REFERENCES

ICOMOS. Australia (1999). *The Australian ICOMOS Charter for the Conservation of Places of Cultural Significance*. Burwood: Australian ICOMOS. (The Burra convention.)

James, S. (1999). Imagining the past: The politics and practicalities of reconstructions in the museum gallery. In N. Merriman (Ed.), *Making early histories in museums*. Leicester: Leicester University Press, pp. 117–135.

Jameson Jr., J. H. (2004). Public archaeology in the United States'. In N. Merriman (Ed.), *Public archaeology*. London and New York: Routledge, pp. 21–58.

Jardine, L. (1996). *Worldly goods*. London: Macmillan.

Jenkins, T. (2005). The censoring of our museums. *New Statesman*, 11 July 2005.

Jones, M. (Ed.). (1990). *Fake?: The art of deception*. London: The British Museum Press.

Jones, S., and Pay, S. (1990). The legacy of Eve. In P. Gathercole and D. Lowenthal (Eds.), *The politics of the past*. London: Unwin, 160–183.

Jordan, D. (2002). Public archaeology–a view from the national council for metal detecting. In P. J. Wise (Ed.), *Public Archaeology: Remains to be Seen, The Museum Archaeologist*, 27, 25–28.

Jordanova, L. (1989). Objects of knowledge: A historical perspective on museums. In P. Vergo (Ed.), *The new museology*. London: Reaktion, pp. 22–40.

Kadrow, K. (1990). The Archaeological Resource Centre. In E. Southworth (Ed.), *Ready for the new millennium? – Futures for Museum Archaeology, The Museum Archaeologist*, 17, 34–36.

Kersel, M. (in press). *Global strategies for protecting against the illicit trade in antiquities and the looting of archaeological sites*.

Kilmister, H. (2003). Visitor perceptions of ancient Egyptian human remains in three United Kingdom museums. *Papers from the Institute of Archaeology*, 14, 57–69.

King, D. (2005). *The Elgin Marbles*. London: Hutchinson.

Kinnes, I. (1992). *Non-megalithic long barrows and allied structures in the British Neolithic, British Museum Occasional Paper 52*. London: British Museum.

Kinnes, I. A., and Longworth, I. H. (1985). *Catalogue of the excavated prehistoric and Romano-British Material in the Greenwell Collection*. London: British Museum Press.

Kinnes, I. A., Longworth, I. M., McIntyre, S. P., Needham, S. P., and Oddy, W. A. (1988). Bush Barrow gold. *Antiquity, 62*, 24–39.

Kitchen, W., and Ronayne, M. (2001). The Ilisu Dam in South East Turkey: archaeology at risk. *Antiquity, 75*(287), 37–8.

Kiyaga-Mulindwa, D., and Segobye, A. K. (1994). Archaeology and education in Botswana. In P. G. Stone and B. L. Molyneax (Eds.), *The Presented Past*. London: Routledge, pp. 46–60.

Knell, S. (Ed.). (1994). *Care of collections*. London: Routledge.

Kruta, V., Frey, O., Raftery, B., and Sazbo, M. (Eds.). (1991). *The Celts*. London: Thames and Hudson.

Lange, A. G. (Ed.). (2004). *Reference Collections Foundations for Future Archaeology*. Amersfoort: ROB.

Lanting, J. N., and van der Waals, J. D. (1972). British beakers from the continent. *Helinium, 12*, 20–46.

Lapourtas, A. (1997). Arthur Evans and his representation of the Minoan civilization at Knossos. In G. T. Denford, (Ed.), *Representing Archaeology in Museums, The Museum Archaeologist, 22*, 71–82.

Legassick, M., and Rassool, C. (2000). *Skeletons in the Cupboard, South African Museums and the Trade in Human Remains 1907–1917*. South Africa: South African Museum, Capetown and McGregor Museum, Kimberley.

Lewis, G. (1992). Museums and their precursors: a brief world survey.In J. M. A. Thompson (Ed.), *Manual of Curatorship, A Guide to Museum Practice*, (2nd ed). Oxford: Museums Association, pp. 5–21.

337

Liddle, P. (2002). Community archaeology in Leicestershire. In P. J. Wise (Ed.), *Public Archaeology: Remains to be Seen, The Museum Archaeologist*, 27, 52–3.

Little, B. J. (Ed.). (2002a). *Public benefits of archaeology*. Gainesville: University Press of Florida.

Little B. J. (2002b). Archaeology as a shared vision. In B. J. Little (Ed.), *Public Benefits of Archaeology*. Gainesville: University Press of Florida, pp. 3–19.

London Museum (1940). *Medieval Catalogue*. London: London Museum.

Lohman, J. and Goodnow, K. (Eds.). (2006). *Human remains and Museum Practice*. Paris: UNESCO.

Longworth, C., and Wood, B. (Eds.). (2000). *Standards in Action, Working with Archaeology*, SMA/MDA.

Lord, B., Dexter Lord, G., and Nicks, J. (1989). *The Cost of Collecting. Collection management in UK Museums*. London: HMSO.

Lotz, C. (2005). Empire building. *Museums Journal*. (December), 30–31.

Lowenthal, D. (1990). Conclusions: Archaeologists and others. In P. Gathercole and D. Lowenthal (Eds.), *The politics of the past*. London: Unwin, pp. 302–314.

Lucy, S., and Herring, C. (1999). Viewing the Dark Ages: The portrayal of early Anglo-Saxon life and material culture in museums. In N. Merriman (Ed.), *Making Early Histories in Museums*. Leicester: Leicester University Press, pp. 74–94.

MacDonald, S. (2000). University museums and the public: The case of the Petrie museum. In P. McManus (Ed.), *Archaeology Displays and the Public*. London: Archetype, pp. 67–86.

MacDonald, S. (2002). Owning ancient Egypt. In P. J. Wise (Ed.), *Public Archaeology: Remains to be Seen, The Museum Archaeologist*, 27, 9–16.

MacDonald, S., and Shaw, C. (2004). 'Uncovering Ancient Egypt: The Petrie Museum and its public. In N. Merriman (Ed.), *Public Archaeology*. London: Routledge.

MacGregor, N., and Williams, J. (2005). The encyclopedic museum, enlightenment ideals, contemporary realities. *Public Archaeology*, 4, 57–59.

MacKenzie, R. (1990). The development of museums in Botswana: Dilemmas and tensions in a front-line state. In P. Gathercole and D. Lowenthal (Eds.), *The politics of the past*. London: Unwin, 203–213.

Malaro, M. C. (1998). *A legal primer on managing museum collections*, Washington, DC and London: Smithsonian Institution Press.

Malbat, R. (1995). Artists as curators. *Museums Journal*, (May), 25–26.

Malone, C. (1989). *Avebury*. London: English Heritage/Batsford.

Martin, D. (2002). Great excavations. *Museums Practice*, 19(7), 1; 21–32.

Masson, P., and Guillot, H. (1994). Archaeofiction with upper primary-school children 1988–1989. In P. G. Stone, and B. L. Molynaeux (Eds.), *The presented past*. London: Routledge, pp. 375–382.

May, S. (1998). *The archaeology of human bones*. London: Routledge.

Mayne, A., and Murray, T. (Eds.). (2001). *The archaeology of urban landscapes, explorations in slumland*. Cambridge, UK: Cambridge University Press.

Mazel, A., and Ritchie, G. (1994). Museums and their messages: The display of the pre- and early colonial past in the museums of South Africa, Botswana and Zimbabwe. In P. G. Stone, and B. L. Molynaeux (Eds.), *The presented past*. London: Routledge, pp. 225–236.

McAdam, E., Nixon, T., Swain, H., and Tomber, R. (Eds.). (2002). *A research framework for London archaeology 2002*. London: Museum of London.

McAtackney, L. (2005). Long Kesh/Maze, an archaeological opportunity. *British Archaeology*, (September–October), 11–14.

McCann, W. J. (1990). Volk und Germanentum: the presentation of the past in Nazi Germany. In P. Gathercole and D. Lowenthal (Eds.), *The politics of the past*. London: Unwin, 74–88.

References

McFarlane, S. (2005). *Ebay.co.uk: A New Era in illicit Trade? Do Public Attitudes Match Archaeological Concerns*, Unpublished MA dissertation from University College London.

McGrail, S. (1991). Finds from maritime sites in Britain. In E. Southworth (Ed.), *What's Mine is Yours – Museum Collecting Policies, The Museum Archaeologist*, 16, 23–29.

McManamon, F. P. (1994). Presenting archaeology to the public in the USA. In P. G. Stone and B. L. Molyneax (Eds.), *The presented past*, London: Routledge, pp. 61–81.

McManus, P. (Ed.). (2000). *Archaeology Displays and the Public*. London: Archetype.

Mepham, L. (2000). Archive deposition: A unit perspective. In P. J. Wise (Ed.), *Significant Others, The Museum Archaeologist*, 25, 7–10.

Merriman, N. (1989). Museum visiting as a cultural phenomenon. In P. Vergo (Ed.), *The new museology*. London: Reaktion, pp. 149–171.

Merriman, N. (1990). Dealing with present issues in the long term: The Peopling of London Project. In E. Southworth (Ed.), *Ready for the New Millennium?–Futures for Museum Archaeology, The Museum Archaeologist*, 17, 4–12.

Merriman, N. (1991). *Beyond the glass case, the heritage and the public in Britain*. Leicester: Leicester University Press.

Merriman, N. (Ed.). (1993a). *The Peopling of London: 1500 of Settlement From Overseas*. London: Museum of London.

Merriman, N. (1993b). 'The use of collections: the need for a positive approach'. In E. Southworth, (Ed.), *Picking up the Pieces–Adapting to Change in Museums and Archaeology, The Museum Archaeologist*, 18, 10–17.

Merriman, N. (Ed.). (1999). *Making Early Histories In Museums*, Leicester: Leicester University Press.

Merriman, N., and Swain, H. (1999). Archaeological archives: Serving the public interest? *European Journal of Archaeology*, 2(2), 249–267.

Merriman, N. (2000). The public interest in archaeology. In P. Wise (Ed.), *Significant Others, The Museum Archaeologist*, 25, 20–25.

Merriman, N. (Ed.). (2004). *Public archaeology*. London: Routledge.

Mikolajczyk, A. (1990). Didactic presentations of the past: Some retrospective considerations in relation to the archaeological and ethnographic museum, Lodz, Poland. In P. Gathercole and D. Lowenthal (Eds.), *The politics of the past*. London: Unwin, pp. 247–256.

Millett, M. with James, S (1983). Excavations at Cowdery's Down, Basingstoke, Hampshire, 1978–81. *Archaeological Journal*, 140, 151–279.

Milne, G. (2001). *Excavations at Medieval Cripplegate, London*. London: English Heritage.

Momin, K. N., and Pratap, A. (1994). Indian museums and the public. In P. G. Stone, and B. L. Molynaeux (Eds.), *The presented past*. London: Routledge, pp. 290–298.

Monaghan, J., and Just, P. (2000). *Social and cultural anthropology, A very short introduction*. Oxford: Oxford University Press.

Morris, J. (2004a). The root of the problem. *Museums Journal*, (September), 10–11.

Morris, J. (2004b). Class divides visitors. *Museums Journal*, (November), 15.

Morris, J. (2006). British Museum steps into a new era of returning remains. *Museums Journal*, (May), 11.

Morris, R. (1993). Archaeology – A causality of the market? *British Archaeology News*, 8, 1–2.

Moser, S. (1998). *Ancestral images, the iconography of human origins*. Thrupp: Sutton.

Moser, S. (1999). The dilemma of didactic displays: Habitat dioramas, life-groups and reconstructions of the past. In N. Merriman (Ed.), *Making early histories in museums*, Leicester: Leicester University Press, pp. 95–116.

REFERENCES

Moser, S. (2003). Representing archaeological knowledge in museums: Exhibiting human origins and strategies for change. *Public Archaeology, 3*, 3–20.

Mouliou, M. (1997). Greek private collecting of antiquities and the museums: Two collectors, two museums and their tales. In G. T. Denford, (Ed.), *Representing Archaeology in Museums, The Museum Archaeologist, 22*, 13–28.

Moussouri, T. (1998). Family agendas and the museum experience. In G. Denford, (Ed.), *Museums for the 21st Century, The Museum Archaeologist, 24*, 20–30.

Museums and Galleries Commission. (1986). *Eligibility criteria for the grant aided storage of excavation archives.* London: Museums and Galleries Commission.

Museums and Galleries Commission. (1992). *Standards in the museum care of archaeological collections.* London: Museums and Galleries Commission.

Museums Association. (MA). (2002). *Code of Ethics for Museums.* London: Museums Association.

Museums Association. (MA). (2005). *Collections for the Future.* London: Museums Association.

Museum of London. (1986). *Discoveries.* London: Museum of London.

Museum of London. (1998). *General Standards for the Preparation of Archaeological Archives Deposited with the Museum of London.* London: Museum of London.

Museum of London. (1999). *Annual Report April 1998–March 1999.* London: Museum of London.

Museum of London Archaeology Service. (2000). *The Archaeology of Greater London.* London: Museum of London Archaeology Service.

Mytum, H., and Waugh, K. (Eds.). (1987). *Rescue Archaeology – What's Next?* Department of Archaeology, University of York Monograph 6. Published jointly by the Department of Archaeology, University of York and Rescue, the British Archaeology Trust.

Nalda, E. (2002). Mexico's archaeological heritage: A convergence and confrontation of interests. In N. Brodie and K. Walker Tubb (Eds.), *Illicit Antiquities*. London: Routledge, pp. 205–227.

National Museum Directors Conference. (NMDC). (2003). *Too Much Stuff*, London: National Museum Directors Conference.

National Museum of Scotland (2004). *Explorer*, 11.

Nørskov, V. (2002). Greek vases for sale, some statistical evidence. In N. Brodie and K. Walker Tubb (Eds.), *Illicit Antiquities*. London: Routledge, pp. 23–37.

Needhma, S. P. (1991). *Excavation and salvage at Runnymede Bridge 1978, The Late Bronze Age Waterfront Site*. London: British Museum.

Nieuwhof, A., and Lange, A. G. (2003). *Op weg Naar Een Nationale Referentiecollectie Archeologie*. Amersfoort: ROB.

Nzewunwa, N. (1990). Cultural education in West Africa: Archaeological perspectives. In P. Gathercole and D. Lowenthal (Eds.), *The politics of the past*. London: Unwin, pp. 189–202.

O' Regan, S. (1990). Maori control of the Maori heritage. In P. Gathercole and D. Lowenthal (Eds.), *The politics of the past*. London: Unwin, pp. 95–106.

Ouma, E., and Abungu, L. (2006). An African renaissance. *Museums Journal*, (June), 18–19.

Owen, J. (1995). *Towards an Accessible Archaeological Archive*, Society of Museum Archaeologists.

Owen, J. (1999). Interaction or tokenism? The role of "hands-on activities" in museum archaeology displays. In N. Merriman (Ed.), *Making early histories in museums*. Leicester: Leicester University Press, pp. 173–189.

Oxford University Press (1976). *The concise Oxford dictionary*, Oxford: Oxford University Press.

Parker Pearson, M. (1993). *Bronze Age Britain*. London: Batsford/English Heritage.

REFERENCES

Parker Pearson, M. (1995). Ethics and the dead in British archaeology. *The Archaeologist, 23*, 17–18.

Pearce, S. (1990). *Archaeological Curatorship.* Leicester: Leicester University Press.

Pearce, S. (1995). *On Collecting: An Investigation into Collecting in the European Tradition.* London: Routledge.

Pearce, S. (1997). Archaeology as collection. In G. T. Denford, (Ed.), *Representing Archaeology in Museums, The Museum Archaeologist, 22*, 6–12.

Pearce, S. (1999). Presenting archaeology. In N. Merriman (Ed.), *Making early histories in museums.* Leicester: Leicester University Press, pp. 12–27.

Peers, L. (2004). Relative values. *Museums Journal,* (September), 18–19.

Perrin, K. (2002). *Archaeological Archives: Documentation, Access, and Deposition.* London: English Heritage.

Pes, J. (2004). Under the wraps, mummy the inside story, British Museum. *Museums Journal,* (September), 40–41.

Pes, J. (2005). Native voices. *Museum Practice,* (Spring), 12–17.

Petrie, W. M. F. (1904). *Methods and aims in archaeology.* New York: Bloom.

Phillipson, D. W. (2003). *Archaeology in Africa and in Museums.* Cambridge, UK: Cambridge University Press.

Piggott, S. (1938). The early Bronze Age in Wessex, *Proceedings of the Prehistoric Society, 4*, 52–106.

Pirie, V. (1985). Woman, heritage and museums. *Archaeological Review from Cambridge, 4*(1), 117–118.

Politis, K. D. (2002). Dealing with the dealers and tomb robbers: The realities of the archaeology of the Ghor es-Safi in Jordan. In N. Brodie and K. Walker Tubb (Eds.), *Illicit antiquities.* London: Routledge, pp. 257–267.

Polk, M., and Schuster, A. (Eds.). (2005). *The looting of the Iraq Museum, Baghdad*. New York: Harry N. Abrams.

Pryor, F. (2001). *Seahenge, new discoveries in Prehistoric Britain*. London: Harper Collins.

Pye, E. (2001). *Caring for the past, issues in conservation for archaeology and museums*. London: James & James.

Rahtz, P. A. (Ed.). (1974). *Rescue archaeology*. London: Penguin.

Ramos, M., and Duganne, D. (2000). *Exploring public perceptions and attitudes about archaeology*. Prepared by Harris Interactives for the Society of American Archaeology, http://www.saa.org.

Rawlings, M. (2005). The last box to be ticked – how archaeological contractors deal with archives. *The Archaeologist*, 58 (Autumn), 33.

Renfrew, A. C. (1968).Wessex without Mycanae. *Annual of the British School at Athens*, 63, 278–285.

Renfrew, C. (2000). *Loot, legitimacy, and ownership*. London: Duckworth.

Renfrew, C., and Bahn, P. (1991). *Archaeology, theory, methods and practice*. London: Thames and Hudson.

Renfrew, C., and Zubrow, E. (Eds.). (1994). *The ancient mind: Elements of cognitive archaeology*, Cambridge, UK: Cambridge University Press.

Renton, D. (2006). The Butrint Museum, Albania: A long road traveled. *Minerva*, 17,(2), 23–24.

Resource (2001). *Renaissance in the regions: A new vision for England's Museums*. London: Resource.

Restall Orr, E. (2004). Honouring the ancient dead. *British Archaeology*, 77, 39.

Restall Orr, E., and Bienkowski, P. (2006). Respect for all. *Museums Journal*, (May), 18.

REFERENCES

Richards, G. (2000). Cultural tourism. In P. McManus (Ed.), *Archaeology displays and the public.* London: Archetype, pp. 1–12.

Roberts, M., and Swain, H. (Eds.). (2001). *The Spitalfields Roman.* London: Museum of London.

Roesdahl, E., Mohen, J-P., and Dillmann, F.-X. (Eds.). (1992). *Les Vikings.* Paris: AFAA.

Ross, C., and Swain, H. (2001). *Museum of London: 25 years.* London: Museum of London.

Rowan, Y., and Baram, U. (2005). *Marketing heritage, archaeology and the consumption of the past.* Walnut Creek: AltaMira Press.

Rowe, M. (2006). Warrior class. *Museums Journal,* (August), 38–39.

Rowsome, P. (2000). *Heart of the city, Roman Medieval and Modern London Revealed by archaeology at 1 Poultry.* London: English Heritage and MoLAS.

The Royal Liverpool Children's Inquiry. (2001). *The report of The Royal Liverpool Children's Inquiry: Summary and recommendations.* London: Stationery Office.

Russell, A. D. (2000). Community archaeology in Southampton. In P. J. Wise (Ed.), *Significant Others, The Museum Archaeologist, 25,* 48–49.

Salinger, J. D. (1951). *The catcher in the rye.* London: Penguin.

Saville, A. (1999). Thinking things over: Aspects of contemporary attitudes towards archaeology, museums and material culture. In N. Merriman (Ed.), *Making early histories in museums.* Leicester: Leicester University Press, pp. 104–209.

Scarre, C. (1990). The western world view in archaeological atlases. In P. Gathercole and D. Lowenthal (Eds.), *The politics of the past.* London: Unwin, pp. 11–18.

Schadla-Hall, T. (1984). Slightly looted: A review of the Jorvik Viking Centre. *Museums Journal 84,* 2 (September), 62–64.

Schadla-Hall, T. (1989). Preserving London's past. *Rescue News, 48*, 1.

Schadla-Hall, T. (1993). Plaiting fog: The search for quality. In E. Southworth, (Ed.), *Picking up the pieces – Adapting to Change in Museums and Archaeology, The Museum Archaeologist, 18*, 1–5.

Schadla-Hall, T. (2000). Public archaeology – Spreading the net wider? In P. J. Wise (Ed.), *Significant Others, The Museum Archaeologist, 25*, 50–58.

Schadla-Hall, T. (2002). Lighting up the past. *Museums Journal*, (December), 38.

Schofield, J. (2005). *Combat archaeology: Material culture and modern conflict.* London: Duckworth.

Schofield, J. (2006). Rethinking heritage management. *British Archaeology*, (July–August), 11.

Shanks, M., and Tilley, C. (1987a). *Social Theory and Archaeology.* Cambridge UK: Polity Press.

Shanks, M., and Tilley, C. (1987b). *Re-constructing archaeology: Theory and practice.* Cambridge, UK: Cambridge University Press.

Sheldon, H. (1989). The curious case of the Queen's Hotel. *Rescue News, 47*, 1.

Shell, C. A., and Robinson, P. (1988). The recent reconstruction of the Bush Barrow lozenge plate. *Antiquity, 62*, 248–260.

Sheppard, F. (1990). *A treasury of London's past.* London: HMSO.

Simmons, D. M. (2000). Archaeology and interpretation at Old Sturbridge Village. In P. McManus (Ed.), *Archaeology displays and the public.* London: Archetype, pp. 29–38.

Skeates, R. (2000). *Debating the archaeological heritage.* London: Duckworth.

Skeates, R. (2002). Speaking for the past in the present. *Public Archaeology, 2*(4), 209–218.

REFERENCES

Skeates, R. (2005). Museum archaeology and the Mediterranean cultural heritage. In E. Blake and A. B. Knapp (Eds.), *The archaeology of Mediterranean prehistory*. Oxford: Blackwell, pp. 303–320.

Smartdz Frost, K. E. (2004). Archaeology and public education in North America. In N. Merriman (Ed.), *Public Archaeology*. London and New York: Routledge, pp. 59–84.

Smith, K. (2004). A monument to neglect. *Museums Journal*, (August), 28–29.

Smith, L. (2002). National archaeology days, how to promote your venue and get your audiences actively involved. In P. J. Wise (Ed.), *Public Archaeology: Remains to be Seen, The Museum Archaeologist, 27*, 3–8.

Smith, M., and Hesse, P. (Eds.). (2005). *23°S Archaeology and environmental history of the southern deserts*. Canberra: National Museum of Australia Press.

Solicari, S. (2005). Interpreting Chinese heritage: A museological observation of China's silk road region and some notes on the Stein textile project at the Victoria & Albert Museum. *Circle of Inner Asian Art, SOAS Newsletter, 20*(July).

Southworth, E. (Ed.). (1990). *Ready for the New Millennium? – Futures for Museum Archaeology, The Museum Archaeologist, 17*.

Southworth, E. (Ed.). (1991). *What's Mine is Yours! – Museum Collecting Policies, The Museum Archaeologist, 16*.

Southworth, E. (Ed.). (1993). *Picking up the Pieces – Adapting to Change in Museums and Archaeology, The Museum Archaeologist, 18*.

Spalding, J. (1999). Scotland's real story hidden in the detail, review of the Museum of Scotland, Edinburgh. *Museums Journal*, (June), 20–21.

Specht, J., and MacLulich, C. (2000). Changes and challenges: The Australian Museum and indigenous communities. In P. McManus (Ed.), *Archaeology displays and the public*. London: Archetype, pp. 39–66.

Spencer Larson, C. (2000). *Skeletons in our closet, revealing our past through bioarchaeology*. Princeton: Princeton University Press.

Spoerry, P. (1993). *Archaeology and legislation in Britain*. Hertford: Rescue.

Staal, G., and de Rijk, M. (2003). *Inside out on site in*. Amsterdam: BIS.

Stanley Price, N. P. (1990). Conservation and information in the display of prehistoric sites. In P. Gathercole and D. Lowenthal (Eds.), *The politics of the past*. London: Unwin, pp. 284–290.

Steel, P. (2004). Close to the bone. *Museums Journal*, (August), 22–25.

Stig Sørenson, M. L. (1999). Archaeology, gender and the museum. In N. Merriman (Ed.), *Making early histories in museums*. Leicester: Leicester University Press, pp. 136–150.

Stone, P. (1990). Life beyond the gallery. Education, archaeology and the new millennium. In E. Southworth (Ed.), *Ready for the New Millennium?–Futures for Museum Archaeology, The Museum Archaeologist*, 17, 53–56.

Stone, P. G. (1994). The re-display of the Alexander Keiller Museum, Avebury, and the National Curriculum in England. In P. G. Stone, and B. L. Molynaeux (Eds.), *The presented past*. London: Routledge, 190–205.

Stone, P. G., and Molyneaux, B. L. (Eds.). (1994). *The presented past*. London: Routledge.

Suenson-Taylor, K., and Swain H. (1999). *Models for the curation of archaeological archives in England* (MGC, unpublished).

Suenson-Taylor, K., Heywood, C., and Dillon, J. (Eds.). (2006). *Whose find is it anyway? Treasure, metal detecting, archaeology and conservation*. London: Institute of Conservation.

Sullivan, L. P., and Childs, T. S. (2003). *Curating archaeological collections*. Walnut Creek: AltaMira Press.

Sussams, K. (2000). Half a million hours: A twenty year archaeology survey of Norfolk. In P. J. Wise, *Significant Others, The Museum Archaeologist*, 25, 39–44.

REFERENCES

Swain, H. (1995). Registration – Are you ready? *The Field Archaeologist*, 24, 6.

Swain, H. (1996). Here comes a national museums crisis. *British Archaeology*, 12, 11.

Swain, H. (1997a). A survey of archaeology in Surrey museums. *Surrey Archaeology Society Collections*, 84, 246–249.

Swain, H. (1997b). Archaeological archive transfer, theory and practice. In G. T. Denford, (Ed.), *Representing Archaeology in Museums, The Museum Archaeologist*, 22, 122–144.

Swain, H. (1998a). *A survey of archaeological archives in England*. London: MGC.

Swain, H. (1998b). Displaying the ancestors. *The Archaeologist*, 33, 14–15.

Swain, H. (2000). Public archaeology and the role of museums. *IFA Yearbook*, 36–37.

Swain, H. (2001). Planning a research agenda for London's archaeology. In P. J. Wise (Ed.)., *Indulgence or Necessity? Research in Museum Archaeology, The Museum Archaeologist*, 26, 56–60.

Swain, H. (2002a). The London Archaeological Archive and Research Centre. *Current Archaeology*, 179, 480–482.

Swain, H. (2002b). The ethics of displaying human remains from British archaeological sites. *Public Archaeology*, 2(2) 95–100.

Swain, H. (2003). London before London. *Minerva*, 14(1), 9–12.

Swain, H. (2004a). High Street Londinium: reconstructing Roman London. In Paul Frodsham (Ed.), *Interpreting the Ambiguous: Archaeology and Interpretation in Early 21st Britain.*, BAR 362, pp. 89–93.

Swain, H. (2004b). The Archaeological Archives Forum. *The Archaeologist*, 53, 31–32.

Swain, H. (2005a). A new medieval gallery for the Museum of London. *The Archaeologist*, 56(Autumn), 22–23.

Swain, H. (2005b). Archaeological archives and our future. *The Archaeologist*, 56(Autumn), 12.

Swain, H., and Werner, A. (1998). London bodies, How the Museum of London is putting our ancestors on display. *Minerva*, 9(6), 16–8.

Sweet, R. (2004). *Antiquaries*. London and New York: Hambledon & London.

Thomas, C. (2004). Life *and Death in London's East End, 2000 Years at Spitalfields*. London: MoLAS.

Thomas, N. (1991). Personal recollection: The museum triangle. In E. Southworth (Ed.), *What's Mine is Yours!–Museum Collecting Policies, The Museum Archaeologist*, 16, 1–8.

Thompson, M. W. (1977). *General Pitt-Rivers, Evolution and Archaeology in the Nineteenth Century*. Bradford-Upon-Avon: Moonraker.

Thompson, J. M. A. (Ed.). (1992). *Manual of curatorship: A guide to museum practice*. (2nd ed.). Oxford: Museums Association.

Tilley, C., Keane, W., Kuechler, S., Rowlands, M., and Spyer, P. (Eds.). (2006). *Handbook of material culture*. London: Sage.

Times Books (1988). *Past worlds. The Times atlas of archaeology*. London: Times Books.

Togola, T. (2002). The rape of Mali's only resource. In N. Brodie and K. Walker Tubb (Eds.), *Illicit antiquities*. London: Routledge, pp. 250–256.

Trigger, B. (1980). Archaeology and the image of the American Indian. *American Antiquity*, 45, 662–676.

Ucko, P. (1987). *Academic Freedom and Apartheid: The Story of the World Archaeological Congress*. London: Duckworth.

Ucko, P. J. (1994). Museums and sites: Cultures of the past within education – Zimbabwe some ten years on. In P. G. Stone, and B. L. Molynaeux, *The presented past*. London: Routledge, pp. 237–282.

REFERENCES

UNESCO (1970). *Protection of mankind's cultural heritage: Sites and Monuments.* Paris: UNESCO.

UNESCO (1999). *International code of ethics for dealers in cultural property.* Paris: UNESCO.

UNIDROIT (1995). *Convention on stolen and illegally exported cultural objects.* Rome: UNIDROIT.

Vergo, P. (Ed.). (1989). *The new museology.* London: Reaktion.

Voss, B. L. (2000). Feminism, queer theories and the archaeological study of past sexualities. *World Archaeology, 32*(2), 180–192.

Vrdoljak, A. F. (2006). *International law, museums and the return of cultural objects.* Cambridge, UK: Cambridge University Press.

Wainwright, G. J. (1989). Saving the Rose. *Antiquity, 63,* 430–435.

Walker Tubb, K. (2002). Point, counterpoint. In N. Brodie and K. Walker Tubb (Eds.), *Illicit antiquities.* London: Routledge, pp. 280–300.

Waller, R. (2000). Community archaeology in an urban environment. In P. J. Wise (Ed.), *Significant Others, The Museum Archaeologist, 25,* 45–47.

Walsh, K. (1990). Postmodernity, the new right and the emergence of heritage. In E. Southworth (Ed.), *Ready for the New Millennium? – Futures for Museum Archaeology, The Museum Archaeologist, 17,* 4–12.

Watkinson, D., and Neal, V. (1998). *First aid for finds.* London: RESCUE and UKIC and Museum of London.

Weeks, J., and Bott, V. (2003). *Scoping Survey of Historic Human Remains in English Museums, Undertaken on Behalf of the Ministerial Working Group on Human Remains* (unpublished but available from the Department of Culture, Media, and Sport website).

Werner, A. (1998). *London bodies.* London: Museum of London.

White, A. J. (Ed.). (1986). *Dust to Dust, Field Archaeology and Museums Conference Proceedings, 2.*

Wilk, C., and Humphrey, N. (Eds.). (2005). *Creating the British galleries at the V&A.* London: V&A Publications.

Willett, F. (1990). Museums: Two cases of reaction to colonialism. In P. Gathercole and D. Lowenthal (Eds.), *The politics of the past.* London: Unwin, pp. 172–183.

Wilson, F. (1995). Silent messages. *Museums Journal,* (May), 27–29.

Wise, A. (1998) Museums and the Archaeology Data Service. In G. Denford (Ed.), *Museums for the 21st Century, The Museum Archaeologist,* 24, 7–9.

Wise, P. J. (Ed.). (2000). *Significant Others, The Museum Archaeologist,* 25.

Wise, P. J. (Ed.). (2001). *Indulgence or Necessity? Research in Museum Archaeology, The Museum Archaeologist,* 26.

Wise, P. J. (Ed.). (2002). *Public Archaeology: Remains to be Seen, The Museum Archaeologist,* 27.

Wise, P. J. (Ed.). (2003). *The Art of Archaeology, The Museum Archaeologist,* 28.

Wood, B. (1997). Does size matter? Effective presentation of archaeology in small museums. In G. T. Denford (Ed.), *Representing Archaeology in Museums, The Museum Archaeologist,* 22, 59–64.

Wood, B., and Cotton, J. (1999). The representation of prehistory in museums. In N. Merriman (Ed.), *Making early histories in museums.* Leicester: Leicester University Press.

Wright, P. (1985). *On living in an old country: The national past in contemporary Britain.* London: Verso.

Zimmerman, S., Dasovich, M., Engstrom, M., and Bradley, L. E. (1994). Listening to the teachers: Warnings about the use of archaeological agenda in classrooms in the United States. In P. G. Stone, and B. L. Molynaeux (Eds.), *The presented past.* London: Routledge, pp. 359–374.

INDEX

Portable Antiquities Scheme,
    xxii, 60, 106, 237, 301, 319
postmodernism, 9, 31
postprocesualism, 31
Potteries Museum.
    Stoke-on-Trent, 314
Prehisto Parc, Tursac, 74, 314
prehistory, 14, 26
*Principles for the Recording of
    Monuments, Groups of Buildings,
    and Sites*, 66
public programmes, 4, 31, 50

Qatar, 83
Quinling Museum, 84, 315

Raiders of the Lost Ark, 55
Receiver of Wreck, 62
reconstructions
    in museum displays, 30
Register of Professional
    Archaeologists, 65
Renaissance, 4, 18, 19, 22, 23
Renaissance in the Regions report,
    174
RESCUE, The British
    Archaeological Trust, 32, 54
Resource. *See* Museums,
    Libraries and Archives
    Council
Roche Abbey, Yorkshire, 261
Roman archaeology, 74
Roman Canterbury, 72
Roman School Box scheme, 275
Romans, 13, 14, 27, 72, 211, 220,
    223, 235, 266, 268, 293
Rome, 4, 19, 23, 36, 70, 74, 94
Roskilde Museum, 315
Roskilde Viking Ship Museum,
    xii, 37, 39, 75, 184, 233, 246,
    247, 281, 315

Royal College of Surgeons
    London, 167
Royal Commission for Ancient
    and Historic Monuments
    Scotland, 117
Royal Commission for Ancient
    and Historic Monuments
    Wales, 117
Royal Liverpool Children's
    Inquiry, 152
Royal Museum Edinburgh, 240,
    311
Runnymede later prehistoric
    site, 178
Rwanda, 79, 305, 311

Saalburg, 74, 315
Sainsbury Centre for Visual Arts,
    30, 315
Salisbury, 212, 222, 232, 244, 316
Schiemann, 24
Schloß Gottorp, 215, 315
Scotland, xxii, 60, 64, 72, 117, 152,
    162, 173, 196, 263, 307, 313
Seattle, 156
Segedunum, 73, 315
Seoul Museum, 85, 315
Shakespeare's Rose Theatre,
    54
Shanks, Michael, 48, 50
Shenyang Museum, 229, 316
Shoreditch Park project, 178, 286
Sicily, 75
Silk Road Cultural Relics
    Museum, 164
Six Nations Museum in
    Onchiota, NY, 80
Smith, Chris, 49
Smithson, James, 29
Smithsonian Institution, 29, 38,
    68, 81, 235, 243, 291, 310, 311